To every Rich B$tch who picks up this book —
may it transform your life, fuel your dreams,
and remind you of how capable
and worthy you truly are.

And to my sister, Kim, whether you knew it
or not, you were always the energetic match
to wealth. I love you.

PREFACE

When I began writing my first book, *She Dares*, in 2016, I was living paycheck to paycheck, with an empty bank account and maxed-out credit cards, all while picking up the pieces after my husband left me for another woman. Honestly, I had every f*cking reason to question my existence — and I did.

My first husband, a law enforcement officer at the time, became the center of a criminal investigation in 2016, just two years after we got married, making the news and facing jail time. Overnight, we lost our primary income and our health insurance. The State Police and FBI raided our home, investigating possible ties to the Russian Mafia, and the unrelenting cruelty of online trolls after he made headlines was devastating to navigate — but not as devastating as the discovery of the affair he was having with his younger coworker.

That season of my life was the most gut-wrenching experience I have ever endured; it was a pain so excruciating that it pushed me to the darkest corners of my mind where I found myself, more than once, questioning whether, at just twenty-nine years old, I could keep going. And though I felt like a woman ripped straight from a *Dateline* episode, waking up to the horrifying revelation that my husband had been living a double life and I was at rock f*cking bottom, it was the catalyst to changing my entire reality.

One day, as I was drowning in self-pity while sobbing on my bedroom floor, a thought struck me — and you'll want to pay attention here because, for the first time in what felt like forever, the thought wasn't about poor little me. An unexpected aha moment pierced through the fog of my pity party, jolting me awake from the hypnosis of despair I had been trapped in:

I have years of training in personal development. I understand the law of attraction and manifestation. I have tools at my disposal and friends who genuinely love me. So, what the f*ck am I doing, feeling this lost?

And that's when it hit me — *if I, with all my training and resources, am suffering this deeply, what chance do other women have? Women who don't have the tools, the knowledge, or the support system I've been fortunate enough to build?*

F*ck. This. In that exact moment, I made a choice — a fierce, life-altering decision to break free from debt and the stress of living paycheck to paycheck, to heal my heart, to rewrite my story, and to inspire others to transform their lives as I had transformed my own. That choice didn't just save my life, it became the unshakable foundation for everything I've built since.

From being the girl who couldn't pay my mortgage or afford everything on my grocery list to making my first million — I've freed myself from debt, traveled first class on my terms, scaled my business, put myself in my dream car, left a marriage that didn't serve me, and moved into a million-dollar home I furnished completely on my own — without needing a single thing from my ex.

Most importantly, I've guided thousands through their own transformations, and if you're reading this, I believe you could be next. Your starting point doesn't define your destination, your vision and actions do.

For anyone who wants to change their life, there's an overwhelming amount of evidence through countless stories that exist of people clawing out of the deepest rock bottoms. Most, if not all, eventually recognize the significance of the moments they once despised as necessary stepping stones for their transformation.

So, whether you're living in your parents' basement, relying on food stamps, at rock bottom, or even doing fine but know there's more for you, this book holds every step I took to create the kind of transformation that has me waking up every day saying, "I f*cking love my life!" It's a master plan to money, abundance, and building a rich life you're obsessed with. If you're here, it's not by accident — this is your chance to begin creating the wealth and fulfillment you deserve.

INTRODUCTION

Welcome to *Rich B$tch Money Goals*, your guide to rewriting the story you tell about money, success, and the abundant life you deserve. This isn't just a book, it's a tool, a road map, and a revolution. I trust you're here because you're ready to transform, to step into the most liberated, unapologetically rich version of yourself.

This book is designed to meet you exactly where you are, whether you're deep in financial struggle, stuck in lack, or ready to elevate your already abundant life. You'll find actionable steps, mindset shifts, and principles that will guide you to become the kind of person who commands wealth and freedom, and not just financially, but in every corner of life.

Read it with intention. Highlight what resonates, revisit the tough parts, and take notes like your life depends on it. Because it does.

Core Principles of This Book

1. **Abundance Is an Inside Job:** Wealth starts in your mind before it shows up in your bank account.
2. **Responsibility, B$tch:** You are the creator of your financial reality. Excuses don't pay bills — ownership does.
3. **Money as Energy:** Money flows to those who respect, value, and work with it — not those who fear or chase it.
4. **Aligned Action:** Manifestation requires movement. Dream big, then do big.
5. **Self-Worth = Net Worth:** Your financial reality mirrors how deeply you value yourself.

The Rich B$tch Principles

Being a Rich B$tch isn't just about money, it's a mindset, a lifestyle, and a choice to live intentionally and unapologetically. Here's the breakdown:

- **R: RESPONSIBILITY** — A Rich B$tch takes 100 percent personal responsibility for her circumstances so that she can change what's not a ten out of ten.

- **I: INTEGRITY** — Every move a Rich B$tch takes has integrity as the foundation.

- **C: COURAGEOUS CONVERSATIONS** — Comfort doesn't define whether a Rich B$tch takes action to lead. She will have every courageous conversation required to create change.

- **H: HEALING (for the highest good)** — A Rich B$tch is in pursuit of healing her life as much as she is in pursuit of growing her bank account.

- **B: BELIEF** — A Rich B$tch believes in herself.

- **I: INVEST** — A Rich B$tch will invest the time and resources required to change her circumstances (both internal and external).

- **T: TRUST** — Trusting our intuition and moving accordingly is a nonnegotiable in this work.

- **C: CONSCIOUS CREATION** — Creating our Rich B$tch life is an everyday move because we understand we are in the driver's seat.

- **H: HEART-CENTERED** — A Rich B$tch is heart-centered in everything she does. Her heart is her true north, her guide, her compass.

LiberateHER: The Mission—Giving Every Woman the Opportunity to Choose Her Rich B$tch Life

This book is more than just pages and chapters, it's part of a movement I founded called *LiberateHER™*. When women heal, rise financially through conscious creation, and lead with their hearts, they transform the world around them. This is about far more than money; it's about reclaiming your power, making pleasure a priority, and stepping fully into the life you were born to lead.

$$\$\$\$$$

I didn't start as a Rich B$tch—I built her. Through relentless self-work, bold action, and unshakable belief—nonnegotiables for building a seven-figure empire, breaking free from debt, and creating a life where wealth, freedom, and love coexist.

Throughout this book, I share stories of my journey through life that most could never even begin to imagine healing from, yet I did. Not only have I healed, but I've refused to be held captive to my past. Instead, I chose to use every hardship as fuel to ignite transformation in others worldwide. I don't just love my life now, I love my past because it shaped me into the woman I am today. And while it's common to feel sorry for those who have endured challenging pasts, I choose to celebrate every opportunity I've had to evolve. It's time to normalize rising from our darkest pains and creating a new life we're obsessed with—no matter where we came from.

I'm not just sharing theory, I'm sharing what's worked for me and the thousands of women I've guided before you. I've lived every word in this book, and I know the way because I've walked it.

Now, it's your turn.

CHAPTER
ONE

CHAPTER 1: KIM

The wealthiest people in the world understand that wealth is an _experience_ of self, not a dollar amount. Evolving from scarcity to abundance happens when you embody self-love, feel worthy to heal, and have the courage to change.

Welcome to the new Era of Becoming the Energetic Match to Wealth.

I am so honored that you're here! Chapter 1 is the foundation of everything _Rich B$tch Money Goals_ stands for. The principles you'll discover will be enriching, life-changing, and challenging.

A rich life is measured by how we experience ourselves, with or without money, which is why we're starting this journey with something deeply personal: the sudden loss of my only sister, Kim. You will soon understand why this has everything to do with you becoming the energetic match to wealth and why this story is the foundation of _Rich B$tch Money Goals_.

So, just as I tell my clients before we embark on something big, I say to you . . .

Let's f*cking go!

$$\$\$\$$$

Two days before Christmas in 2021, a single phone call altered the course of my thriving business, reshaped my perspective on money, and redefined the soul-level work I was meant to fulfill. Clients were hiring me from all over the world to support the growth of their businesses. They saw the financial success I created while having fun and wanted the same results.

By this time, I had identified a gap in the entrepreneurial space that explained why some coaches succeeded while others did not.

Everyone wanted to learn business strategies (the "secret") they believed would make them rich, but that wasn't step one. Many entrepreneurs believed it was and, as a result, ended up running in circles, getting nowhere.

On December 23, 2021, my work — especially around money teachings — became personal on a level I never knew existed. From that day forward, a principle now deeply woven into my mission, *Your Next Business Strategy Is a Personal One™*, was born from the ashes.

I was standing in my kitchen with my twin brother and his wife, who had flown into Detroit from Orlando for the holidays. We were enjoying each other's company, warmed by the fireplace against the dark, cold winter, and making tea when his phone rang.

As my brother answered, I watched his expression change, and even with the phone pressed firmly against his ear, I could hear my mom sobbing in the background. I instantly fell to my knees. The sound of anguish that erupted from my mouth, as if my body were purging the shock from my system, echoed throughout the otherwise silent house. One minute, laughter and holiday excitement had filled the air as we planned our family schedule for Christmas Day. The next, we were frantically racing to my sister's condo where her boyfriend had found her lifeless on her bedroom floor.

When we arrived, the police and first responders were already inside, and despite my desperate pleas to see my sister, the officer blocking the doorway wouldn't let me in. I stood in the cold December air, closed my already swollen, bloodshot eyes as more tears streamed down my face, and wondered how we would tell her twelve-year-old son, right before Christmas, that the center of his world was gone forever.

At this point, you're probably wondering what this has to do with you, with money, or with becoming the energetic match to wealth.

Because you're reading this, I'm assuming you want to create wealth and likely believe that having more money will solve most, if not all, of your problems.

I'm telling you, it won't.

That's why you're here, right? To figure out how to create abundance in your life? To find a way out of struggling? How many books on money have you read before this one, and how many have made a difference for you?

Are you rich yet?

The Rich B$tch principles you'll be learning focus on *how* I went from debt to generating seven figures, on wealth frequency, on soul alignment, and on the importance of who you choose to become in the process of change. This is not about a quick fix, it's about a sustainable one. It's about wealth as an ongoing state of mind — the embodiment of wealth as the catalyst for external prosperity.

So, let me repeat:

The wealthiest people in the world understand that wealth is an *experience* of self, not a dollar amount. Evolving from scarcity to abundance happens when you embody self-love, feel worthy to heal, and have the courage to change.

This means that money cannot be your source of happiness or your "why." Not because I'm saying it can't, but because anything external that you try to build your sense of self on — gratitude, wealth, happiness, worthiness — is like trying to build a house on quicksand. It's unstable; sooner or later, you'll confront this fact: building anything on an unstable foundation never lasts.

The Rich B$tch community knows that true wealth is how we *experience* ourselves. Internal success creates our external results, and a regulated nervous system is worth its weight in gold. I know it's unsexy to hear, but you can't bypass the internal work if you're trying to create your highest timeline in life, business, wealth, and beyond.

So, what exactly does this have to do with my sister and with you?

Absolutely everything.

My sister, probably like you, was all these things, yet she *never* believed it. She was beautiful, intelligent, creative, gifted, loved, and funny. She was highly extroverted, and I always thought she had star qualities.

Growing up, I wanted to be just like her. Until I didn't.

I could never understand how someone who outwardly seemed to have it all — the athleticism, the looks, the brains, the boyfriend, access to money, and life experiences I could only dream of — could hate herself so much.

That is, until I, too, came to hate myself.

Although we both experienced unworthiness and a lack of self-love, eventually falling into separate addictions, the difference between my sister and me was that I engaged in transformational work at seventeen. I began attending countless in-person seminars, always the youngest there. It altered the course of my life, putting me on a path of healing, accelerated growth, and, ultimately, my life's work.

My sister, however, did not. Instead, she turned to drugs to numb the profound cellular pain she felt, as being sober felt too heavy.

At the intersection of choice, the fork in the road we all face at one point or another: to heal or self-sabotage — I chose left, and she chose right.

**Numbing doesn't protect us from pain,
it keeps us from feeling alive, creative, and liberated.**

Despite my sister's addiction, which began with a Vicodin prescription after her wisdom teeth were removed and eventually ended with heroin, she always managed to attract wealth into her life through the men she dated and the opportunities she manifested. At the time, I envied what she could buy and the trips she was gifted.

While she was flying somewhere tropical, I could barely afford a road trip. And even when I did, I stressed over the cost of gas from point A to point B.

However, I quickly realized that no amount of money (and trust me, she had access to a lot at times) could make up for her lack of self-love. No vacation, fancy dinner, purse, boat ride, salon day, cosmetic procedure, cash on hand, or luxury item could fill the deepening hole in her heart.

If money or material possessions could have saved her, this chapter wouldn't exist.

She looked to the external world for answers (as most of us have been conditioned to do), avoiding the internal work required to change.

In some ways, money killed her as much as fentanyl did. Because what does a drug addict do when they come into cash? They seek out and buy more drugs.

There's a saying that money doesn't change who you are, but it does amplify it. So, if you're not actively working to overcome self-hatred, insecurities, shame, guilt, fears, judgment, unworthiness, lack, and negative learned behaviors — and you start generating abundance — money might fill your bank account, but it will never fill an internal void. So, sure, you'll have more money, but you'll be far from wealthy.

I highlight this because of my sister, and it's evident in the entrepreneurial space. I have witnessed women go from debt to creating financial overflow, yet they're still f*cking broke because their sense of self remains unchanged: shattered, not healed. And it's not money that repairs that — it's self-love.

When women celebrate massive financial wins yet still feel inadequate or accumulate wealth while constantly comparing themselves to others — feeling insecure, unworthy, or competitive — they may have more in the bank, but what good is it if their inner self is fragmented? A void of self-love keeps us experiencing lack and separation, no matter what possessions we own. Hopefully, you're beginning to see why *Your Next Business Strategy Is a Personal One,* just like your next wealth strategy, is a personal one.

I want you to embody the Rich B$tch principles to create a new experience of being healed *and* wealthy, recognizing that wealth is an inside job.

I know you want to make more money, have the freedom to do as you wish, and have limitless funds to experience more of life or simply find relief in paying bills and providing for your family. There are endless ways to make more money. Becoming a Rich B$tch is about more than that. It's about taking personal responsibility and ownership of your life, *being* the catalyst for change, generating an overflow of internal love, and allowing that overflow to manifest as external richness.

It's also about holding yourself accountable for all the ways you hold yourself back so that you can f*cking do something about it.

To become the energetic match for wealth, you must prioritize and learn to love yourself. You won't complete this book or do the homework if you're stuck in self-hate or are unconsciously self-sabotaging your success.

You'll have to demonstrate a level of self-love bigger than your ego. You'll have to stop quitting on yourself when it gets hard, when you feel uncomfortable, when you doubt yourself, or when that familiar internal voice starts to scream "Just give up; you're not good enough, you're a fraud, this will never work for you!"

Limiting beliefs will inevitably arise, and when they do, you'll need willpower greater than your addiction to believing the thoughts that have held you back for years.

This work is the work of love — the unbecoming of all you're not and the becoming of who you truly are.

Fair Warning: Just like entrepreneurship, this work is not for the faint of heart.

This is why **RICH B$TCH** stands for a woman who takes (personal) **R**esponsibility for her success, leads with **I**ntegrity, prioritizes **C**ourageous **C**onversations (when it's right, not when it's easy), **H**eals for the highest good, **B**elieves in herself, **I**nvests in herself, **T**rusts herself, **C**onsciously **C**reates her life, and is **H**eart-centered in her pursuit of wealth.

These principles will change your life if you apply them. If you catch yourself reacting to someone or something as your old self normally would, regulate, and then ask yourself, "What would the Rich B$tch version of me do instead?"

Next, you'll have to move accordingly as you discover the answer to that question daily. Why? Because insight without action makes no f*cking difference.

Before my sister passed away, I wrote her a poem. It sat in my iPhone's Notes section for months before I found the courage to share it with her. The poem expressed the loss of my sister to addiction; my pain, concern, and the unconditional love I had for her despite her choices. It also expressed my hope that someday she would heal and discover self-love.

I sent it to her in September 2021.

She cried, expressing both her love for me and her gratitude for the poem. Tragically, the addict won the battle, and my sister passed away three months later.

I felt called to share this poem with you because nearly everyone has an addiction — to someone or something — that keeps them anchored to the past, even when they long for change. Addictions can take many forms: sex, drugs, alcohol, constant complaining, endless social-media scrolling, validation-seeking, food, toxic relationships, suffering, self-loathing, codependency, and more.

A Rich B$tch must confront and transcend all self-imposed limitations to become the energetic match to wealth.

Dear Addict,

It's my sister you took, and I now know you better than the memories of a once happy girl sadly trapped in your hook. I know your lies, self-hatred, desperation, and pain. I know you're consumed on a fix with no concern for others when it comes to achieving an empty, self-centered gain. I don't know how you help her, but she chooses you every time. I'm afraid she is unaware of everything you cost her and fear the day she can't pay your fine. Is permanent death worth your temporary high? Is one more fix necessary just to get by? I dread the day I answer my phone just to hear on the other end cries. No words will be needed because I'll know the unavoidable day has arrived. You took her spirit while her heart was beating, and though she is alive, she appears dead. I hope I remember to tell her everything I never said. Dear Sister, I've missed you. Where did you go? Will you ever come back, or does the addict forever run the show? Dear Sister, I'm not mad. I know your actions stem from deep-rooted pain. But I've experienced trauma too, and I overcame without drugs; why couldn't you do the same? Dear Sister, what about your son? Why wasn't he your reason to stay clean? Why can't you see clearly? Addiction is so mean. Dear Sister, I love you. And one day, you'll know, whether in heaven or on earth, you've always been worthy enough to let your addiction go.

I know my sister found her worthiness in heaven. My only wish is that she could have felt it when she was still alive. And so, to you, my sister on this Rich B$tch journey . . .

**Find your worthiness and self-love, and bring your
Rich B$tch dreams to life while you're still here.**

A CHANNELED MESSAGE: Days before this book was published, a message came through me, urging me to tell you about a song called "Rose" by Ayla Schafer. I invite you to experience it now, preferably in video form on YouTube. Trust that there's a reason for you to hear it. When the song is over, return and complete this day.

$$$

Worthiness is possible, and wealth is inevitable when you claim it. I know this truth, and it's time for you to know it too.

You are worthy.

You're worthy simply because you exist.

You're worthy to receive.

You're worthy to create the life of your dreams.

You're worthy of setting strong, healthy boundaries that respect your time, energy, and focus, and everything you value.

You're worthy of change.

You're worthy to heal, forgive, be forgiven, let go, and overcome.

You're worthy of outgrowing relationships and friendships.

You're worthy of investing in yourself.

You're worthy of a Rich B$tch life.

You're worthy of walking the path of your highest truth and highest self.

You're worthy of loving yourself deeply.

You're worthy of success.

You're worthy of being in the Rich B$tch community, surrounded by others who are actively growing, just like you.

You're worthy of a loving partnership that honors your authentic self and invites you back to your truest essence.

You're worthy of living a life you love and creatively expressing yourself in exciting ways.

You're worthy of giving and receiving love, embodying the principles of a Rich B$tch, and writing an entirely new story for yourself.

Your next business strategy, just like your next wealth strategy, is a f*cking personal one.

$$$

Rich B$tch Homework: Let It Flow

Your Rich B$tch journey is just beginning. You have the potential to profoundly change your life if you commit to showing up fully for yourself.

You may be feeling a range of unexpected emotions right now. I encourage you to journal about anything that arises. Let it flow — release anything that no longer serves you.

Click on the following QR code to hear my personal message before officially beginning your Rich B$tch journey.

I love you. LFG!

xx Kyera Kacey,
Founder of LiberateHER™

CHAPTER
TWO

RICH
B$TCH MONEY GOALS

CHAPTER 2: RICH B$TCH RESPONSIBILITY

Taking Rich B$tch responsibility means claiming the driver's seat of your life and declaring, "I'm the one." No more whining from the back seat, no more blaming the detours — because you're the one holding the wheel, and you're in control of where this ride is going.

In my early twenties, I attended a three-day seminar on transformation. During one of the sessions, a man from the audience volunteered to go on stage, then shared how his uncle had molested him as a child. Understandably so, years later, he was still consumed by rage.

As the seminar leader attempted to facilitate a breakthrough by asking deeper questions, the participant grew significantly more agitated. Ultimately, he stormed off the stage, yelling profanities for the entire room to hear on his way out the door. While most people were looking around with discomfort, unsure of what to do, I immediately stood up and chased after him.

"Hey, wait up!" I yelled at him as he made his way to his car. He turned around and looked at me, his eyes holding back tears. "I want to share something with you," I said in between catching my breath.

When I was fifteen years old, I was raped by not one, not two, but three men simultaneously. At nineteen years old, I did something uncommon and healed myself entirely from that experience.

The man from the seminar allowed me to get in his car and sit in the parking lot with him, where he spent the first several minutes shouting that his uncle deserved to die. When he finished, I shared my experience at fifteen years old, how I healed at nineteen, and that I only wanted to help.

It is said that people can only accept, believe, and surrender to information equal to their emotional state. Though I had good intentions, his readiness to hear anything outside his anger wasn't there.

> *Most people are fighting for their limitations. If you're going to become the energetic match for wealth, it's imperative that you draw a line in the sand and choose a side. Fight for your past, or change for your Rich B$tch future.*

Despite sharing my own story and how I overcame the darkness that often follows rape, he refused to let go of his anger. He stood firm, saying he wouldn't give his uncle the satisfaction of his forgiveness.

That's understandable, right? I mean, he was molested by his uncle.

His reactions, anger, rage . . . they're all valid.

His pain is justified.

One hundred percent.

That's not the issue.

The issue is this . . .

Justified or not, valid or not, his way of *being* in life (rage-filled) due to what happened to him as a child is holding him hostage to a reoccurring experience of hatred and shame. Whether he knows it or not, those repetitive thoughts and feelings are his hell, his prison, the bars he lives behind, and yet he's the one holding the keys to get out.

Let's review a powerful statement from the previous chapter.

The wealthiest people in the world understand wealth is an experience of self, not a dollar amount. Evolving from scarcity to abundance happens when you embody self-love, feel worthy to heal, and have the courage to change.

You've experienced painful events throughout your life, and though **you may not have caused the wound, the experience you're left with is now your responsibility to heal.**

That's a tough pill to swallow.

I know because I, too, had a hard time swallowing it, and I've had women tell me to go f*ck myself for saying the same thing.

Let's be clear: this isn't about excusing an injustice or letting anyone off the hook. This is about taking responsibility for your life and refusing to let the pain someone else caused have the power to control you. The cards you were dealt may not be fair, but staying angry doesn't hurt *them*, it keeps *you* chained to the past. Forgiveness isn't for them, it's for *you* — to cut the cord, reclaim your power, and ensure your future is shaped by your Rich B$tch desires, not the wounds of your past.

This is why the **R** in **R**ICH B$TCH stands for (personal) **R**esponsibility.

When I was nineteen years old, my choice to heal from the shame and anger I was carrying after being raped happened when the Universe showed me who I would be in the future if I continued down the same path I was on.

I was attending another transformational seminar, and as usual, I was the youngest person there.

This time was different, though. For some reason, I was highly present to everyone around me on this particular day, and because of that, I had a wake-up call.

You don't just miss 100 percent of the shots you never take, you miss 100 percent of the shots you never see.

I noticed a theme from the energy and look on the participants' faces. Mostly, they looked stressed the f*ck out and unhappy.

So, I was sitting in a room of 150 people at nineteen years old, watching men and women in their thirties to seventies, when I thought, *Oh my God. That's going to be me in twenty years if I don't heal my trauma.*

That moment was like being presented with the opportunity to try hardcore drugs for the first time, but before you do, you're shown someone who has been doing drugs for years, and suddenly, your life flashes before your eyes.

At nineteen, I was a ticking time bomb, holding myself hostage to a moment in time when the only actual place "being raped" continued to exist was in my mind. I allowed being raped to define my life, shape my future, and dictate every present moment.

I convinced myself that being too nice, trusting, and naive got me into trouble. So, instead of being friendly, I displayed anger and a rough-around-the-edges attitude (you know, massive resting bitch face) to get people to leave me alone.

It was an act I became really good at, but it wasn't one I enjoyed. I convinced myself I'd be safer — what an illusion — if people were too uncomfortable to approach me.

And in some ways, it worked. The payoff of being an angry teenager was that most people left me alone. But the cost? The cost was everything I truly wanted: love, connection, joy, self-love, laughter, and peace of mind. In trying to protect myself, I had unknowingly locked myself out of the life I desperately longed for.

Sitting in my chair, still observing the other participants, I had a flashback of younger Kyera in elementary school, the one who questioned why adults always looked (and felt . . . I'm very psychic) unhappy but said, "Everything's fine" when asked if they were okay.

At that moment, all I had to do was look at my life to know the answer.

I need to make something crystal clear . . .

You do NOT need to change.

You don't need to heal, forgive, "get over," find peace, move on, create wealth, etc.

You don't *need* to do anything.

You, as you are right now, are perfect.

I only share this story (with more to come) to highlight how I've overcome trauma and changed my life so that you can see a new possibility for yourself and dive deeper into the Rich B$tch principles if what *and how* I've created my success inspires you to dream bigger or do the same.

LiberateHER is about the power of choice, and we stand for giving every woman the opportunity *to choose* her Rich B$tch life.

So, if you've experienced injustice and want to keep your story about it, the experience, and the aftermath, you're free to do so. I only want you to know that healing is possible, and the side effects of healing provide you with a clean slate from which to create your most prosperous f*cking life.

Teaching you how to become the energetic match to wealth without your healed and happy era turned on is not the Rich B$tch vibe.

Internal success = external results. (You'll see this occasionally throughout the book to remind you of the true meaning of wealth and the prosperity that follows the work of change.)

So, how did I do it? How did I heal myself at just nineteen years old from an experience that most people take to their graves?

The first step was becoming aware of *how* my personality (resentful, angry, and closed off) negatively impacted my life.

The second step was having the desire to change.

The third step (a defining moment) was making a choice.

To choose anything in life is to select freely and after consideration. This meant that I considered what I would have to give up to be free from the chains of my past. I would have to give up being a victim, being angry, and telling a disempowered story. (I was justified in my victim story and my anger, but it wasn't giving me the outcome I wanted.)

I would have to give up protecting myself and learn to open my heart again. (I was justified in being closed off, but that wasn't making me happy.)

I considered what it meant to take personal responsibility for my life experience moving forward, regardless of what happened in my past or how I got here.

I had to be willing to let go of my abusers, and I was evolved enough at the time to recognize I was worthy of that, and so were they.

The fourth step (a crucial one) is the **C** in B$T**C**H, **C**onsciously **C**reate, but we'll save that conversation for a later chapter.

At nineteen, I realized something profound and life-altering. I (just like you) had to go first to do significant work in the world and facilitate change, and someone had to play the role of "abuser" for me to have the opportunity to heal my life so I could teach this work to others.

Your life experiences are not an accident.

Our soul contracts — spiritual agreements made with another soul before birth — are designed with precision and love to support mutual growth in this human experience. Yet, the flipside is that they honor free will, allowing us to choose evolution or remain stagnant. These agreements shape key relationships — some offering deep love and support, while others challenge you through pain or heartbreak, pushing you to choose self-love over self-abandonment. Every soul you encounter plays a role in your evolution, mirroring the lessons you need to learn, until you consciously break old cycles and step into your power. How do we learn to forgive if we have nothing to forgive? How can we be an example of change without extraordinary opportunities to stand in our power?

The guy on your first date pressuring you to go back to his place after dinner for a drink isn't a jerk, he's a soul contract that agreed to play this exact role (*for* you) so that you had an opportunity to speak your truth and trust your intuition despite any discomfort you feel standing up for yourself.

If you missed the mark in a past life, consider this one your chance to course-correct. Life is giving you opportunities — right here, right now — to try again, to grow, and to create the alignment you may have missed before. Every challenge, every lesson, is a doorway inviting you to rewrite the script.

The boss who won't give you a raise and walks all over you? Soul contract. His role? The one who gifts you the opportunity to raise your standards and trust your intuition that it's time to pour energy into your dreams of entrepreneurship.

The parent who couldn't love you the way you craved? The one who you're still upset with forty years later? Soul contract.

The miscarriage you're still grieving? Soul contract.

The ex who cheated on you and "destroyed your life"? Soul contract.

So, here you are, likely considering whether to keep reading this book or burn it to the ground because I've either moved you to tears or pissed you off.

Me in your life? Soul contract.

It's all ... by ... design.

So, if you're going to become the energetic match to wealth through the Rich B$tch principles, you must take personal responsibility for your experience of life moving forward.

The power here is that *you* get to choose, and there's no right or wrong.

There's only an experience that you're left with depending on which road you go down, and if, at any point in time, you don't love the experience you're in, you can choose to change it.

At nineteen, I took a hard look at the direction my life was headed, and I knew I didn't love it. I wanted more: I wanted to love myself, love men, love people. I wanted to trust again, to experience pleasure, to be a woman who embraced intimacy instead of fearing it because of what had happened to me.

So, I made a decision. I changed my life. And here's the part that might surprise you: I did it without drugs, without medication, without years of therapy. I shifted my reality with more ease than we're ever told is possible. It took work, but it was simpler than we're led to believe — and that's a truth more people need to hear.

If you continue this journey with me, I'll take that as a sign you're choosing your Rich B$tch future over your past and say congratulations, today is your day.

$$$

Rich B$tch Homework: Owning Your Life, Unlocking Your Wealth

1. **THE LIFE AUDIT**

    Take fifteen minutes to write down the key areas of your life: business, finances, relationships, health, and self-care. For each area, ask yourself:

    - Am I taking full responsibility here, or am I blaming, avoiding, or waiting for something outside of me to change?
    - What specific actions can I take to step into my power and improve this area?

2. **REWRITE THE BLAME STORY**

    Identify one situation where you've been blaming someone or something else for your current reality. Write it out. Then rewrite the story from a Rich B$tch perspective by taking ownership of your role. For example: "I'm not stuck; I'm in charge of finding a new opportunity."

3. **OWNERSHIP IN ACTION**

    Choose one tangible step you'll take this week to own your power in an area where you've been avoiding responsibility. Maybe it's creating a plan to move your body daily, having a courageous conversation, or dedicating time to your passion project. Make it specific, then commit to taking action.

Personal responsibility is your gateway to wealth. When you stop waiting for someone else to fix your life and own every part of it, you unlock the power to create massive abundance. The question isn't "Who will do this for me?" it's "What am I doing today to make it happen?"

CHAPTER THREE

RICH
B$TCH
MONEY GOALS

CHAPTER 3: A RICH B$TCH LEADS WITH INTEGRITY

Integrity is the ultimate Rich B$tch flex — it aligns your actions with your values, makes you magnetic to abundance, and builds the kind of trust that screams "I'm unstoppable, and so is my bank account!"

From my Rich B$tch experience, lacking integrity — not walking your talk or honoring your truth — is like putting up a giant Do Not Enter sign for cash. Money's like "Oh, you're not serious? Cool, I'll find someone who is." People can smell misalignment from a mile away, and trust me, it's not a good scent. If you're not embodying what you preach, don't be surprised when abundance swipes left! Integrity isn't just nice to have, it's your golden ticket to making it rain.

Furthermore, it's time to stop saying yes to things we don't actually want to say yes to. You know, like the birthday parties you have no desire to attend, or that second date when you already know you'll be running for the hills.

The truth, however unsexy it may sound, is this: When you betray the direction your heart is calling you toward, you fracture your integrity. And when your integrity is compromised, your energy weakens, your magnetism fades, and the doors to abundance slam shut. Your heart is never wrong — it's your compass, your source of power. Ignore it, and you scatter your potential. Honor it, and you unlock the limitless flow of opportunity, alignment, and success.

But let's be clear: Integrity isn't about chasing every impulse or letting temporary frustration dictate your actions. It's about showing up with Rich B$tch energy that commands wealth in every sense: wealth of character, wealth of focus, and wealth of results.

It's not about skipping the gym because you don't feel like going or abandoning goals when motivation dips. True integrity is about staying connected to your deeper truth — the values, desires, and intentions that align with your highest self and your greatest vision.

When you dismiss or suppress how you genuinely feel, you create internal resistance, which blocks the flow of energy and opportunity. But when you honor those feelings, even when they're uncomfortable, you create a pathway to greater clarity, self-trust, and alignment. And that alignment? That's where your magnetism and abundance truly thrive.

Someone recently asked me, "If integrity is about honoring your word and commitments, then how do you justify your second divorce?" Easy. I'm married to myself above all else. Integrity starts with me, and I'm not going to act against my heart or stay in something where the frequency has shifted and alignment no longer exists.

Now, does this mean I dismiss my obligations? Absolutely not. If you commit to something — like signing up for a program with terms and conditions, or a contract — and later decide it's no longer aligned, integrity doesn't give you permission to just walk away and ghost your commitments.

It *does* mean, however, that you can honor your truth while honoring your word. You can exit gracefully, owning the agreements you made, fulfilling payments you committed to (even if you decide not to use the service), and taking full responsibility for your choice to pivot. True integrity is about owning it all: your desires, your decisions, and the follow-through that reflects the wealth of your character and the energy you want to embody.

When you stay rooted in this kind of integrity, you create the kind of clean, magnetic energy that attracts abundance effortlessly. So, stop saying yes to what isn't real for you — it's not just your time you're wasting, it's your power.

Let me spill some tea on how integrity and cash flow are basically the ultimate power couple — like Beyoncé and Jay-Z, but for your bank account.

I have a story for you, and I'm about to say something that might give you the *ick* . . .

Network Marketing!

Stay with me . . . I promise this isn't a "Hey girl, wanna join my team?" pitch. This is a story about doing network marketing (NWM) the Rich B$tch way, where integrity meets authenticity, and a side hustle becomes a money magnet.

I'm sharing this story because *millions* of women globally are stepping into entrepreneurship through this very model. For many, it's the key to financial freedom. Whether it's layered in as a side hustle or built into a full-time empire, this model often serves as an entry point into a world many never thought possible: owning their own time, rewriting their money stories, and claiming their power.

This is also about more than just income streams, it's about reclaiming sovereignty in a way that honors who you are, aligning with abundance and *integrity*. Let's acknowledge the past stigma, the eye rolls, the skepticism that often surrounds it. Why? Because hiding from uncomfortable truths never leads to empowerment. I've always believed that the most transformative paths often challenge the status quo. This model has been a launchpad for countless women to step into their worth, rewrite their narratives, and build wealth on their own terms.

It's also been a major turnoff for some. And I love to shine a light on what we've been told to keep in the shadows. Taboo conversations have the power to change lives, and this story is a testament to that. So, whether you've walked this path or are just curious, lean into the message: Abundance is your birthright, and integrity is the foundation that builds it.

Okay, let me explain.

The *ick* of network marketing — the thing that makes people roll their eyes and mutter, "Oh great, another pyramid scheme!"

First, let's clear the air: almost all network marketing opportunities (otherwise known as multi-level marketing, MLM) are NOT pyramid schemes. Pyramid schemes are highly illegal and get shut down by the Federal Trade Commission very quickly. But let's be honest: some people make it *feel* that way. With their integrity meter way off the charts, people can feel their dissonance from a mile away.

Then you add in people who have wrongfully labeled the entire industry as a scam based on the structure looking like a "pyramid," and now millions of people have blindly adopted this blanket statement because they don't do their own due diligence and research.

In fact, if you think of any traditional job, there is a CEO at the top, then C-level suite executives, some district managers below them and a level of managers below them, then hundreds of hard-working employees at the very bottom. If you look at this structure it resembles . . . you got it, a pyramid. No matter how hard that forty-hours-a-week employee works they will never make as much as the CEO. However, we are conditioned to approve these models of business structure every day. This is all about perspective.

Now, that's neither here nor there. The point is, the integrity of the business industry got a bad rap for a select few companies who didn't comply with regulations and "scammed" the average person. Now the integrity of the entire industry gets canceled.

And then there are those who sell the pipe dream — parading flashy cars, shiny checks, and curated lifestyles that might be nothing more than smoke and mirrors. Let's call it what it is: a lack of integrity, especially when they claim results they haven't earned. On the other side, you have individuals who buy into illusion, never put in the real work, and then point fingers, blaming the opportunity instead of owning their personal responsibility. Both sides miss the truth: Success is built on authenticity, aligned effort, and unwavering accountability, not shortcuts or excuses.

And then there are the reps who've been taught outdated, transactional tactics that make network marketing feel robotic and inauthentic. You know the ones: sliding into your DMs with "Hey girl, long time no talk! Wanna change your life?" (Sure, Susie, it's been a decade since high school — tell me about your magic protein shake.) The problem is glaring: Their approach compromises genuine connection because they're operating from a script, not from integrity. And, as a result, they wonder why they can't attract a single soul to their "team." Energy doesn't lie — when your values and methods don't align, the results speak for themselves.

You can see how easy it is for an entire business model to need damage control.

Now to share my personal experience . . .

Over the years, I've been pitched MLM opportunities more times than I can count, and every single time, I've said no faster than I can demolish a pizza — and trust me, that's a skill I've perfected.

While leading a retreat in Tulum back in 2023, a dear friend, passionate and convincing, approached me with a product she was partnered with. She shared how it could not only benefit me personally but also align perfectly with the work I was already doing. I trusted her deeply and had witnessed her incredible success in network marketing over the years. But at that moment, I was laser-focused on my current programs and had absolutely no interest in adding another stream of income.

That is, until nine months later when she brought it up again. This time, she framed it differently, explaining how this business model could solve a real problem for women in my community.

Suddenly, my perspective shifted. It wasn't just about adding another income stream for myself anymore, it was about creating something meaningful that aligned with my purpose. I saw the opportunity as a vehicle to amplify my mission: giving every woman the opportunity to choose her Rich B$tch life. It clicked. Now, the idea wasn't just appealing, it was fully aligned with my integrity and the vision I hold for the women I serve.

In 2020, when the world went into lockdown, a massive opportunity exploded in the coaching industry: working from home while getting highly paid to guide and inspire others. It sounded like the dream for so many. But here's the catch: while many had the best intentions, too many jumped into coaching without being fully ready or aligned with their true purpose.

The result? A wave of well-meaning women left feeling stuck, broke, and unsure how to actually create success in their coaching businesses.

But what if there was another way? A way that not only supported their purpose but also provided the structure, alignment, and tools to thrive?

What if the women who desired the entrepreneurial life (but weren't meant to run a coaching business) could instead sell a product they genuinely loved — something that added value — and could bring in additional income with ease? Think about it. Women are *always* chatting, sharing recommendations, and connecting. Why not do it with intention? Why not sell while serving? It's a way to align passion with purpose and create an income stream without the pressure of trying to "figure it all out" overnight.

I mean, you're literally selling every day, whether you realize it or not. Wouldn't you rather get paid for it? Let me break this down for you because I know the minute people hear NWM/MLM, they roll their eyes and feel some kind of way. But stick with me here; I promise this will make a light bulb go off.

I have an obsession with candles. I don't just like them, I *love* them. I burn them daily, but not just any candles — only clean, non-toxic beeswax candles from a company called Big Dipper Wax Works. Why? Because their products and their story align with my Rich B$tch standards, and I'm bougie when it comes to certain products.

Whenever I get a new order, I'm so excited that I post an unboxing message on Instagram. It takes me maybe sixty seconds to upload a story, and every single time, someone slides into my DMs asking for more information about the company and my recommendations. I happily share, and a week later, they're back, showing off the candles they bought.

I don't get paid for that. I don't earn a commission, and I'm not affiliated with Big Dipper Wax Works. I just authentically *love* their products, and because of that, sharing them feels natural, effortless, and genuine.

This is precisely how conscious network marketing *should* be. It's not about spamming people or chasing numbers, it's about loving a product so much that sharing it is second nature. When you lead with that kind of integrity and authenticity, not only does it feel good but your bank account will reflect it.

What's a product you're so obsessed with that you can't stop telling your friends about? And what do they do? They go buy it. Why? Because they trust you, they feel your authentic excitement for something, and now they want it! Hello?! That's the power of sharing with integrity and intention, except you can actually get paid for it.

**Wealth is everywhere — surrounding you,
waiting for you to see it. It's time to open your eyes
to new possibilities of earning money beyond
what you've ever known or done before.**

So, you may have guessed it by the way I lined up this story . . . I decided to try the product for myself. I've always stood firm on one thing: I will never sell something I don't love or believe in. If it weren't something I would genuinely use and didn't see the benefit, it would never touch my offerings. This was about integrity, not just business. After trying the product and ultimately falling in love with it, I decided to step in as a business builder for the network marketing company my friend was affiliated with, so I joined her team.

Now, because I've always shown up with integrity and transparency, my audience already trusted me. They knew that if I was speaking about something, it wasn't just hype — my words carried real weight.

In my first month of my new venture within network marketing, I generated an additional six thousand dollars from just one post, one story, and one sixty-minute Zoom call. (For some people, an additional four figures each month would be f*cking life-changing.) The key? Integrity as my foundation — it's what made it all possible.

I in RICH B$TCH stands for Integrity.

Let's talk about how integrity and wealth are total besties, shall we? Imagine trying to build a thriving business or make serious bank without integrity. It's like trying to bake a cake without flour — sure, you might end up with *something*, but it's not gonna rise, and nobody's coming back for seconds. Your cake sucks, Lisa! I'm just kidding. Kind of. Sort of. Not really . . .

Integrity is the secret ingredient that makes your wealth sustainable. It's about showing up, keeping your promises, and delivering value people can trust. When your energy is aligned and you're walking your talk, people feel that, and trust equals cash flow. No trust? No dough. Simple math.

Now, let's be real: We've all seen someone try to hustle without integrity. The pushy sales pitches, the overpromises, the "this opportunity is closing in ten minutes!" vibes. Cringe-worthy, right? Nobody wants to buy from someone who feels shady or desperate. Integrity isn't just the high road, it's the shortcut to building a brand people can't wait to support.

Here's the fun part: Integrity doesn't mean boring. It means you're out here being your badass, authentic self, selling things you actually love, and *meaning it* when you speak. When you're grounded in that energy, wealth flows naturally, and you don't even have to chase it.

Integrity makes you magnetic. Wealth follows energy, and when your energy says "I'm legit and I care," it's like money can't help but slide into your DMs. It's not just about making sales, it's about building a legacy of trust, loyalty, and abundance. It's all about embodying the "I" in Rich B$tch: Integrity. Because without it, you're just another Lisa with a dry, flat cake.

$$$

Rich B$tch Homework: Mastering the Art of Integrity

1. **WALK YOUR TALK AUDIT**

   Write down three areas of your life (business, relationships, health, etc.) and ask yourself:

   - Am I showing up in alignment with what I say I value?
   - Are there places where my actions don't match my words?
   - What small shifts can I make to close that gap starting today?

2. PROMISE TRACKER

For the next week, commit to keeping every promise you make — to yourself and others. Whether it's completing a task, meeting a deadline, or sticking to a personal goal, track your follow-through. Reflect: How does it feel to be impeccable with your word?

3. INTEGRITY IN ACTION

Identify one situation this week where you can choose integrity over convenience or fear. This could be being honest in a tough conversation, delivering what you promised, or making an aligned decision even if it's uncomfortable.

4. MONEY + INTEGRITY CONNECTION

Journal about a time when you embodied integrity and saw financial or relational rewards. Then, write about a time when you didn't — and what it cost you. Reflect on how staying aligned impacts not just your bank account but also your overall energy.

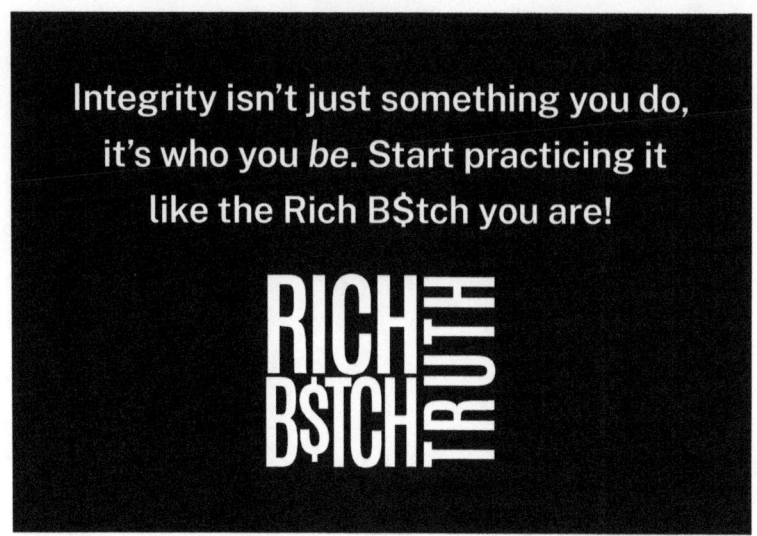

Integrity isn't just something you do, it's who you *be*. Start practicing it like the Rich B$tch you are!

RICH B$TCH TRUTH

CHAPTER
FOUR

RICH
B$TCH MONEY GOALS

CHAPTER 4: COURAGEOUS CONVERSATIONS

Courageous conversations are your golden ticket to more wealth and richness in every area of life. Speaking your truth realigns your energy, sets the vibe for abundance, and screams to the Universe, "I'm ready for more!" The richer your conversations, the richer your life — and your bank account — becomes.

"I want a divorce," I said to my husband, who sat quietly on the couch beside me.

During this time, my business was thriving, and though it had just been another six-figure month in sales, I felt myself hitting the glass ceiling. I knew my next business strategy wasn't about marketing, scaling, or systems. It was personal.

I had already invested countless hours and hundreds of thousands of dollars in private mentorship and knew one thing for certain: no external strategy would move the needle until I addressed the core. Every energetic leak had to be sealed, and every part of my life needed to align with the energy I wanted to embody.

That meant taking a raw, unfiltered look at every area of my life that wasn't a ten out of ten. Every draining relationship, every misaligned situation, and every place pulling me out of my power had to be addressed head-on. Liberation wasn't just a desire, it was nonnegotiable.

This wasn't just a business move. It was a reclamation.

The words *I want a divorce* hung in the air, but as they left my mouth, I felt a wave of nausea mixed with a strange sense of relief. Finally, the truth — the thing that had been eating away at me for weeks — was out. The weight of holding it in was gone, replaced by the bittersweet freedom that comes with speaking something you can't take back.

In many ways, this moment felt harder than my first divorce six years earlier. That time, the choice wasn't mine. My first husband made it for both of us when he had an affair and left me for another woman. I didn't have to wrestle with the guilt or the responsibility of initiating the end of a marriage.

This time, it was my choice, my decision, my voice shattering the life we'd built together. But with that truth came a deep, undeniable clarity: courageous conversations — the ones you fear the most — set you free.

My second husband wasn't cheating, and he wasn't leaving me for another woman. He had a secure job, and we lived in a beautiful home. But beneath the surface, our marriage was neither secure nor beautiful. It was on life support — an empty partnership surviving on habit, not love. And deep in my soul, I knew that once the door to fixing it had fully closed, there was only one option: I had to leave.

Christmas was two weeks away, and only a week had passed since we laid my sister to rest — a moment delayed for a year by COVID before we could finally place her ashes in their final resting place.

It was, without question, the worst f*cking time to move out of my marital home and ask for a divorce. But the "right" time is an illusion — a convenient excuse that keeps people stuck, paralyzed by fear, and avoiding the aligned action they *know* they need to take.

When we delay what we know we're meant to do in our soul, it's never because we're waiting for the perfect moment, it's because we're afraid: afraid of the fallout, the unknown, the discomfort of dismantling what's already fractured. But delaying only prolongs the inevitable.

When we delay something we know we're meant to do, it's always rooted in fear.

Fear that it's terrible timing.
Fear of what others might think.
Fear of change.
Fear of the unknown.
Fear of loss.
Fear of the emotional discomfort that comes with it.
Fear of making a mistake.

The list could go on forever. Fear loves to dress up as "logic" or "waiting for the right moment," but the truth? It's just holding us hostage.

To delay what our heart knows to be true is pure fear, plain and simple. Because here's the thing: There's no good f*cking time to have a conversation that causes pain and flips everyone's world upside down.

Yes, Christmas was two weeks away. But if it weren't Christmas, it would've been New Year's. If not New Year's, then Valentine's Day, Easter, someone's birthday, or a friend's wedding. There's never a good time, never a perfect moment. There's only now — and the courage to act, even when it's messy.

Your heart is a straight shooter; you can follow its guidance or delay out of fear.

It became impossible for me to advocate self-expression and liberation in my work while lacking those very things in my marriage. Once it became clear that the door had closed on us working through our differences, I had to confront the integrity of my work head-on. How could I preach freedom if I wasn't living it?

The thought of hurting my husband by asking for a divorce weighed heavily on me. It wasn't just heartbreak, though, I was terrified: terrified of stepping into the unknown, facing life without him, and lying awake during the quiet, lonely nights when I'd have no choice but to confront myself. But deep down, I knew that the discomfort of facing my truth was the price of reclaiming my freedom, alignment, and power. Sometimes the hardest choices are the ones that lead us back to ourselves.

The conversation, though painful, was also honest, necessary, and unavoidable. And on the other side of my fear and heartbreak was something I longed for: liberation.

The **C** in RI**C**H B$TCH stands for **C**ourageous **C**onversations.

The hard truths we speak, no matter how uncomfortable, are the ones that set us free and realign our energy. And that alignment, the act of setting the frequency right, is essential in becoming an energetic match to wealth. Truth clears the path for abundance to flow.

Do you know what an energetic leak is? If not, let me paint you a picture because I guarantee you have at least one, and it's likely your million-dollar cock block.

An energetic leak is subtle at first, like a slow drip from a pipe hidden behind the walls. You don't notice it right away. Life keeps moving, and things feel fine, until one day you come home and your house is completely flooded. Everything is soaked, ruined; the damage is overwhelming. That's precisely what an unchecked energetic leak does. It seeps into the foundations of your life, quietly stealing your focus, drive, and energy.

Maybe it's the toxic relationship you've been too afraid to confront. Maybe it's the pattern of people-pleasing that's draining your energy. Or maybe it's the unresolved trauma you've been stuffing down because it feels too big to face. Whatever it is, those leaks thrive in silence, avoidance, and fear of courageous conversations. But the longer you avoid those hard talks (with others and yourself) the more you let the leak grow, costing you your power, your peace, and your Rich B$tch era.

Courageous conversations are how you take back your energy. They're the tools that allow you to patch the leak and heal the root cause. They might feel messy or uncomfortable, but they're the gateway to reclaiming your power. When you step into your truth, address what's been draining you, and refuse to stay stuck in avoidance, you take back control. That's when the flood stops — and the abundance and success start flowing in.

A courageous conversation isn't just about words, it's about energy. When you step into a difficult discussion with clarity and authenticity, you reset the energetic frequency between you and the other person. Think of it like tuning a radio: when you're avoiding the truth, holding on to resentment, or staying stuck in assumptions, the frequency is static filled, disjointed, and chaotic. Nothing flows. But when you dare to address what's out of alignment, you clear the static and dial into harmony.

Every unspoken truth or unresolved tension creates an energetic leak — a drag on your mental, emotional, and even physical state. It holds you back from your highest potential because your energy is scattered, tied up in avoidance or unspoken conflict. A courageous conversation is how you take back that energy. It's a moment when you declare, "I'm done carrying this weight" and consciously choose alignment over resistance.

When you show up for a courageous conversation, you set the tone for honesty, mutual respect, and resolution. This act alone raises the frequency of the relationship or situation. Whether it's with a partner, a colleague, a client, a best friend, or even yourself, that new frequency becomes a match for truth, healing, and forward momentum.

Rich B$tch courageous conversations are the ultimate key to unlocking wealth because they clear the blocks standing between you and your abundance. Every time you avoid a hard truth or sidestep a necessary conversation, you're creating an energetic leak, one that drains your focus, your confidence, and your ability to show up fully. But when you step into courage and speak your truth, no matter how uncomfortable, you realign your energy and take back your power. Courageous conversations aren't just about addressing what's wrong, they're about creating what's right. They set the frequency for clarity, integrity, and alignment, all of which are essential for attracting and holding wealth. When you're willing to say what needs to be said, you prove to yourself and the Universe that you're ready for the next level. And trust me, wealth follows that kind of power.

Asking for a divorce was one of the most painful and terrifying decisions I've ever made. But it was also the most loving choice — not just for me, but for him too. It's a truth we often overlook: When we honor what is deeply right for us, we create space for others to find their own freedom as well.

Chances are, you've avoided difficult conversations because you're afraid of causing hurt or conflict. Or maybe you've never been taught how to have courageous conversations at all. When something is your highest truth, when it aligns with what's deeply right for you, it will ultimately liberate everyone involved.

Truth has a way of cutting through the illusions we cling to. It might be messy, even painful at the moment, but it clears the path for authenticity, growth, and healing on both sides. Trust that when you act from a place of love and integrity, even the hardest choices can become acts of grace.

And this ties directly to money and your cash flow. Just like a river won't flow freely if it's dammed up, your financial abundance can't flow when you're blocking yourself with fear, avoidance, or dishonesty.

Avoiding difficult conversations, staying in misaligned situations, or clinging to what no longer serves you creates energetic resistance. When you're holding on to what isn't true for you — whether it's a relationship, a job, or even outdated beliefs about money — you're cutting yourself off from the natural flow of abundance that's always available to you.

Money, like energy, thrives in clarity and alignment. When you have the courage to address what is out of integrity in your life, you remove the blockages that choke your flow. That's when things begin to shift: opportunities appear, ideas spark, and your cash flow mirrors the freedom you've created within.

So, yes, having those hard conversations isn't just about emotional or personal alignment, it's about opening the floodgates for all forms of abundance to find you. Freedom in truth leads to freedom in all things — including your finances.

Before I sat my husband down and asked for a divorce, I asked myself a question that shifted everything: *How could I powerfully complete this marriage?*

I didn't want this to be a breakup filled with blame, resentment, or bitterness. So, I took time to reflect on what I truly wanted — not just in the divorce, but in how we transitioned into a new normal without each other. I committed to creating the possibility of a divorce that held love and respect at its core.

When I finally sat down with him, I made a conscious decision: I would not bring up a single thing he had done "wrong." I left my list of grievances — the "you did this" or "you didn't do that" — to myself. Instead, I chose to take full responsibility for my feelings, my needs, and my decisions.

The truth was, we had shared so many incredible memories. No matter how much we had drifted apart, this man had brought some of my biggest bucket list dreams to life. He gave the very best of himself — with what he knew and what he had. And it wasn't like I stopped loving him. I loved him, *and* we weren't happy. I loved him, *and* while opposites might attract, they don't always make the best life partners.

Loving him made the courageous conversation so much harder to have. But it was also that love that gave me the courage to have it. I loved him enough to set us both free. He deserved to be with a woman he didn't want to change, and I deserved to be with a man who didn't ask me to.

So, while his best ultimately wasn't enough for us, because we both needed things the other couldn't give, I could still honor the love we once shared. That love didn't have to be destroyed in the process of ending the marriage. Instead, it became the foundation for how we chose to move forward. Because love doesn't have to be a casualty of change. Sometimes it's the reason for it.

Facing the reality of our disconnection was hard. But by leading with integrity and love, I opened the door for us both to step into a future that felt truer to who we had become.

That's not to say that finding a new normal with one another was easy or smooth sailing 100 percent of the time. It wasn't. But it was *damn good* for a lot of it, and I'm incredibly proud of how we chose to navigate the breakdown.

Although LiberateHER came to life almost two years later, its roots were planted in that moment — when I chose to embody the very truth I stand for today: the truth that courageous conversations, rooted in love and integrity, are the foundation for Rich B$tch transformation.

This is why your next wealth strategy isn't just financial, it's deeply personal. It starts with having the courageous conversations you've been avoiding. Whether it's with a partner, a client, a boss, or even yourself, setting the frequency right is the first step to opening the doors to abundance.

Wealth doesn't begin in the bank account, it begins in the energy you hold and the truth you live. Align that, then watch the rest fall into place.

So, the next time you feel the weight of something unsaid, and the energy is off, remember this: Your courage is the key to setting the frequency right. One honest, intentional conversation can transform the dynamic with others and your internal energy, freeing you to move forward with clarity and power.

Oh, and to give you hope, my first divorce and my second were worlds apart from a financial standpoint. But the lesson in that transformation lies in a vow I made to myself: Never again would I find myself in a position where I couldn't provide for my own needs, pay my mortgage, or afford the care I required — especially in the hardest moments.

That vow became my turning point. I committed to changing my circumstances, not through luck or waiting for someone to save me, but by doing the deep, uncomfortable work to reclaim my power and rewrite my story.

And because of that work, I moved myself into a million-dollar home, paid six months of the lease upfront without blinking, and furnished it brand new from top to bottom, not because I "needed" luxury to prove anything, but because I could. And because I was no longer living a life built on fear, scarcity, or survival.

This isn't just about financial wins, it's about what is possible when you decide to take full ownership of your life, no matter how impossible it might seem in the moment.

$$$

Rich B$tch Homework: Courageous Conversations That Unlock Wealth

1. **IDENTIFY THE ENERGETIC LEAK**

   Think of one area in your life where avoidance is draining your energy — this could be a tough conversation with a client, partner, friend, or team member. Write it down. Be honest: Where are you holding back, and how is this affecting your energy, focus, or ability to show up fully?

2. **CONNECT THE DOTS TO MONEY**

   Reflect on how this unresolved situation might be costing you financially. Is it:

   - Distracting you from scaling your business?
   - Keeping you from fully showing up for your offers?
   - Sabotaging your confidence when pitching or creating?

   Write down at least three ways this energetic drain is blocking abundance.

3. **CLARIFY YOUR INTENT**

   Ask yourself: What do I need to say in this conversation to feel clear, aligned, and powerful again? What outcome would leave me feeling lighter, focused, and more magnetic to money? Write out your intention for the conversation — this is your *why*.

4. **PREPARE WITH INTEGRITY AND ABUNDANCE**

   Plan what you'll say, focusing on honesty and alignment. Approach the conversation with a mindset of abundance: "I'm clearing this to make space for more wealth and opportunities." Practice aloud if needed, but keep it real — this isn't about perfection, it's about truth.

5. **TAKE ACTION IN THE NEXT FORTY-EIGHT HOURS**

   Schedule the conversation and commit to having it within the next two days. The longer you wait, the more energy you lose, and the less money you call in. A Rich B$tch doesn't delay when her wealth is on the line.

6. **NOTICE THE SHIFT**

   After the conversation, reflect on how your energy feels. Lighter? More focused? More powerful? Journal about the clarity or relief you've gained and how this is freeing you to focus on creating and attracting wealth.

7. **CELEBRATE THE RIPPLE EFFECT**

   Watch what happens next. Do opportunities flow more easily? Do you feel more confident in business? Pay attention to the shifts that come from clearing this block, then celebrate every win — even small ones.

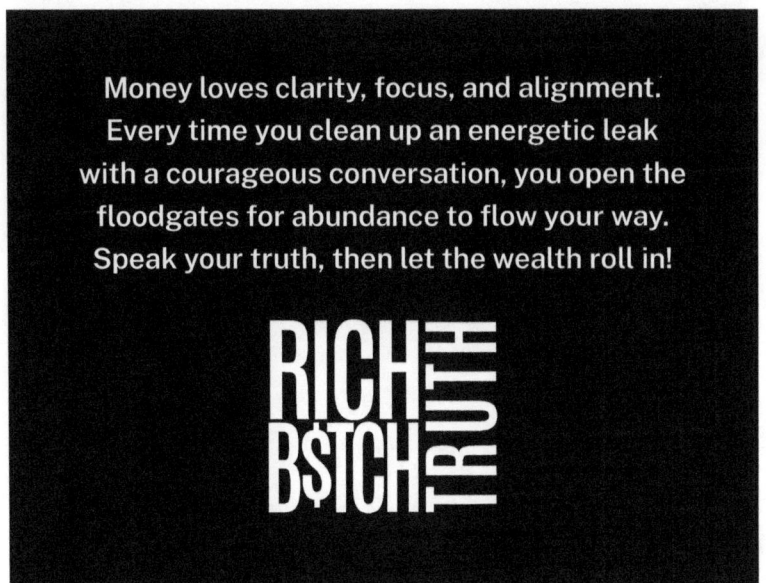

Money loves clarity, focus, and alignment. Every time you clean up an energetic leak with a courageous conversation, you open the floodgates for abundance to flow your way. Speak your truth, then let the wealth roll in!

RICH B$TCH TRUTH

CHAPTER
FIVE

**RICH
B$TCH** MONEY GOALS

CHAPTER 5: HEALING (FOR THE HIGHEST GOOD)

Healing isn't just personal, it's strategic. It aligns you with clarity, confidence, and the unapologetic power to call in wealth and opportunities that reflect your worth. When you heal, you rise — and so does your bank account.

After my sister's death, I found myself so f*cking bored and deeply turned off by everyone around me in their endless obsession with money, especially the relentless push to chase more of it. Everywhere I turned, it seemed like women online were fixated on making quick cash, but so few of them were rooted in the depth of true, internal wealth — the kind that can't be measured in dollars.

The same female coaches who preached self-love and women's empowerment were often the ones shaming me, whether for not wearing a bra, for swearing too much, or for celebrating a milestone. I'd see bios that read "Helping you BOOST your confidence and live BOLDLY," only to find a post from that same person saying "I wish some coaches would stop going on about how much money they make. We get it; you're a rock star . . . but how about sharing something that adds value, that inspires, that feeds our souls?"

Heal, but don't heal TOO much.
Be confident, but not TOO confident.
Get out of debt, turn your life around, Sis — just don't "brag" about it.
Be bold, just not TOO bold.

Are you f*cking kidding me?

I guarantee that entrepreneurs who positioned themselves as advocates for something (like boosting confidence) but turned around and shamed women for being "too much" likely experienced massive financial caps and money leaks in their businesses. Misaligned energy always shows up in results — whether it's unhealed judgment or scarcity disguised as authority, the disconnect will cost you.

When unhealed coaches or professionals show up in their work without doing their own inner healing, they dilute the impact they're meant to create. That's not true wealth, it's survival disguised as service. Wealth demands embodiment — it demands that you lead yourself before you ever attempt to lead others.

The nine Rich B$tch principles are about building unshakable foundations, internally and externally, so the work you do, the relationships you nurture, and the abundance you create are all aligned with the highest version of yourself. Wealth isn't just in what you earn, it's in the energy you *are*. And if you're not whole within, your external "success" will never hold.

Wealth flows to integrity, not contradictions.

People often tell me, "I follow you because I want your level of confidence and your success." And just as often, it's the opposite: "I'm here because you trigger the f*ck out of me and I didn't initially like you." The truth is, if you look at me today and think, *Wow, she's confident,* or *The audacity she has to wear that,* just know this: The self-love you see now is the result of deep, intentional work — because I once knew what it was like to be consumed by self-hate. Transformation isn't magic, it's earned.

But it begged the question: Would the women who are triggered by me or quick to judge see me differently if they knew I once took a razor blade to my skin as a teenager and carved the word *hate* above my belly button, leaving a scar I carry to this day? Would my self-love and liberation be more acceptable to them then?

There was a time when I was worlds apart from the woman I am today, a time when thoughts of suicide and hopelessness crowded out any hint of joy. So, when my self-love triggers someone, I don't take it personally because their reaction has nothing to do with me and everything to do with them. I know because I've been there.

Money in the bank, with mental health in the red, doesn't make us rich. How we experience ourselves — our thoughts, our emotions — inevitably impacts everyone around us. This is why wealth without the conversation of healing doesn't solve a deeper problem. It's why I felt called to address something bigger.

The **H** in RICH B$TCH stands for **H**ealing — for the Highest Good.

"Healing for the Highest Good" became the force that drove me to overcome my addiction to cutting in my early twenties. I had always felt called to bring transformational work to the world, to help others at the deepest level. But to do that, I first had to confront and conquer my own struggles.

That struggle began with emotional pain rooted in my psychic sensitivity. As a young empath, I didn't know how to separate my emotions from the energies around me. I absorbed others' pain, anger, and tension, and, unable to release it, I felt it all build up in my body — a tightening in my stomach, a constant ball of unprocessed anger and sadness.

One day, as teenagers, a friend and I tried to give ourselves tattoos using dull scissors and ink from a pen. I remember feeling the sting, and though it didn't turn into a real tattoo, I discovered something: pain on my skin had the power to cut through the intensity inside me. It gave me a brief relief, a strange escape from the emotional overload I carried but didn't know how to release.

Whenever I had these overwhelming, empathic moments — holding on to others' emotions with no way to let them go — I'd eventually find myself alone in the bathroom, going through a process that became routine. I would take a razor blade to my body, replacing the inner pain with a physical one that, strangely, felt easier to manage. Those moments left me with scars, marks all over my body, each one a reminder of the weight I was carrying and the temporary relief I found from transferring the pain.

That was my addiction, my only outlet until I learned to approach healing differently.

A Rich B$tch embodies unshakable power, unbreakable integrity, and unapologetic healing. She doesn't just talk transformation, she is the transformation.

I know you're here because you want more wealth, abundance, and richness in your life, but what's the deeper *why* driving your desire to change? For me, facing that question was a turning point.

How could I teach the work of transformation if I was still engaging in self-harm?

The decision to heal came easily because I valued my life's work more than I valued cutting myself; it was the execution that was hard. Let's talk about the "how."

The first step? I made a choice — to change, to overcome, and to teach my work with authenticity. If I was going to talk about self-love, I better damn well have it for myself.

It's always easier said than done, because if you've ever tried to overcome something, change, or achieve a goal, you know old patterns don't just disappear. Destructive habits often dig in deeper, growing louder and more seductive. That's exactly what happened to me.

It took only a small trigger to bring back my urge to self-harm, and suddenly I was locked in a battle between my commitment to change and the painful voices urging *Who the f*ck cares? Just make the pain go away.*

My feelings pushed me to do it; my commitment told me not to. The truth was, I didn't know how to stop. So, in a moment of absolute frustration and rage with no certainty of how to NOT cut myself to "feel" better, I yelled out loud to the Universe, "YOU F*CKING TELL ME HOW I'M SUPPOSED TO STOP THEN BECAUSE I DON'T KNOW WHAT TO DO!"

I took a deep breath and, overwhelmed, began to cry.

Eventually, I stopped, wiped my tears, and just sat there, looking around my bedroom, feeling helpless, until something caught my eye: a colorful book on a nearby shelf. Intuition nudged me to get up, walk over, and open it.

It was *Oh, The Places You'll Go* by Dr. Seuss.

Interesting. I couldn't remember when I'd received the book, but I knew it was a gift I'd never opened — until that day.

I sat down on my bed and began to read. It was full of bright colors, happy rhymes, and a childlike cadence that calmed me. But what really grabbed me was the message. If you've ever read *Oh, The Places You'll Go*, you know it's a call to rise to own your power, to face life's twists head-on, and to refuse to quit, no matter how tough the road gets. It's a reminder that the only thing standing between you and your wildest dreams is your willingness to keep moving forward.

By the time I reached the end, something incredible had happened. My urge to cut had completely dissolved. For the first time in years, I hadn't given in to my addiction.

Every obstacle you face isn't here to stop you — it's here to shape you, to burn away what no longer serves and ignite the fire of transformation within. Trust this process! Every step, every challenge, is aligning you with your highest good, calling you to heal, grow, and step boldly into the Rich B$tch life you're destined to create. This is *your* journey, and it's time to claim it.

One of the core principles of manifestation is knowing precisely what you want but letting go of the "how." I knew that I wanted to impact lives around the world, and I knew I had to overcome my addiction to do that at the highest level (and I wanted to), but I would *never* have guessed that a children's book, a Dr. Seuss book, would be the medicine I needed. It was, and it worked.

So, here's what I did:

I promised myself that anytime I felt the urge to cut, before acting on it, I would read *Oh, The Places You'll Go* from start to finish. That was it. My one commitment. Simple but powerful. But I knew it wouldn't be enough on its own.

When you commit to change, you have to set yourself up for success. You have to anticipate the moments when keeping your word will be hardest.

Oh, The Places You'll Go is a large book. What if I felt triggered but wasn't home to read it? I couldn't carry it with me everywhere I went. So, with limited access to the internet on my cell phone at the time, I had only one option: I decided to memorize the entire book. Page by page, line by line, I committed to knowing it by heart.

In the Rich B$tch community, we call this the "1 percent" mentality: the discipline, courage, and integrity to honor your word and do whatever it takes to create change or bring your vision to life.

I relapsed only once. When I did, I didn't beat myself up or carry guilt, I simply forgave myself and started over.

Eventually, I no longer needed to recite the book because I no longer felt the urge to cut. I began channeling my energy into martial arts and running, which gave me new, healthy outlets. I kept attending in-person seminars and events, surrounding myself with people committed to transformation.

Overcoming the hardest aspects of my life didn't require years of therapy, antidepressants, inner-child work, or past-life regression. It required personal responsibility, a willingness to change, a clear vision for my future, and an unbreakable commitment every single day to show up as the future me.

Healing trauma is like unlocking a hidden vault within yourself that's been holding back more wealth, creativity, and potential than you even knew existed. Trauma has a sneaky way of keeping you in survival mode, a mode where all energy goes toward getting by, staying small, and avoiding risk. When you heal, you break out of this limitation, and suddenly, the energy that used to go into fear and protection is freed up to fuel your ambitions and attract opportunities; it allows you to see yourself as the empowered creator of your reality. Wealth is about flow, and trauma blocks that flow. Heal the trauma and you'll feel the wealth moving toward you with momentum you never imagined.

As you release old patterns and wounds, your relationship with money itself transforms. Think about it. Trauma often teaches us we're not safe, not enough, or that we have to work twice as hard to earn our worth. This belief runs through everything — how we spend, save, and even imagine wealth. When you heal, you shed those beliefs and replace them with a mindset of abundance, trust, and worthiness. You start treating money as a natural reflection of your value rather than a scarce resource you have to struggle for. Wealth grows because you're no longer holding on with fear but are instead moving with intention and a sense of empowerment.

Healing trauma also opens up your capacity to take risks and seize opportunities that once felt out of reach. Trauma wires you for caution, keeping you trapped in familiar, "safe" patterns that might feel comfortable but limit your growth. When you heal, you start choosing from a place of confidence and possibility, seeing opportunities where others see threats. You'll have the courage to bet on yourself, make moves that align with your higher purpose, and step into arenas that once felt intimidating. True wealth comes from expanding into the unknown, and that expansion is only possible when you've broken the chains that trauma once held on you.

There's also the undeniable truth that healing changes the way you connect with others. When you heal, you step into your relationships with openness, trust, and an authentic presence that naturally attracts people, resources, and support. People are drawn to those who radiate inner wealth, and that energy starts to compound — partners, collaborators, mentors, and clients appear because they feel the strength and clarity in you. Wealth grows exponentially when your network and relationships flourish, and healing is the cornerstone of building those powerful connections.

Healing for the highest good ignites creativity, which is one of the most potent sources of wealth creation. Trauma drains creative energy, keeping you locked in repetitive thoughts and cycles. When you heal, you liberate that energy, then your mind is free to imagine, innovate, and create. You're open to ideas, solutions, and inspirations that seemed unreachable before. Your uniqueness and gifts can finally come through fully, and when you're creating from a place of alignment and healed energy, wealth flows as a natural byproduct. Trauma healing doesn't just generate wealth, it transforms you into a magnet for it. So, step up, do the work, and watch your life expand in every possible way.

And here's the reality: A healed leader is magnetic and inspiring in a way that few others can be. When you've done the work to break free from old wounds, you lead with an energy that people trust instinctively. They feel your authenticity, your strength, and your clarity, and they're drawn to it. Healed leaders don't just set the vision, they embody it, showing others what's possible when you operate from wholeness and purpose. This isn't just leadership, it's an invitation for you to step into your own power.

The impact of a healed leader goes far beyond just inspiration. It's transformative. When you step into your power and heal, you don't just rise, you create a ripple effect that shifts everything around you. That's the energy we cultivate in the Rich B$tch community.

Here, it's not just about building success, it's about doing the inner work, breaking generational cycles, and showing up as the most aligned, unstoppable version of yourself. This isn't surface-level motivation — it's deep, unshakable healing that allows you to lead your life, your business, and your relationships for the highest good.

The Rich B$tch community is a movement of women owning their worth, rewriting their stories, and leading with fierce authenticity. Together, we're not just making big waves, we're changing f*cking tides.

$$$

Rich B$tch Homework: Healing for the Highest Good

1. **IDENTIFY WHAT'S HOLDING YOU BACK**

   Take fifteen minutes to journal about what you're ready to heal so you can step into the next level of your Rich B$tch energy.

2. **FORGIVENESS INVENTORY**

   Write down three things or people you need to forgive — including yourself. Next to each, write how holding on to this pain has blocked your abundance or drained your power. Then, declare: "I choose to release this and make space for wealth and alignment."

3. **ENERGY CLEARING RITUAL**

   Choose one healing activity to clear stagnant energy. This could be journaling, meditating, breathwork, EFT (Emotional Freedom Technique), or even a symbolic act like burning a letter that represents what you're releasing. Do it with intention, knowing you're clearing space for abundance.

4. ANCHOR YOUR HIGHEST GOOD

Write an affirmation or mantra that reflects your healed, wealthy self. Examples:

- I am free, whole, and open to limitless abundance.
- I release what no longer serves me and make space for wealth in all forms.

Repeat it daily to anchor your energy in healing and prosperity.

5. RICH B$TCH ACTION

Identify one aligned action you can take this week that reflects your healed self. Maybe it's setting a boundary, saying yes to an opportunity, or investing in yourself. Commit to it and do it, knowing this is how you embody your Rich B$tch energy.

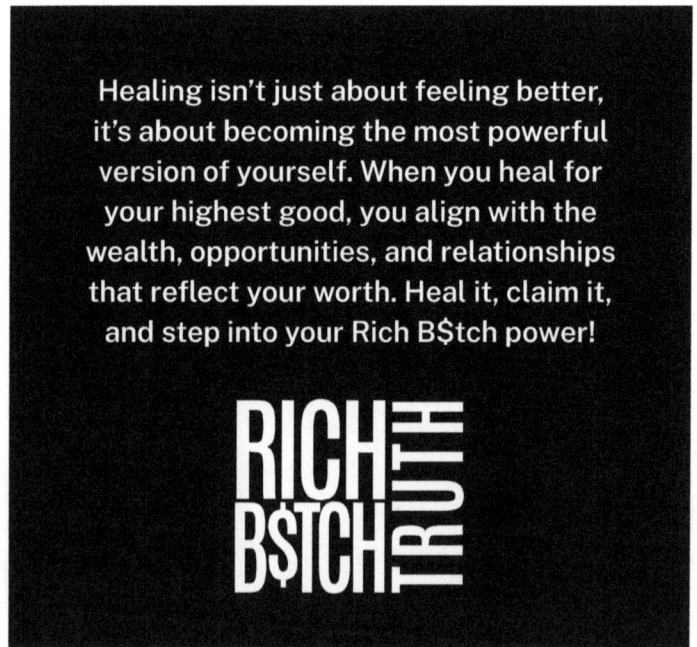

Healing isn't just about feeling better, it's about becoming the most powerful version of yourself. When you heal for your highest good, you align with the wealth, opportunities, and relationships that reflect your worth. Heal it, claim it, and step into your Rich B$tch power!

RICH B$TCH TRUTH

CHAPTER
SIX

RICH
B$TCH MONEY GOALS

CHAPTER 6: A RICH B$TCH BELIEVES IN HERSELF

When you believe, *really* believe, that you can create anything you desire, something magical happens. Manifestations stop feeling like distant "what-ifs" floating in the cosmos — they become *real*. Dreams materialize the moment your mind fully accepts they are possible.

The unsexy secret to becoming an energetic match to wealth? **Belief.**

Not half-assed belief, not "I'll believe when I see it" energy. No, I'm talking about fierce, bulletproof, nobody-can-tell-me-otherwise belief. This belief fuels consistent, bold, aligned action, especially when fear, doubt, or obstacles try to knock you off course.

Over the years, I've given thousands of channeled readings, and here's a sneak peek at the kind of questions I get about wealth:

- Will I be successful?
- What's my purpose?
- Will I become a millionaire?
- When will I get clients?
- Should I leave my nine-to-five to pursue my dreams?

But all these questions boil down to one core plea: "Do you believe in me?"

Or even deeper:

- "Do you think I have what it takes to succeed?"
- "Can I fulfill my soul mission and still be safe?"
- "Am I truly capable of making millions and living the life I desire?"

But let me tell you a truth you *need* to hear: The answer to those questions doesn't lie with me, it's already inside you. You already *know* the truth, but when we're in the middle of change and life feels messy, we look for permission slips from the world because we don't trust ourselves yet.

Let me share a story to show you how powerful belief can be.

Years ago, a woman came to me for a reading. The second I connected to her energy, I knew she was a healer, but she was stuck in a traditional nine-to-five that was draining the life out of her. Now, let me preface this by saying not everyone is meant to leave their job. Some people are thriving exactly where they are. But this woman? Her soul was practically *screaming* to break free and step into her calling.

When I told her what I saw — her self-employed, facilitating healing work, creating a flexible and fulfilling life — she started to cry. She told me she hated her job and had always felt she was a healer but didn't trust herself enough to go for it.

She already knew what she wanted. She didn't need me to tell her. What she needed was someone to remind her of her own potential and the highest timeline she could choose to step into.

The **B** in RICH **B$TCH** stands for **B**elief.

Belief is your superpower.

It's the invisible force shaping your life, day by day, choice by choice.

When you believe in yourself, you stop settling for less than you deserve. When you don't, you'll unconsciously sabotage yourself or stay stuck in the same soul-crushing cycles.

WHEN YOU BELIEVE IN YOURSELF:

- You *know* you're worthy of everything you desire — and more.
- You magnetize abundance, love, and prosperity like the Rich B$tch you are.
- You'll say "hell yes" to what lights you up and a simple "thank you, but I graciously decline" to what drains you.

But when you don't? You'll keep manifesting proof that you're unworthy. That's the hard truth.

And the worst part? Instead of building belief within yourself, you'll start asking others to believe in you. Spoiler alert: That never works.

Asking someone else to believe in you is like borrowing a charger for a dying phone. Sure, it gives you a little juice, but as soon as you unplug, you're right back to empty. The real power? That comes from building your own internal battery — permanently charged and unstoppable.

During my travels in 2023, just days before leading a retreat in Ireland, a client arrived ahead of the group for a VIP day. I asked if she wanted to keep it low-key or go out dancing since we had a spa experience booked the next day — she chose fun, and that's exactly what we had.

After an incredible dinner, we walked into a club, let the locals spoil us with shots, danced like we were headlining the place, and shut it down like it was our job. At 3 a.m., we hopped into a taxi back to our hotel — joined by a charming Irishman who had been hitting on me all night and was absolutely *speechless* when I finally agreed to let him come back with me. After countless "Come on, when in Ireland!" attempts to wear me down, I finally laughed and said, "You know what? F*ck it — when in Ireland."

Then, in the harsh reality of better lighting, I asked his age and nearly choked when he casually admitted he was just twenty-five. Meh. What's a ten-year age difference anyway? He still ended up in my room because, well, *when in Ireland.* And although his accent was so thick I could barely understand him, we laughed, we lived, and we had the time of our damn lives.

So much fun, in fact, that before flying back to the States, I got "when in Ireland" tattooed on my left arm in the Irish language — a phrase that became the retreat's official motto. But as I sat with him at 7 a.m., looking like last night's party in human form while he waited for his taxi, he shared his story. He worked brutal hours, commuting two hours each way for a paycheck of just two thousand sterling (about $2,500 USD) a month. With a tired shrug, he sighed, "That'll be my life, just getting by, but what can you do?"

And in that moment, it hit me like a freight train. This wasn't just his story, this was the silent epidemic of *settling.* The quiet resignation that convinces people life is something to *endure* rather than something they have the power to change.

And you know what? He was right — *unless* he chose to believe otherwise. His life would remain exactly as he expected because belief shapes reality, and belief is *that* powerful.

Your belief, or lack of it, is the engine powering your life. Whether you're accelerating toward success, stuck idling in the same struggles, or sliding into reverse, your beliefs (conscious or unconscious) are behind the wheel, steering your destiny.

For example: If you're living paycheck to paycheck, you might secretly believe you're only worth "just enough" to survive. Your thoughts will reflect that belief, and your actions (or inaction) will create a reality that reinforces it.

The good news? You can flip the script.

HERE'S THE BOTTOM LINE:

If you want to create wealth, abundance, and freedom, you've got to believe in yourself. Fiercely. Boldly. Unapologetically.

We've all seen people with insane talent but zero confidence fizzle out before they even start. On the flip side, we've seen people with average skills but *unshakable belief* crush it.

A Rich B$tch believes in herself.

The most common limiting belief I see when someone asks, "Do you believe in me?" is this deeply ingrained, unconscious thought:

"Success can happen for her, but it can't happen for me."

Let's break it down. It's so much easier to believe someone else can have it all — be something, do something, create their dream life, find the one, change their circumstances, manifest their desires — than to believe you can.

At the root of it, your inner dialogue boils down to one of two stories:

1. *It can happen for her, but not for me.*
2. *If she can do it, I can do it too.*

Let me tell you something. When you choose to believe in yourself — and I'm not talking about some halfhearted, lukewarm belief, but that fierce, full-bodied certainty — you become unstoppable. You transform into a woman who makes extraordinary things happen.

And here's the magic! People notice when you step into that energy. They're drawn to you like a magnet. Do you know why? Because a woman in her power, who's unapologetically turned on by her own life, is radiant. She's irresistible.

Belief is energy. And not just any energy, a potent, magnetic force. And energy doesn't lie. You can't fake it. It just is.

Think about it. You've been around someone oozing frustration or irritation. They don't have to say a word, yet you feel it. The same goes for a woman who believes in herself. Her energy speaks volumes without her saying a damn thing.

Whether you realize it or not, you have an energetic signature. That energy defines how you show up in the world.

To achieve greatness — against all odds — and create the rich, extraordinary life you desire, you need sustained belief. This isn't just about fleeting confidence, it's about unwavering, soul-deep conviction.

Confidence is magnetic. When someone fully believes in themselves, it's a reminder of what's possible for the rest of us. Their success whispers "If she can do it, I can do it too."

That's why people gravitate toward someone who embodies belief. Their energy is electric, inspiring, and contagious. If you're a coach or a leader, this is why people will want to work with you. They sense your belief and want to tap into it for themselves.

This is the magic of proximity — being around people who are thriving naturally expands your own potential. On the flip side, surrounding yourself with people who are stuck in their limitations will shrink your energy.

Belief is contagious. A Rich B$tch knows this and embodies it. She speaks and acts with certainty. She doesn't ask for permission or wait for validation. She sure as hell doesn't need anyone else to believe in her — she's got that handled.

Her bold actions don't just create results, they make a statement. To those sitting on the sidelines playing it safe, she says, "Watch me."

And let's be clear! Anyone criticizing her will only ever do so from the sidelines.

When you believe in yourself, you don't just change your life, you break generational patterns. You become the energetic match for wealth, success, and freedom. And in doing so, you serve the collective by showing others what's possible.

This isn't just about wealth. It's about the ripple effect of standing in your power. It's about showing up, speaking up, and shining so bright that you give others permission to do the same.

Believe in yourself, then watch the entire world shift to meet your power.

Here's a powerful example of how belief, or the lack of it, determines success:

In winter 2021, I had two women invest in private mentorship with me at the same time. They couldn't have been more different. One client, in her late twenties, had all the outward advantages: a polished website, experience running an online business, and a sizable social media following. The other, in her fifties, was starting from scratch. She had no website, no branding, a minimal social media presence, and limited tech knowledge.

On the surface, most people would assume my younger client had the upper hand. But here's where things got interesting.

Despite her lack of resources, my older client had something far more powerful than a polished online presence: She had unshakable belief. She trusted in her ability to succeed, no matter what.

My younger client, on the other hand, struggled to embody that same belief. She was caught up in doubt, questioning every move despite the tools and experience she already had.

Let me tell you this: The foundation of success isn't built on websites or followers, it's built on belief — the Rich B$tch kind of belief.

When my older client started mentorship, she confidently declared, "I'm going to make a f*ck ton of money during our time together." And guess what? She did exactly that.

In just six weeks, she earned $24,000 — without a website, without ads, without overcomplicating it. How? She embodied the B in Rich B$tch: absolute belief in herself. She knew she could manifest and create whatever the f*ck she wanted, and that energy paved the way for her success.

Meanwhile, despite all her external advantages, my younger client struggled to make the same progress because she was stuck in lack — doubting her worth, offers, and ability to succeed.

This is a common trap in the online coaching world. So many women create from lack, basing their offers on what they think people will or won't buy, pay, or invest in. They shape their prices and programs around others' perceived limitations instead of their own soul alignment.

I teach my clients to do the opposite. I show them how to create from desire, not from lack or fear. Pricing your offers from a place of belief, based on what *you* want, is where the magic happens.

My older client did exactly that. She released a group program that lit her soul on fire. It was fun, exciting, and liberating. Her business became an extension of her magic, her zone of genius. She wasn't worrying about who would join or whether people would invest. She was too busy celebrating how much she *loved* her offer. She embodied the energy of success before she had the results, and the results followed.

Her success wasn't a fluke. It was the direct result of declaring her vision, believing in it fully, and creating from a place of joy and alignment. She wasn't chasing success, it was chasing her. And when you believe in yourself like that — when you embody the energy of already having what you desire — you don't just create results, you create results that feel effortless.

Belief isn't just an ingredient in success, it's the whole damn recipe.

What's stopping you from embodying that kind of belief today? What offer, decision, or dream would you finally say yes to if you trusted yourself fully?

The Rich B$tch way is simple: Declare it done. Believe it's yours. Take intuitive action. And watch the magic unfold.

$$$

Rich B$tch Homework: Work on Your Belief

- If you fully believed in yourself, what would you say yes (or no) to?
- What actions would you take that you've been avoiding?
- How would it feel to no longer need validation or permission?
- How would you show up if you already had everything you desire?

Now take a moment. Place one hand on your heart and the other on your belly. Breathe deeply and slowly. Feel into your body and tell yourself: "I believe in you."

Don't just say it, feel it. Let it sink in. Repeat it over and over until it becomes your truth.

Next, create a mantra and commit to it for yourself. Here's an example: "I am an energetic match to wealth and abundance. The more I believe in myself, the more unstoppable I become."

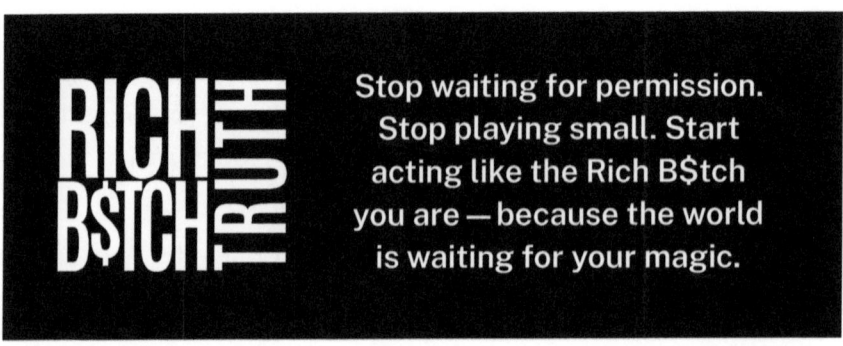

RICH B$TCH TRUTH

Stop waiting for permission. Stop playing small. Start acting like the Rich B$tch you are — because the world is waiting for your magic.

CHAPTER
SEVEN

CHAPTER 7: A RICH B$TCH INVESTS IN HERSELF

There's no Shaman named Becky, no healer deep in the jungle, no Guru clutching crystals, and no Ayahuasca ceremony that will magically compensate for a lack of wealth or self-love. Rich B$tch work demands daily devotion — a relentless commitment to recognizing and healing your negative, limiting beliefs and reframing them every single motherf*cking time they arise.

Rich B$tch work is not for the faint of heart. It's far easier to remain in unconscious belief, avoiding the discomfort of confronting how toxic our self-talk, beliefs, and projections have become.

You are the most significant nonnegotiable investment you will ever make in this life. Until you recognize your worthiness and the power of your truth, you will continue "investing" in a negative bank account of self-doubt and limitation.

The I in RICH B$TCH stands for Invest.

Investing in yourself is not a one-time decision, it's an ongoing choice. It's an initiation into living the life of a Rich B$tch, a declaration that you are ready to rise above scarcity and mediocrity. It's time to love yourself enough to bet on you.

It's also time to release the people you wanted to believe in you (like your parents or others you sought validation from) who couldn't or wouldn't. **This journey is about you choosing you.** It's about investing in yourself as the foundation of your Rich B$tch future. Two nonnegotiable investments I made that helped me rise out of debt and create a seven-figure business were:

1. Time
2. Money

Let's start with money.

In 2017, after years of seeing clients in an office and charging $70 an hour, I decided to pivot and create an online coaching business. With nothing but determination and good old Google to guide me, I stepped into the unknown. At the time, I was fresh out of a divorce and flat-out broke. Not "a little tight on cash" broke, I'm talking "say a Hail Mary before you check your bank account" broke.

Here's what that looked like:

- My mom stepping in to help cover my monthly mortgage.
- A pile of unopened bills sitting on the counter, each one a trigger for panic attacks.
- Grocery shopping that felt more like a battlefield than a routine errand, where I regularly returned items to the shelf because I couldn't afford to keep everything in my cart.

I lived in a constant state of survival, trying to catch my breath while simultaneously trying to build something out of nothing. It was stressful, humbling, and at times, defeating.

But it was also the exact fire that forged my transformation.

I was quickly sliding deeper into debt, and the weight of it was dragging me into depression.

After two years of trying to get my online coaching business off the ground by myself, I had little to show for it: no new clients, barely any income, and an all-too-easy trigger response whenever I saw other women celebrating their business wins and six-figure months. I *knew* that if it was possible for them, it was possible for me. Yet no matter what I tried, nothing seemed to work.

Frustrated and exhausted, I began analyzing the successful coaches I admired, trying to distill what they had in common. The answer was glaringly obvious: **They all invested in themselves.**

And here's the commonality among them — they openly shared making those investments when they "didn't have the money."

I get it — investing in yourself when you feel financially strapped can be *triggering*. But here's the hard truth: Waiting for the perfect moment or for excess money to magically appear isn't exactly the path forward. At least for me it never was.

There's a reason Tony Robbins famously said, "It's not the lack of resources; it's your lack of resourcefulness that stops you."

Maybe you don't have piles of extra cash lying around right now. That's okay. **Resourcefulness doesn't mean you wait, it means you create.**

Here's an example to drive it home: I once heard about someone who sold their car just to use the money to invest in their dreams. Extreme? Sure. But they chose their future over their current comfort.

Investing isn't just about money, it's about committing to your growth, your vision, and your potential. It's about making the bold decision to bet on *yourself*.

Now, I'm not suggesting you sell your car, but I *am* saying there's always a way forward if you're willing to get resourceful and see what's available. Infinite potentials exist, but you have to move beyond your doubt and limiting beliefs to uncover them. As I often tell my clients, when it feels like every door is closed, you're likely overlooking the one that's waiting to open.

I began to see investing as more than just a transaction. It became an initiation, a challenge disguised as an opportunity to lean into growth, trust my intuition, and step into my next level.

Most people don't trust their intuition enough to act on it, especially when it comes to money. They overanalyze, rationalize, or doubt themselves right out of expansion.

But when you break it down, investing isn't about the exact dollar amount or the specific thing you invest in, it's about believing in yourself enough to take that leap — it's about releasing money with trust and the knowledge that it's not just an expense but an act of self-faith. It's about standing in the power of who you are now — capable, worthy, and ready — and trusting in the person you're becoming: the one who has already manifested the desires you're working toward.

Here's the key difference between those who create extraordinary results and those who don't:

- They're willing to observe what's holding them back.
- They trust their inner voice over their fears.
- They take inspired action on that guidance without hesitation.

This work is for the bold. It's for you, if you choose to lean in.

You're an energetic match to the moves you make.

Your current reality doesn't lie — it's a direct reflection of the choices you've made, the energy you've embodied, and the actions you've taken (or avoided).

So, ask yourself:

- What do I truly desire?
- What am I doing to bring it into existence?
- Most importantly, **who am I *being*** in the process?

Are you stuck on the hamster wheel of old patterns, repeating the same behaviors and expecting different results? Or are you stepping boldly into the unknown, navigating the discomfort of growth, self-regulating through uncertainty, and trusting your intuition to guide you toward your next-level self?

You cannot create a new reality by staying in the energy of your old one.

$$$

SIDENOTE FOR ENTREPRENEURS: If you're unwilling to invest in yourself or your business, how can you expect your clients to do so with you? We lead by example. We go first. If you want others to say yes to you, you have to show them what saying yes to yourself looks like.

$$$

Rich B$tch moves demand courage, faith, and aligned action. Your desires are already available to you. Are you ready to rise to meet them? Waiting for someone else to choose you is a losing game — it keeps your worth tied to external validation. That's not the Rich B$tch way.

Choose yourself first. Choose your dreams, your growth, your abundance, your joy. When you decide you are worthy, everything else aligns.

The world reflects how you treat yourself. When you claim your desires unapologetically and move with conviction, you radiate the energy that draws in the people, opportunities, and experiences meant for you.

You are the first and most important "yes" in your life. The rest will follow.

When you invest your hard-earned money into something that truly matters, it transforms how you show up. You approach it with a deeper commitment and a heightened sense of responsibility because you've made it personal.

Think about it. How many free courses or webinars have you signed up for and abandoned halfway through? Probably more than you'd like to admit. Now, imagine investing $20,000 instead of $100. Imagine that money came from your own pocket, not borrowed. You'd be all in, wouldn't you?

It's not that the resources aren't there. You could hit YouTube, grab books at the library, or ask local entrepreneurs for advice. All of it is free or low cost. So, the question is: **Why aren't you where you want to be yet?**

I'm not saying you *can't* do it on your own — you absolutely can. But the truth is, investing in yourself isn't just about learning new strategies or gaining access to a mentor, it's a symbolic act. It's the moment you declare: "I am worthy. I am capable. I am ready."

Investing is an initiation. It's the beginning of a new chapter. It's you saying goodbye to the story of "It works for her, but not for me," and hello to "It's my time now."

So, ask yourself: What am I waiting for?

In 2019, my journey into true success began. I had reached a tipping point when the fear of my business staying stuck outweighed the fear of my bank account going into the red. That realization led me to take a bold leap: investing in a coach who I believed could help me grow, even if it meant going back into debt to do so.

With three maxed-out credit cards, I made a $20,000 investment in private mentorship. Sure, I could have sought out a cheaper coach, but my intuition was clear: "He's the one." As wild as it seemed at the time, I trusted it.

The weeks that followed were a whirlwind as I worked to regulate my nervous system — it wasn't a familiar experience then. But here's what I learned: We have the power to self-regulate and find our center, even as we take bold, Rich B$tch moves. It's part of the process, part of the initiation.

As I worked to overcome my self-imposed limitations, I wasn't waiting to feel good enough, or ready, or for some external proof that success was guaranteed. Instead, I stepped into the identity of someone already successful. I acted in alignment with my new belief, consciously creating the business of my dreams in real time.

Here's the epiphany that changed everything: **You're never truly "ready." You're either willing or you're not.**

If you're serious about becoming a Rich B$tch, waiting is no longer an option. Look around: How far has waiting gotten you?

Yes, I was fearful before and after making my first significant investment. Like most people, I rode the emotional roller coaster of doubt, excitement, and everything in between. But beneath it all, I was hopeful. Despite the uncertainty, something about it felt innately aligned, a soul-level "yes" that was impossible to ignore.

And yes, my friends and family thought I was crazy. But "crazy" is a compliment. It's a sign that you're breaking free from the confines of what society tells you is "normal." When someone calls you crazy for the bold, Rich B$tch moves you're making, take it as confirmation that you're on the right path, stepping into a life far beyond the matrix of mediocrity.

Also, do yourself a massive favor: Keep your bold, daring moves to yourself unless you're sharing them with someone just as audacious and visionary as you are. Speaking from experience, opening up to those who haven't tapped into their own inner courage or abundance mindset often invites the projections of their fears and limitations. If you're not hyper-aware, their doubts can infiltrate your energy, leaving you second-guessing your intuitive "yes." Worse, it could cause you to back out of what you know is your highest truth — and for an empath like me, that's a hard no.

Most people, even those closest to you, won't fully grasp your dreams. They likely won't have the capacity to support you in the ways you deeply crave or need, especially if they haven't done the inner work to liberate themselves. But a Rich B$tch? She doesn't let that stop her. When her internal compass points toward expansion, she doesn't require validation, approval, or permission. She trusts herself. She says yes. And she moves forward — fearlessly.

When I invested $20,000 in my mentor, I quickly realized he handed me the exact steps he had used to scale his business into a multiple seven-figure empire. The blueprint was right there, laid out perfectly. But all that knowledge, strategy, and insight wouldn't mean a damn thing unless I worked on my **internal beliefs** — about myself, about money, and about what I was truly worthy of receiving.

This brings us to the second, equally critical investment: **Time.**

Time may not cost you a dime, but it is the most valuable asset you have. It's the currency you trade daily to create the life you desire. If you're serious about becoming the energetic match to wealth, **investing your time in Rich B$tch work is nonnegotiable.**

Now, let me drop this truth bomb about wealth: Your external wealth is a mirror. It reflects your self-worth, your self-love, and your frequency. When you commit your time to do this work — uncovering limiting beliefs, dismantling old stories, and stepping into elevated emotions — you'll notice the external world start to match your inner transformation.

You want wealth? **Start by investing in your internal reality.** That's where the magic begins.

According to the National Endowment for Financial Education, a staggering 70 percent of lottery winners end up broke, and a third eventually declare bankruptcy. While many factors contribute to this outcome, one truth stands out: If you make or suddenly come into a large sum of money, yet your money mindset is stuck in lack, negativity, or fear, that money will vanish faster than it appeared.

And there it is — the real battle you're facing. Not external circumstances, not even money itself, but the part of you that resists stepping into your greatness, the part that delays, doubts, or dismisses your desire for an abundant life, keeping it on the back burner.

It takes awareness — and let's be real: guts — to uncover the thoughts, beliefs, and patterns you've been operating from that continue to hold you back. The moment you confront that internal resistance and choose to do the work, you'll stop money from being fleeting and start becoming the energetic match to wealth that flows effortlessly.

Abundance begins where resistance ends.

Belief in yourself might seem complicated, but it doesn't have to be. Humans are creatures of habit, shaped by their environment, upbringing, and the social norms of the circles they move within. Look around your life, and you'll likely notice patterns: you spend your days in similar ways, your thoughts are often repetitive, and much of your belief system is inherited from your childhood, society, and the people with whom you surround yourself. Want proof? Bring up a topic like politics, sports, religion, or anything remotely controversial, and watch how quickly someone agrees or disagrees with you. It's a reflection of the conditioning that runs so deeply that we often mistake it for our truth.

You must invest time in reconditioning your belief system and creating new patterns of thought and routines that empower you. This isn't just a nice-to-have, it's a nonnegotiable if you want lasting success and abundance. The payoff for this work is life-changing, not just in the short term but for your future self.

Why? Because if you don't take the time to reprogram your mind and beliefs, you might achieve what you think you want — like a sudden influx of money — only to find it slipping through your fingers. Why? Because psychologically, physically, and energetically, you won't feel comfortable holding on to it. You'll unconsciously sabotage what you've worked so hard to gain because the foundation of your beliefs hasn't caught up with your desires.

The work isn't just about creating wealth or success, it's about **becoming the person who can sustain and grow it.**

Let's break it down. Imagine a woman who's spent her life in toxic relationships. Then, one day, she finds herself in a healthy one. What happens? She unconsciously sabotages it — not because she doesn't want happiness, but because it feels so unfamiliar, so far outside her norm, that she doesn't know how to act or even think within it. It's not aligned with her current identity.

Or consider the friend who always seems to attract the "bad guy" — the one who cheats, lies, and breaks her heart repeatedly. Despite saying she wants true love and happiness, she keeps ending up in the same situation. Why? Because drama, betrayal, and toxicity are what she knows. They're her *normal.* Unconsciously, she's more comfortable with chaos than peace, more at ease with heartbreak than genuine love. This isn't because she doesn't want love, it's because her patterns, beliefs, and energy don't align with receiving it. Her identity, rooted in false beliefs like *I'm not worth it, I don't deserve love,* or *I'll always be hurt* continues to attract what reinforces those beliefs.

Why does this happen? Because, healthy or not, the familiar feels safe. The familiar is predictable. And if she can predict it, she feels a false sense of control, and even when that "control" guarantees heartbreak, it feels less terrifying than stepping into the unknown.

It's a self-fulfilling cycle. Her beliefs shape her reality. The drama, betrayal, and toxicity become proof that her limiting beliefs are true. Breaking that cycle requires the courage to step out of the familiar and consciously choose a new identity, one rooted in worthiness, self-love, and the belief that she is capable of and deserving of more.

If lack has been your normal, the idea of abundance may feel unsafe, even if it's what you consciously say you want. This is especially true if you've spent years living paycheck to paycheck, operating in survival mode, or growing up in a household where scarcity was the baseline belief system. Statements like "Money doesn't grow on trees," "Take the job for the health insurance," or "Wealthy people are bad" may have shaped your understanding of money and kept you tethered to an outdated paradigm. Let's call it what it is: old, limiting programming.

Why does this happen?

Because your external life reflects your internal beliefs. Sit with that. Really let it land.

Now, say this out loud: "What I see and experience in the outside world mirrors what I think and feel about myself."

You don't attract what you want through wishful thinking alone, you attract it by *who you are being.*

If your internal state is:

- **Financially broke**, your bank account and lifestyle will align with that energy.
- **Unlovable**, your relationships will mirror that belief by draining you, being imbalanced, or never quite meeting your needs. You might even unconsciously push love away.
- **A victim**, your life will feel like a series of never-ending challenges, and the blame will always lie outside of you.

$$\$\$\$$$

AN IMPORTANT SIDENOTE: If you're a victim of abuse, this isn't about blaming you for someone else's harmful actions. Seeking help and support from trusted authorities, friends, or shelters is one of the bravest and most self-loving actions you can take. There is no shame in reaching out, and you deserve safety, respect, and healing.

$$\$\$\$$$

Back to self-limiting beliefs.

It's important to understand that breaking free of these patterns takes *time and commitment*. After all, you didn't become who you are overnight — you've spent years unknowingly rehearsing these beliefs and behaviors.

In fact, Dr. Joe Dispenza claimed in his book *Breaking the Habit of Being Yourself* (Hay House, 2013) that nearly 100 percent of who we are by the age of thirty-five is determined by our beliefs, emotions, and other characteristics that work together to form our identity.

In other words, the 5 percent of your conscious mind that wants to change is working against the 95 percent of your subconscious programming. Do the math — that's a massive uphill battle.

The good news? You have the power to change the equation. It starts with the daily choice to commit to your growth and invest in becoming the Rich B$tch version of yourself. It's not easy, but it's worth it. The life you're working toward is closer than you think — it just requires consistency, courage, and a willingness to rewire those beliefs one day at a time.

If you can memorize lack, you can unlearn it. And if you can unlearn it, you can embody abundance.

The manifestation of your dreams demands time, focus, and deliberate investment. It's not optional, it's essential.

Here's why: Your ego's primary role is self-preservation, which means it's hardwired to focus on fear. Fear doesn't quietly knock and wait for you to notice it, it demands your attention, takes center stage, and shouts louder than your desires ever will. Because of this, your dreams often feel like they're competing with fear for space in your mind and energy.

Fear thrives on instinct. It's immediate, reactive, and persistent. Your desires, on the other hand, require intention, presence, and commitment. They ask you to pause, trust, and move beyond fear's grasp, which is exactly why your Rich B$tch future self demands *ongoing* investment of time, energy, and focus.

The formula is simple: High-vibrational energy, thoughts, and aligned actions = the manifestation of abundance, wealth, and your desires.

By consistently investing in restructuring your beliefs, elevating your thoughts, and making bold moves that align with the life you want to create, you become the embodiment of your future Rich B$tch self. And when you embody her — fully, unapologetically — she's no longer competing for space in your life. She *is* your life. You are no longer separate from the wealth, freedom, and joy you desire, you *are* the energy that creates it.

Your job? Choose her daily. Align with her fiercely. Let her lead.

$$$

Rich B$tch Homework: Invest in Your Future

1. **WHAT INVESTMENT HAVE YOU BEEN DELAYING?**
   - Is there a program you've been dreaming of joining?
   - A trip that keeps calling your name?
   - A luxury item like a handbag or jewelry that makes your heart skip a beat?

2. **ACTION**

   Invest in yourself today, and let it feel lighthearted and exciting. This doesn't have to break the bank — it could mean:

   - Setting aside $5 with a commitment to add to it weekly.
   - Scheduling a manicure or spa day, even if that's new for you.
   - Taking a walk while daydreaming about the ways you'll invest and grow your money.

   The point is to act. Show the Universe, and yourself, that you're prioritizing YOU.

3. WHO OR WHAT WOULD YOU JOYFULLY SPEND MONEY ON?

Let your imagination run wild here. Pretend you've just hit the jackpot. Write down five ways or people you'd lovingly, joyfully, and gratefully release your money to:

- Would you buy your parents a house?
- Donate to your favorite charity?
- Splurge on a dream car or wardrobe?
- Build a business?
- Host a retreat for your favorite people?

Go all out. Feel the joy of releasing money with intention and excitement.

4. DAILY DEVOTION TO INVESTING IN YOURSELF

Ask yourself:

- What would it take to invest in myself daily?
- What habits, rituals, or routines could I create that affirm my worthiness?
- What limiting beliefs am I holding on to, and how can I lovingly reframe them into empowering truths?

For example:

- Limiting belief: "I'll never have enough money to invest in the things I love."
- Reframe: "I am an abundant creator, and I always find ways to prioritize my desires and growth."

RICH B$TCH TRUTH

Make investing in yourself a daily habit, whether it's time, money, or energy. If you're not willing to invest in yourself, why should the Universe? Money, time, energy — put them where your future is, not where your fears are. A Rich B$tch doesn't wait for change — she funds it, fuels it, and becomes it.

CHAPTER
EIGHT

RICH
B$TCH MONEY GOALS

CHAPTER 8: A RICH B$TCH TRUSTS HERSELF

Trusting your intuition over logic isn't optional, it's the gateway to embodying your Rich B$tch future.

At some point, you've been hit with a million-dollar idea — probably more than one! Whether inventing the next big thing, launching a podcast, writing a book, creating an app, solving a problem, or boldly saying yes to something wild and exciting, it wasn't just a random thought. It was your intuition throwing glitter bombs of genius your way.

So, where's the problem?

You didn't trust yourself enough to follow through on your million-dollar idea, or you handed over your power by seeking validation from someone else — and let them talk you out of it (hello, self-doubt). Maybe you ignored your idea so many times that your intuition lost its charge, and now you struggle to recognize when it's calling. Or worse, maybe you gaslit yourself into thinking it wasn't your intuition at all, leaving you stuck in a loop of fear and regret.

Do you resonate with this?

If your answer is yes, let's acknowledge how powerful it is that you're here, investing your time and energy into learning to become the energetic match to wealth through the Rich B$tch principles. Divine timing is never random, and the fact that you're moving through these lessons right now is no coincidence. You are already aligned with the possibilities laid out in this work. Let's lean in and trust that truth.

Let me share a story about trusting intuition and watching it pay off.

In November 2021, I opened enrollment for my first-ever year-long program: The Abundant Woman Project. I did something radically different: I announced it with minimal details on my social media channels. No flashy landing page, no exhaustive bullet-point list breaking down what participants would get. This approach flew in the face of what was considered "best practice" in the online coaching industry. At the time, releasing a high-ticket program this way was not just unconventional but unheard of and definitely not recommended.

Logically, I understood why the industry leaned heavily on structured launches and detailed outlines, just as I'm sure you do. But my intuition? It was pulling me in a completely different direction.

I felt guided to go against common practice, even when logic whispered caution. And if you've been in my world for a while, you already know I'm relentless about one principle: **intuition over logic, always.**

This was one of those pivotal moments when intuition became the loudest voice in the room — and I decided to trust it.

I intuitively *knew* The Abundant Woman Project would be a $10K investment. I knew how many group calls would happen each month, and I had absolute clarity that the women who joined would experience profound transformations in their businesses. But there was a catch: for this to happen, they had to make the bold move — the leap of faith — to trust the year-long process.

Beyond that, I didn't have a master plan, I only knew that more details would reveal themselves to me over time. The guidance I was receiving was crystal clear: trust the desire I felt and release the program in a way that aligned deeply with me, even if it defied conventional wisdom.

I didn't want to convince anyone to invest $10K by over-explaining why they *should*. That's the old paradigm of sales — a belief system rooted in convincing, justifying, and over-proving. Instead, I trusted that the right women would feel the intuitive pull and say yes without needing to be sold on the details.

As I sat down to script a post, logic tried to intervene, but the stress and resistance I felt in my body were undeniable. My intuition wasn't having it, and I couldn't come up with anything to say that felt true. That's when I realized this process would only succeed if I led from trust, not tactics.

Remember, your business is an extension of who you're being — a direct reflection of your energy. Creating from a "turned-off" frequency, one filled with resistance, stress, or obligation, is the *opposite* of the Rich B$tch vibe. Your body is your most powerful guide, so when it's giving you a full-body "no," trust it completely. That "no" is your inner wisdom protecting your alignment. Listen, pivot, and only create from your highest truth.

When I closed my eyes and meditated on how to release The Abundant Woman Project, clarity struck like lightning: publish a simple post and go live to speak directly from my heart. I envisioned this as more than just an offer — it was an invitation for women to trust their intuition as deeply as I was trusting mine. Immediately, I felt a surge of alignment and excitement.

I was being called to lead by example, anchoring myself in intuitive trust and holding space for others to rise into that same energy. This wasn't just strategy, it was the law of attraction at its finest — pure alignment with my highest truth.

Let's also highlight the B in B$tch: Belief. I believed with every fiber of my being in myself and The Abundant Woman Project. It wasn't just a program, it was an energetic extension of my essence. There was no resistance to the $10K investment, no doubt about releasing it without a landing page, and no question in my mind that the right women would feel the call, invest boldly, and transform. This is the magnetic power of belief in action.

Furthermore, I knew intuitively that the collective energy of the women who joined The Abundant Woman Project would shape and amplify the experience. Trying to map out a rigid, month-by-month plan ahead of time would have been entirely misaligned. This program was designed to flow with the unique energies and needs of the group, not to conform to a pre-set structure.

I trusted that our collective energies would organically guide us exactly where we needed to go, and I knew this truth deep in my core. By releasing the need to plan every detail meticulously, I embraced divine timing and leaned into the magic of intuitive creation.

One of the ways I activate transformation in those who step into my world is by creating opportunities — portals, if you will — that call them to trust their intuition deeply. These are not ordinary offers. Women have said yes to investing thousands of dollars without knowing every detail, relying solely on their inner guidance. The most extraordinary? A woman claimed my $47K "trust offer." She had no idea what she was signing up for except two VIP days with me. Beyond that, all she knew was the price and her deep calling to say yes. She moved in perfect rhythm with her intuition.

Is this uncommon? Absolutely. But that's the point.

These offers aren't about comfort or convention, they're about breaking through the layers of doubt, overthinking, and fear that keep you disconnected from your body, heart, and inner knowing. They serve as a mirror, reflecting your capacity to trust yourself in ways that society has conditioned you to ignore.

Not everyone will feel ready to claim these offers — they'll feel too vulnerable, uncomfortable, or unaligned. That's okay. I fully understand that much of the world continues to deny its own intuition, staying locked in logic and fear. But for those who say yes, the experience is life-altering. It's a reclamation of self-trust and a profound alignment with their highest truth.

While I offer plenty of detailed programs and offers, my trust offers, and the way I sell them, are intentionally designed to call women forward in a unique way. They encourage you to go inward for the answer instead of relying on logic or waiting to be convinced by a traditional sales page or pitch. This approach isn't about external validation or persuasion, it's an invitation for you to reconnect with your own inner knowing.

Your intuition speaks a language that only you can truly understand. It isn't meant to be dissected, debated, or weighed in on by anyone else. It's sacred. It's yours. And honoring it is the ultimate act of self-trust. When you listen and act from this place, you're not just making a choice, you're transforming your life.

The **T** in RICH B$TCH stands for **T**rust.

Trusting your intuition is a prerequisite to becoming a Rich B$tch.

When I announced my decision to release a $10K program without sharing detailed deliverables, several people were quick to tell me I was making a mistake. They insisted I should include a landing page — a place for women to "learn more." Their concerns were rooted in their belief that no one would sign up without a clear outline. But that was their reality, their truth, not mine.

Your conviction and belief in yourself will define these moments.

Thankfully, I wasn't swayed by their fear-based projections. Why? Because I trust myself. I trust my intuition completely, knowing it has *never* steered me wrong. It might lead me somewhere unexpected, but it's always for the highest good.

This isn't to say our friends and family are wrong to voice their concerns. Often, they communicate through their own fear filters, projecting their worries onto us. That's human. But this is where your discernment becomes vital.

Ultimately, your choices belong to you, whether or not others approve or support them. Trust yourself. Honor your path. Only *you* know what's aligned for your highest truth.

The bottom line? Your desires exist because they are meant to be realized. They are your compass, guiding you toward expansion when you boldly align with them.

When I envisioned The Abundant Woman Project, my desire was clear: to work with women who intuitively *knew* they were meant to be part of it, women who didn't need convincing, persuasion, or a checklist of deliverables to trust the pull.

Creating a sales page for those who needed to be "sold" would have attracted misaligned clients, women who didn't fully trust themselves or the process. That wasn't my vision. My desire was for alignment, trust, and the freedom to create from my fullest, most authentic self-expression. And because I led with that level of clarity and certainty, I attracted women ready to do the same. By trusting myself, I inspired them to trust their intuition. Whether they realized it or not, their *yes* to The Abundant Woman Project was also a profound *yes* to themselves — a declaration of their own worth and power.

Before I even released a landing page, The Abundant Woman Project closed six figures in sales.

This is the power of trust, alignment, and leading from your highest truth.

Trusting your intuition — your highest truth — always yields the greatest results.

To trust your intuition, you must first learn to tune in to how it speaks to you. Let's explore how to distinguish between your intuitive "yes" and your intuitive "no," as this is a common area of confusion for many. You're not alone in wondering about this — I get asked about it often. While the line between the two can feel subtle, the sensations they evoke are distinct when you learn to recognize them.

Intuition often guides you toward something that stirs both *excitement* and *uncertainty*. It's not a logical certainty but rather a visceral pull that feels alive in your body. Think of it as a "hell yes" that comes with butterflies in your stomach or a sense of being called forward, even if fear or doubt lingers about the unknown.

A hallmark of the intuitive yes is repetition. If an idea or desire keeps surfacing no matter how much you try to dismiss it, that's your inner knowing saying, *Pay attention. This is for you.*

You may hear yourself think or say:

- *YES, I want this, but I'm scared.*
- *YES, this feels right, but what if it doesn't work out?*

The fear and uncertainty don't cancel the *yes,* they simply reflect your awareness of stepping into something bigger than yourself. Trust that pull. The yes will guide you toward expansion, breaking you free from the ordinary and mundane.

By contrast, an intuitive "no" often feels like resistance, contraction, or heaviness in your body. It may appear as:

- A tightness in your chest.
- A sinking feeling in your stomach.
- A sense of dread or anxiety that won't subside.

Where your intuitive yes feels expansive and exciting despite the uncertainty, an intuitive no feels like a firm, immovable block. It's a firm, unshakable knowing that says, *This isn't for you.*

Trust your inner wisdom.

The key to honoring your intuition is allowing these sensations to guide you without overthinking. Logic often tries to override what your body and heart already know, but your intuition exists beyond the mind.

When you feel a "yes" stirring excitement within you, lean into it, even if the path ahead is unclear. Conversely, when you sense a "no," honor it, even if it defies conventional logic or expectations. Your intuition is always working for your highest good. The more you practice listening and trusting, the clearer its voice becomes and the easier it is to move in alignment with your truth.

An intuitive yes often comes with a side of fear — not because it's wrong, but because it's unfamiliar. Venturing into the unknown, where outcomes aren't guaranteed, naturally triggers discomfort. This is your nervous system reacting to uncharted territory, not a sign that you're making the wrong decision.

Lean into this truth: Discomfort is often the price of expansion. Your intuitive yes is a catalyst for growth, guiding you toward new opportunities and possibilities that stretch your limits. Feel the fear, acknowledge the uncertainty, and move forward anyway. Trust that your intuitive yes is the compass pointing you toward the next level of your Rich B$tch life.

An intuitive yes is a lightning bolt of truth, a powerful catalyst for transformation. You might not always have the words to articulate it, but you'll feel it deep in your core. It's the undeniable pull toward something greater, a nudge from your future self to step into expansion.

On the other hand, an intuitive no offers clarity wrapped in relief. It's the unmistakable exhale of freedom when you release a misaligned opportunity, trusting that it wasn't meant for your path.

Both are gifts — one propels you forward, the other protects your alignment. Listen to them both.

Let me tell you about a time my intuitive no came through loud and clear — only for me to ignore it completely. Spoiler alert: It ended in a dating disaster and with the cops driving me home. Buckle up; it's a juicy one.

Ignoring your intuition isn't just about the lesson you *will* learn, it's about the drama you might accidentally create along the way. Trust me, I learned the hard way, and by the end of the night, I had an epic story, a clear message from the Universe, and a ride in a police car to seal the deal.

Sometimes life gives you loud, flashing neon signs to say no, and when you override them? Well, let's just say the Universe doesn't mess around.

In true Rich B$tch fashion, I decided to get the windows tinted on my SUV — a little upgrade to match my vibe. When I walked into the local detailing shop, I was greeted by a ridiculously handsome employee. No wedding ring? Check. Friendly? Double check. Let's just say the conversation flowed as easily as the service.

Later, I received a text that my SUV was ready for pickup. Innocent enough, right? Wrong. That single text turned into a flirty back-and-forth exchange, and before I knew it, the handsome employee was inviting me to Chicago for the weekend. He'd be traveling there to deliver a Porsche he was selling, and apparently, he wanted some company.

Naturally, I did my due diligence and asked about his relationship status. Single, he confirmed, and so the texting continued. Now, let me be clear: The idea of spontaneously driving to Chicago with someone I hardly knew? Crazy. But a little part of me was tempted.

Here's where the story takes a turn. As I entertained the idea, a subtle discomfort began to creep into my body. It wasn't loud or obvious, but it was there — a quiet yet undeniable feeling. That's the power of an intuitive no. I couldn't explain it logically, and there was no concrete reason to say no, but the fact that my body was sending even the faintest signal of hesitation told me everything

I needed to make a decision. Sometimes the slightest discomfort is your intuition waving a red flag, and you have to trust it, even if you can't rationalize it.

I decided Chicago wasn't happening — but I agreed to go on a date with him once he returned. Normally, this wouldn't even be up for debate. But I justified it. After all, we'd already met, he seemed reputable as an employee at an established business, and — let's be honest — he already had my address. Against my usual instincts, I let him pick me up.

He kept the destination a mystery, which I initially thought was charming. But as we drove, something shifted. He took me further away from my city than expected, and a thought crept in: *Is he taking me out here so no one sees us together?*

That quiet discomfort from before was now growing louder. My body tensed, and my intuition went off: *Something's not right.* And yet, I dismissed the signs again and again. Why? Because the logical mind can be a master manipulator, convincing you to override your instincts. But let me tell you, this is a crash course in why you should *never* ignore the voice of your intuition.

The moment we arrived at our destination, I tried to shake off the uneasiness. There were enjoyable moments, sure, but something still felt . . . off. I couldn't quite put my finger on it, but the tension in my body told me it was real.

After a final round of pool, he offered to grab dinner, but it was late, and I wanted to head home. Still, he insisted on ordering carryout so I'd have something to eat later. At that point, I was tired and ready for the night to end, but I agreed.

When we pulled up to the restaurant, he parked the truck and went inside to grab the food. A few minutes passed while I distracted myself with my phone. That's when it happened. The passenger door suddenly flung open with violent force. Before I could process what was happening, a woman started screaming at the top of her lungs.

"I'm his wife! Get the f*ck out of the car!"

And then — before I could even respond — she grabbed my head and slammed it against the interior.

By the time he ran back to the truck and pulled her off me, the chaos had spiraled into a full-blown nightmare. One minute I was watching him knock her to the ground with his fist, and the next, I was in *her* car, attempting to reason with her.

But reasoning wasn't on her agenda.

With her baby in the back seat and adrenaline clouding her judgment, she took off, declaring, "You're coming back to my house."

My discomfort quickly turned to alarm as I realized she was not thinking rationally. I demanded, "Pull over and let me out!" but she ignored me. As the tension escalated, I started planning to call 911, my heart racing, when I saw flashing lights in the rearview mirror.

*Thank f*cking God*, I thought as multiple police cars surrounded the vehicle and pulled us over.

Two officers approached, one on each side of the car, and forced her to roll down the passenger window. One shone a flashlight in my face and asked, "Are you all right?"

"No, I'm not all right!" I exclaimed without hesitation. "This woman assaulted me and practically kidnapped me!"

I explained the entire situation to the cops and showed the wife the texts where her husband had explicitly claimed to be single. I declined to press charges and felt a wave of relief when they drove me home.

Before the encounter ended, the cops turned to me with stern advice: "Next time, don't let someone pick you up from your home if you don't know them well."

Lesson learned, loud and clear.

This wasn't just about safety, it was a wake-up call about trusting my intuition and setting firm boundaries. Sometimes the Universe delivers the lesson dramatically, but the message remains the same: *Trust yourself.*

But the story didn't end there.

An hour later, the wife contacted me on social media. I chose to respond, and we ended up talking. I provided her again with proof of his texts where he claimed to be single, and she dropped a bombshell of her own: I was the *thirteenth* woman she had caught him cheating with.

Thirteenth.

Let's pause here and talk about something so many women wrestle with: the lack of belief in their worthiness to receive love of the highest kind. This woman had been repeatedly betrayed, yet she stayed, clinging to a relationship that diminished her.

Unhealthy relationships are a recurring pattern for many women, rooted in old stories, limiting beliefs, and fear of stepping into the unknown. It's heartbreaking and infuriating to witness — and yet, so f*cking common.

Ladies, let's be real: **Settling for less than you deserve is not the Rich B$tch vibe.** Healing starts with recognizing your worth and refusing to entertain anything less than extraordinary love, the kind that honors your heart, respects your soul, and matches your highest truth.

As I pointed out in Chapter 1, money alone doesn't make us wealthy, nor does it solve the deep-rooted issues we carry within ourselves.

This woman, who told me she was earning over $20K a month through her own business, clearly had the financial means to provide for herself. She was more than capable of leaving her abusive marriage should she choose to. But she stayed.

Why?

Because money isn't enough when our self-worth is in deficit.

Her continual choice to remain in this toxic relationship reflected her internal belief system — a belief that she isn't worthy of something better. And here's the harsh truth: **When we don't believe we are worthy, we unconsciously create a reality that confirms it.**

It's not the lack of money that holds us captive in these cycles, it's the lack of belief in ourselves. Until we confront and reprogram those self-limiting beliefs, no amount of money, success, or external validation will liberate us. You see, abundance starts from within. It's born from a deep sense of worthiness and self-love, the kind that no paycheck or bank balance can buy. When we don't believe we deserve better, life has a way of mirroring that belief right back to us, again and again, until we finally wake up and reclaim our power.

Real wealth is knowing your worth and building your life from that truth.

A Rich B$tch trusts herself.

An intuitive "no" can be a nuanced experience, even when your curiosity or excitement is piqued. It may surface as a physical discomfort: a churning in your stomach, sudden headaches, nausea, or a general feeling of unease. Perhaps you notice a loss of appetite, bowel changes, confusion, or a nagging irritation that doesn't dissipate until you realign with your intuitive "yes."

Distinguishing between an intuitive "yes" and "no" can feel overwhelming, particularly if self-trust isn't a muscle you've strengthened. Many of us have been conditioned to dismiss our inner knowing, silencing it to prioritize the comfort or validation of others. This practice leaves us disconnected from one of our most powerful guides: ourselves.

The more you listen to and honor your intuition, the more natural it becomes to trust its voice. It's a skill, one that requires intention and repetition. With each moment you say yes to what feels aligned and no to what doesn't, you reconnect with your power.

Your intuition *always* has your back. Learning to trust it is about undoing years of conditioning and choosing to believe in the wisdom of your inner compass.

Start this practice by paying attention to how you feel when faced with choices. The excitement of a "yes," even in the presence of uncertainty or fear, feels alive in your body. Meanwhile, a "no" often brings a sense of relief or an undeniable dissonance that's impossible to ignore.

Trusting yourself begins with noticing these sensations and clearly articulating your highest truth in every area of your life and business — because that's what a Rich B$tch does unapologetically.

Your intuitive yes is your soul's compass, a deep knowing that transcends logic and speaks directly to your essence. It may not align with what others deem practical, but to your feelings, it makes all the sense in the world. Your next level of leadership, your expansion into wealth, and your embodiment of power are all unlocked through honoring this truth. Your intuition isn't just a whisper, it's your ultimate Rich B$tch guide.

$$$

Rich B$tch Homework: Trust Your Intuition

1. **REFLECTION ON TRUST**
   - How does your current reality reflect your level of trust in yourself — or the absence of it?
   - Are you following your intuition (those inner nudges), or are you allowing the noise around you and internal fear to dictate your choices? Be honest.

2. **IDENTIFY YOUR INTUITIVE "YES"**
   - What excites you, brings you joy, and fills you with peace when you say yes?
   - Reflect on how your intuitive "yes" feels in your body. Is it lightness, ease, a sense of alignment?

3. **REVISIT PAST NUDGES**
   - Think back to moments when your intuition guided you with ideas. What were they?
   - Do you still feel those nudges? If so, why haven't you acted on them?

4. **ASSESS ALIGNMENT**
   - What changes must be made in your life and business to create alignment?
   - What no longer feels true, and what needs to shift for you to fully embody your highest truth?

5. **TAKE INSPIRED ACTION**
   Now that you've identified what needs to change to create alignment — and you know that your next level of leadership is rooted in trusting your intuition — ask yourself:
   - What action do I need to take right now that's rooted in trust?
   - How can I honor my intuition and highest truth starting today?

Your intuition is your built-in wealth strategy — trust it, move with it, and watch the Universe rearrange itself in your favor. A Rich B$tch doesn't second-guess; she decides, acts, and receives without apology.

CHAPTER NINE

RICH
B$TCH MONEY GOALS

CHAPTER 9: A RICH B$TCH CONSCIOUSLY CREATES HER LIFE

Consciously creating is vital to becoming an energetic match to wealth because it aligns your thoughts, emotions, and actions with abundance. When you create with intention and clarity, you shift from passively hoping for success to actively embodying the energy that attracts it.

One day, I came across an Instagram story from a well-known influencer mocking women who call themselves "conscious coaches." While I'd never use that title myself, the concept of "consciously creating" is far too important — imperative, even — to dismiss. In fact, it's what the "C" in my acronym B$TCH stands for because throughout my journey from drowning in debt to building a seven-figure business, consciously creating my reality, my business (and success) wasn't just a choice, it was nonnegotiable.

If you want to binge-watch *Bridgerton* on Netflix, you need Wi-Fi — or you're just staring at the loading screen, wondering if Lady Whistledown will ever spill the tea. The same goes for becoming an energetic match to wealth: you need clear intention and awareness to keep the signal strong and the energy flowing. Without consciously creating, your dreams are like a buffering episode: stuck in limbo, never fully coming to life. If you're not tuning into your vision, you're running on autopilot, stuck in outdated programming, while everyone else is already on the next season.

Today, I'm celebrating a conscious creator, the OG Rich B$tch herself — my mom — who's just as out of her mind as I am. You know the saying, "She got it from her mama." Well, when it comes to manifestation and making crazy moves, I certainly did.

Back in 2010, my mom put her house on the market at a price that completely defied her realtor's recommendation. The realtor, armed with "expert" advice about the location and comps, insisted the house wouldn't sell for her asking price and repeatedly pressured her to lower it.

But my mom? She's the kind of manifestation queen who doesn't buy into anyone else's limiting beliefs — expert or not. She knew her worth, trusted her intuition, and held an unshakable belief that the house would sell exactly as she envisioned. Not once did she waver.

That's the magic of a conscious creator — someone who sets the standard, trusts the process, and refuses to compromise their vision. My mom taught me that belief is the foundation of creation, and when you stand firm in what you know is possible, the Universe rises to meet you.

Before I go on, let me share a bit of history that worked in my favor. When I was in elementary school, my parents divorced, and some years later, my mom married an Irishman who deeply understood and practiced the principles of the law of attraction. Through him, my mom learned the art of aligning her energy with her desires, and not just as an idea but as a way of being.

She didn't just believe in these principles, she *embodied* them. She became a master of holding the energy of her desires as though they were already done. So, when it came to selling her house, she didn't just hope for the price she wanted, she energetically claimed it.

This is the perfect example of how the law of attraction works: When your energy is fully aligned with what you desire, the Universe moves to match it. My mom had already primed herself to receive that exact outcome, and of course, that's exactly what happened!

Before I understood what my mom was practicing, I used to think she was just lucky. But now I know luck had nothing to do with it — she was consciously creating her life. She chose her desires, acted "as if," and fully embodied the principles of a Rich B$tch by trusting her intuition and taking inspired action. Every time she had the opportunity to prove the power of thought and manifestation, she seized it. When her intuition nudged her, she didn't hesitate, she leaped.

One iconic example of her Rich B$tch energy happened while we were living in Ireland. Lyons Tea held a contest to give away a car to the person who came up with the best slogan. Naturally, my mom jumped in with absolute confidence and submitted her idea: "Tea so good, you can even drink and drive!"

You can probably guess how the story ends: she rolled into our driveway in a brand-new silver car. That's the power of aligned energy, trust, and a little humor to go with it! My mom taught me that life doesn't just happen to you, you consciously create it — one bold decision at a time.

How did my mom embody the energy and beliefs of a conscious creator? She knew what she wanted, trusted her intuition, and aligned her thoughts, feelings, and actions with the outcomes she desired. She didn't hope for things to happen, she believed, acted, and lived as though they were already done. She stayed focused, took daily action, and held unwavering faith in her ability to create the life she envisioned.

So, how do you embody the energy of a conscious creator? Start with clarity. To consciously create your life, you must first *know* what you truly desire — and that desire has to come from your heart, not your fear or external pressures.

To jump-start your awareness, ask yourself:

- What do I truly want in life?
- What can I change? (If you think you're confused, you're not. Confusion is an illusion. If I asked what you don't like about your current circumstances, you could list them all. You're just too focused on what you *don't* want instead of everything you *do*.)
- Am I actually prioritizing my goals? Or am I busy binge-watching Netflix and scrolling social media?

Your life isn't going to create itself. It's time to get honest, get clear, and get moving.

It would have been easy for my mom to defer to her realtor's advice and lower the price of her home, trusting the "expert" who presented hard data about the surrounding area. But that's not who my mom is. While the realtor may have been an expert in real estate, my mom is an expert in something far more powerful: consciously creating and calling her desires into existence.

To follow the realtor's advice would have been the "normal" thing to do, but anyone who knows my mom knows she's anything but ordinary. She doesn't settle for average outcomes, she creates extraordinary ones because she refuses to let outside opinions dictate her reality.

The truth is, if you're not embodying the principles of a Rich B$tch with confidence, clarity, and unwavering belief, you'll find yourself easily swayed when someone tells you that your dreams are impossible. And when that "someone" is a person of authority, like an expert or a professional, the temptation to shrink and give in becomes even stronger.

If you don't anchor yourself in your own belief and power, you'll fall prey to the fear and limitations others project onto you. But when you stand firm in your truth, like my mom, you create results that defy the ordinary.

The **C** in RICH B$TCH stands for **C**onsciously **C**reating.

Henry Ford once said, "Whether you think you can or think you can't — you're right." This timeless truth forces us to confront some powerful questions about belief, trust, and resilience:

- Can you trust yourself and believe in your ability to create your desires, even when others are rooting against you?
- Can you hold firm to your vision, rooted in unwavering energy, when the world tells you it can't be done?
- Can you act on your intuition when it challenges popular opinions or breaks from the crowd?
- How long can you hold your vision without surrendering to impatience, simply because it hasn't manifested as quickly as you wanted?
- And most importantly, how steadfast can you remain in trust before the whispers of doubt start to creep in?

Your ability to answer these questions with conviction determines whether you're living as a conscious creator or merely reacting to the world around you. True creation requires resilience, trust, and the audacity to believe in your vision when no one else does.

Holding your vision and mastering the ability to trust, act, and believe — despite doubt or external noise — is part of the work.

Beyond consciously creating your desires with clear intention, adding visual cues as daily reminders is a game-changer. These cues anchor you in the energy of "as if" your desire is already done. They're powerful tools for stepping into your future self — the version of you who has already manifested what you want.

For example, when I was drowning in debt, I had a vision of one hundred thousand dollars. That number felt exhilarating, liberating, and completely life-changing. Visualizing it wasn't just daydreaming, it was a way to start embodying the energy of abundance, even when my reality screamed otherwise.

This practice isn't about hoping, it's about becoming.

In 2016, I made a bold decision: I would consciously create $100K in my bank account. This wasn't a vague wish—I committed to making it real by starting and ending every day with visualization.

To anchor my intention, I grabbed a black Sharpie, added five zeros to a one-dollar bill, and transformed it into $100,000. I taped it to the ceiling above my bed so it was the first thing I saw every morning and the last thing I saw each night.

Every time I looked at that $100,000 bill, I moved into a state of excitement and gratitude, as if the money was already mine. I imagined grocery shopping without hesitation—no longer putting items back on the shelf, feeling the lightness of financial freedom and the thrill of overflow instead of lack.

For those moments, I wasn't broke—I was one hundred thousand dollars richer. I felt it. I embodied it. My imagination didn't just lift me out of my reality, it rewired it.

And now? That $100,000 is no longer a fake bill on my ceiling. It's a reality.

As the conscious creator of your life, you don't let anyone dictate what's possible. You hold the power, which means you're fully responsible for the external manifestations of your world.

A Rich B$tch doesn't blame others for her financial situation, nor does she walk around like Eeyore — the gloomy, defeated donkey from *Winnie the Pooh*. That energy has no place here.

Instead, a Rich B$tch takes ownership of her life—her destiny, emotions, bank account, business, relationships, health, home, and every desire she holds. She knows that accountability is her superpower and claims responsibility for the totality of her experience.

And let's be clear: A Rich B$tch creates from abundance, not lack. She's not chasing more because she feels empty, she's creating because it's fun, exciting, and aligned with her desires. The Rich B$tch mindset is all about owning your power and playing life at the highest level — because you *can*.

The more I consciously create my reality, the more abundance I generate. Say it with me and let it sink in: **The more I consciously create my reality, the more abundance I generate.**

In time, every Rich B$tch discovers that life is just a game, a game where she's both the player and the creator. So, the real questions are: How big can you dream? How bold can you go? Because the only limits are the ones you place on yourself.

$$$

Rich B$tch Homework: Consciously Create

1. **ACKNOWLEDGE YOUR MANIFESTATION**

   Reflect on and celebrate a manifestation you consciously created and feel proud of. Own your power!

2. **DREAM BIG**

   Write down the top five things you plan to create as an experience. No limits — let your imagination run wild.

3. **MANIFESTATION MAGIC WITH A DOLLAR BILL**

   Take out a dollar bill and a black Sharpie. Add zeros, transform it into your desired amount, and tape it somewhere you'll see it every day. Once it's done, snap a picture and tag me on Instagram **@kyerakacey** — I can't wait to celebrate with you!

4. STAY INSPIRED WITH VISUAL CUES

Explore creative ways to remind yourself that your desires are already done. Some ideas:

- Write affirmations on sticky notes and put them around your home, car, or workspace.
- Set reminders on your phone to nudge you back into alignment throughout the day.
- Create a vision board or collage of your desires to keep your energy focused and inspired.

Consciously creating
your Rich B$tch era requires
resilience, trust, and the audacity
to believe in your vision
when no one else does.

CHAPTER
TEN

RICH
B$TCH MONEY GOALS

CHAPTER 10: A RICH B$TCH IS HEART-CENTERED (AND UNCOMPROMISING)

A Rich B$tch makes decisions from her heart, knowing love is the highest frequency from which to create. Your heart holds the key to answers that your logical mind could never fathom. Your heart will never steer you wrong.

Living in fear and unconsciousness is the path of least resistance, and for many, it's all they've ever known. Survival-based choices might feel instinctive, but they keep you small, stuck, and handing over your power to circumstances or people unworthy of it. Wake up — your life doesn't belong to fear or anyone else. It's time to reclaim what's yours.

Anyone can slip between higher and lower frequencies in a single day — that's the dance of being human. Fear and logic might pull you out of heart-centeredness, but it's not about perfection, it's about awareness. This is the work: catching yourself, choosing again, and rising stronger every time.

Let's rewind to 2016. It was a year when survival mode gripped me, pulling me into the fear-driven spiral of fight-or-flight. My first divorce triggered that response, a raw and primal instinct to protect, defend, and simply get through. It was a storm that tested me, but it also cracked me open to the work of transformation on a deeper level.

My body wasn't whispering, it was screaming, begging for me to listen. Constant sickness, an overload of cortisol, a battered immune system, and relentless eczema that left me scratching my feet until they bled were just the start. Head-to-toe hives and sleep deprivation pushed me further into the chaos, and I became a walking reminder of what happens when life falls out of alignment. My body's breakdown wasn't a punishment, it was a wake-up call — a sign that something had to change.

According to HeartMath Institute (https://www.heartmath.com/), there is scientific proof behind our difficulty to think clearly when dealing with emotional stress. Erratic neural signals travel from our heart-rhythm to our brain and actually reinforce our feelings of negativity. Because of the heightened state of stress I was surviving in, my continued focus on lack created a larger field of fear around me, and because we can only see equal to our emotional state, I couldn't see a way out of the nightmare I was living in.

Nightmares are a part of us and created within us. But at the same time, we have the power to liberate ourselves from them by waking up. So, how do we wake up? I'll get to that later on.

Now, I want to preface what I'm about to share by clearly stating that I do not judge anyone who chooses the path I'm going to speak about. Nothing that follows this statement is about shame or being good, bad, right, or wrong — it is about being heart conscious and lovingly understanding that every individual on the planet has a sacred yes and a sacred no in addition to free will. So, I honor without judgment your free will to choose what's right for you, just as I honor my own free will. What I'm about to discuss is about what's true and a sacred no or yes strictly for me.

While I was in my twenties, women I deeply loved were working at strip clubs to earn money. Driven by a deep sense of low self-worth, survival, and escapism through drug use, I witnessed them immersing themselves in a world of unhealthy self-expression and fear-based choices. Upon seeing this, I vowed to myself to never become part of this scene or to contribute to the environment or lifestyle in any way. For me, it was nonnegotiable; it was an absolute no.

Remember what I said previously? During times of stress, our ability to think clearly or make effective decisions is limited.

At the lowest point in my life, following my divorce, I couldn't see any other way out of my nightmare but to join this lifestyle; it seemed like a viable answer. I had tunnel vision regarding my problems and was desperate to make money quickly as my bills piled up. I needed to find a way to survive. So, one summer afternoon I drove to downtown Detroit, reluctantly walked into a strip club for an interview and was hired on the spot.

When I returned to my car, despite how sunny it was outside, everything around me felt so dim and dark. I drove home in silence, tears falling from my face.

A Rich B$tch will never compromise her soul's highest truth.

As divine intervention would have it, I had an intuitive nudge and decided to schedule an appointment with my energy practitioner prior to my start date at the club. Sharon had been a steady presence in my life since my late teens, she knew me well, and I wholeheartedly trusted her.

During our session, I was vulnerable and shared that I'd been hired to work at a strip club in the city, and while I knew she would definitely not love the idea, I anticipated some level of understanding and support around my decision, that is until she said, "Kyera, if you do this, you will throw away everything you believe in and have worked so hard for while compromising your energy."

There was no softness to her words or gentleness in her energy. She was firm as she spoke with a fierce love for my highest truth.

In thinking back on it, Sharon fulfilled an important role for me that day. She pointed out to me where I had compromised my standards.

$$$

SIDENOTE: I hope you have someone in your life who will hold you to high standards, tell you the things you most need to hear at times you most need to hear them (even if you resist the truth in the moment), and highlight your greatness when you've lost sight of it. If you don't, now is the time to raise your standards and know that you are deserving of people who love you enough to call you forward.

$$$

We've all experienced moments in life when we've lost our way and forgot who we are. Certain souls are put on our path to light a match for us when we are in a dark place, illuminating a way forward we forgot was available to us.

I was angry at her reaction and became defensive, but the truth was, I had gone to her to seek her approval, her permission. I wanted her to help justify my decision to work at a strip club even though I was incredibly uncomfortable at the thought. Instead, she reflected back to me my truth, a truth my soul resonated with.

She was right. I was on a precipice, choosing between ultimate self-sacrifice (for me) on a path to compromising myself and self-love of the highest kind on a path to divine manifestation.

This brings me to my next point: No amount of money made in lack or fear will ever make you rich. We are either empowered — rooted in our heart center on our path to creating wealth and creating a life filled with love and desire — or we are unconsciously powerless to our circumstances, letting other people and fear dictate our choices and our lives, taking on the role of victim.

The **H** in RICH B$TCH stands for **H**eart-centered.

A Rich B$tch does not compromise her values, sacrifice her safety, or ignore her truth in the pursuit of making money. Instead, she trusts in divine timing, believes in her intuition, and holds herself in the highest embodiment, in alignment with her heart center and desires. As she moves, the Universe moves with her.

I returned home from my appointment with Sharon feeling confused and hopeless. *What had happened to my life? To my vision? To my dreams? How did I get here?*

I completely broke down. I had no idea what my next move would be or how I would continue to survive on my own. Too exhausted to move, I took a deep breath and sank into my white couch.

As I laid there and focused on my breath to calm my nervous system, the noise in my head began to quiet and soften. Then, out of nowhere, in what felt like the first time in a long time, I could suddenly sense the consciousness of my heart. Seconds later, it was accompanied by the presence of angelic energy surrounding me, and in that moment, I knew I was being reminded I was safe.

Although I couldn't see it at first, the answer was obvious. I knew it wasn't a heart-centered decision to put myself in an environment that made me extremely uncomfortable, not to mention one that would compromise my health and safety, and knowing this truth became enough. I made a firm decision to close the door to working at the strip club, which resulted in a sense of immediate relief (another perfect example of what can happen when we honor our intuition).

A few days later, I met up with one of my best friends, Trish, and reluctantly shared everything that had happened. What occurred next felt like nothing short of a miracle.

After I relayed all that had transpired in the previous days, Trish looked me in the eyes and asked, "Kyera, how much do you need to get by for a couple of months so you can rest your mind and body?"

At first, I didn't know what to say. I just stood there and stared at her.

The point is, by honoring my heart and saying no, closing a door that wasn't aligned with my future, the Universe moved with me through Trish, and it was a move I never could have predicted or foreseen. This is the magic that's available to you when you make heart-centered decisions. This is how we become the energetic match to wealth.

Often, your "no" is actually highlighting your soul's "yes." Your greatest desires will never require you to step out of alignment to reach them. In fact, doing so will lead you down a road that doesn't feel good toward a dead end. If you move in faith, the Universe will have your back.

Heart-centered action, truth, and alignment in everything that we do, teach, and preach is the way of the Rich B$tch.

One of my proudest moments came several years later. Trish came to my house for a visit. Waiting for her on my kitchen counter was a tiny silver box with a beautiful red bow and her name on it. Confused, as it wasn't her birthday or a holiday, she asked, "What's this?"

"Open it!" I encouraged with excitement. I cannot convey how overflowing with joy I was in this moment.

With piqued curiosity and a smile on her face, I watched her open it. Then, a moment of confusion hit when she found a check inside. As she read the amount on the check, the exact amount she had gifted me when I was in debt and greatly struggling, tears filled her eyes and we both began to cry. She reminded me that what she had given me was a gift and that it never needed to be repaid.

I reminded her that although I knew this, I was now in a place in my life where writing a four-figure check was effortless, and more importantly, it brought me immense joy to repay her (not to mention I felt like it was the right thing to do).

Let this be a reminder that where you are now is the beginning of an end . . . and the birth of something extraordinary. Allow for the truth of your heart to take the wheel and trust in the direction it leads you. You may not have all the details your logical mind insists upon you having, but you will be guided toward your highest good.

$$$

Rich B$tch Homework: Becoming Heart-Centered

1. **FOLLOW YOUR HEART**

    What is your heart guiding you to do? When you hear the answer, move accordingly. If this answer doesn't come easily to you, then you'll want to practice heart connection (see #2) and ask what she desires. Please don't judge yourself if this connection doesn't seem to happen immediately. Give her your time, grace, kindness, undivided attention, and the space to answer.

2. **FOCUS**

    Practice spending a minimum of five minutes each day connecting with your fourth center (your heart) by focusing your attention there. I like to place one hand on my heart and the other on or below my belly button (your center of safety). As I do this, I close my eyes, breathe, and give all my attention to her.

Rich B$tch desires demand alignment, not sacrifice. The moment you think you have to betray your truth to get them, you've stepped out of wealth frequency. True abundance is a match for who you are, not what you fear.

CHAPTER
ELEVEN

RICH
B$TCH MONEY GOALS

CHAPTER 11: BILLS

Wealth is your Rich B$tch birthright, and financial overflow is your natural state. Money moves for you because you decide it does. You are not just attracting abundance — you are the force that creates it.

How does this statement make you feel? "A rich woman pays her bills with ease and gratitude."

Does it spark annoyance? Failure? Regret? Frustration? Or does it inspire hope, hope for a day when paying a bill feels like an act of gratitude? Maybe it leaves you confused. You may be thinking: *Who in the world feels grateful for paying bills?*

Here's what I've learned about becoming an energetic match to wealth and creating opportunities that invite more money into my life — like clients unexpectedly reaching out, eager to work with me: **Our entire relationship with money matters.**

It's not enough to feel abundant and grateful only when money flows in. True wealth consciousness means cultivating that same abundance and gratitude as money flows out. Paying bills becomes an act of trust, a knowing that there's always more than enough for those who align themselves with the frequency of abundance.

When you wake up in the morning, do you panic and question whether there's enough air to breathe? Of course not. You simply wake up and breathe — without doubt, without worry.

Now imagine feeling that way about money. Imagine waking up, living your day, and going to bed at night without the weight of financial anxiety. No stress, no second-guessing if there will be enough. Just trust and ease.

It's a powerful thought, isn't it? But let me share something that once held me back from creating that sense of ease in my own life.

Back when I was drowning in debt and stuck in a scarcity mindset, I had a deeply toxic relationship with my bills. I resented them.

If this resonates, you're not alone. Bills are a source of stress for so many people. But they don't have to be.

What changed for me? I'll tell you — it wasn't about making more money right away. It started with shifting my *energy* around money, bills, and abundance. That shift was everything.

Here's an example: One day, after returning home from work, I sifted through the mail and came across yet another overdue notice from the chiropractor's office. I didn't even bother to open it. I rolled my eyes, irritated and exasperated, like an entitled teenager.

Instead of dealing with it, I did what I'd been doing for months: I tore it up and threw it in the trash (yes, cringe-worthy, I know). Ripping up those bills instead of watching them pile up felt like a temporary fix. It gave me fleeting relief, dulling the sting of stress and anxiety. But let's be real: it didn't make the bills go away. The past-due notices kept coming, no matter how many I ripped up.

I longed for the day when I could receive a bill, open it without flinching, and pay it with ease. Yet my avoidance and refusal to take responsibility only delayed that reality — and actively blocked abundance from flowing into my life.

It wasn't just bills I avoided. I dreaded checking my bank account balance. I'd hold my breath every time I logged in online, bracing myself for what I might find. Then I'd try to convince myself that everything was fine, but deep down, I didn't believe it.

I hadn't yet decided, really decided, that I could change my money story. I didn't believe I was capable of creating wealth, let alone worthy of it. I was stuck in the mindset of "It can happen for everyone else, but not for me."

Instead of wealth consciousness, I lived in resistance. And we all know the truth: What you resist persists.

Why is that? Because resistance creates focus, and whatever you give energy to expands. This quote, often attributed to Eckhart Tolle, puts it perfectly: "Whatever you accept completely will take you to peace, including the acceptance that you cannot accept, that you are in resistance."

That hit me hard. **The moment I started shifting from avoidance and resistance to responsibility and acceptance, my entire relationship with money began to change.** That's when abundance could finally find its way to me.

Fast-forward to 2020. I was on the phone with a client navigating a divorce, and she shared something profoundly tied to the theme of this chapter. Before her husband's affair, she had always carried a deep, gnawing fear of infidelity. She admitted it was one of her worst nightmares, a thought she couldn't shake. She obsessed over the idea so much that she would often find herself imagining what it would feel like if it happened.

She vividly described how, time and again, she would generate the emotions of betrayal — the heartbreak, the anger, the devastation — as if it were real. But it wasn't her reality. Not yet. All those feelings were self-created in her mind, and in her mental rehearsals, she kept seeing her husband as the betrayer.

After reflecting on this, she gave a resigned laugh and said, "Kyera, it's almost as if I manifested it."

Her words carried weight because they spoke to a truth so many of us overlook: Where we place our energy, consciously or unconsciously, shapes our reality. What we fixate on, especially with strong emotional charge, has a way of materializing in our lives. This is why awareness is everything.

You've heard it time and time again: Whatever you focus on, you attract. But can you think of a moment in your life when this rang true, even if it didn't feel good?

The brain cannot tell the difference between a thought and an actual experience. When you mentally rehearse something enough and feel the emotions as though it's real, you create an energetic blueprint, a field of information, that becomes a match for that imagined experience to manifest in your physical reality.

If you understand the law of attraction, you know this principle doesn't discriminate. It doesn't differentiate between what you *want* and what you *fear*. It simply responds to the energy you emit — the thoughts you think, the feelings you feel, and the beliefs you hold. This means that even when you're fixated on something you don't want to have happen, you may unconsciously be drawing it closer. People do this every day without realizing it.

But here's the good news: If you have the power to attract the things you resist and fear most, then you absolutely have the power to attract your wildest dreams and deepest desires. You can call in a rich, unapologetic, motherf*cking life. It's not only possible, it's inevitable when you align with it.

As you step into your Rich B$tch self, it's crucial to recognize this: What you resist must ultimately be mastered. When you spend your days fixating on worst-case scenarios — whether it's not being able to pay a bill, losing your home to foreclosure, or any other fear — you are feeding energy into the field where those potentials exist. And whatever you feed, grows.

To align yourself with wealth, you must stop resisting and avoiding the very things tied to your financial reality: your bills, taxes, debts, or even checking your bank account. Avoidance keeps you stuck in scarcity, and awareness sets you free.

Back when I was receiving those past-due notices from the chiropractor's office, I was living paycheck to paycheck. The truth is, I could have made different choices. I could have created a plan to set money aside until I had enough to pay the bill. Or I could have picked up the phone and called the office, asking for a payment arrangement to chip away at the balance over time.

But I didn't. I avoided it, convinced that I couldn't handle it. That avoidance only blocked me from stepping into my power and becoming an energetic match for wealth. The shift began when I faced what I had been resisting and realized I had far more options than I'd allowed myself to see.

Either of those actions — saving up to pay the bill or asking for a payment plan — would have aligned me with integrity and personal responsibility. But instead, for months, I opened those past-due notices and felt anger, as though my circumstances were the chiropractor's fault, as if *they* were somehow making my life harder.

Looking back, I see now that I could have made a completely different choice. I could have decided, right then and there, that even if I didn't know how I was going to get out of debt or create financial freedom, I was going to do it. I could have declared to the Universe (God, Jesus, angels, spirit guides — whatever you believe in and call upon) that I was ready for help and was committed to turning my life around.

The first step in any transformation is choosing. It's deciding, with conviction, what you're ready to heal, release, and change. It's declaring for yourself that you are worthy of a new reality. All potentials exist. Every possibility, every version of you, is already waiting in the quantum field. But nothing changes until *you* choose. Choose the potential you want to bring to life, and watch the Universe rise to meet you.

Once I realized that avoiding and resisting my bills was never going to set me free, I thought, *Enough is enough.* I made a conscious choice to heal my relationship with money, specifically around receiving bills and releasing money. That internal shift alone, the decision to stop resisting and start facing my financial reality, created a ripple effect.

The Universe met my decision with undeniable support: I received unexpected money in the mail. It was just enough to cover my outstanding balance with the chiropractor's office.

For a brief moment, I thought about how nice it would be to buy a new pair of shoes. But deep down, I knew that paying off my debt was the most abundant choice I could make. Aligning with integrity felt better than any fleeting indulgence could.

Reflecting on this, I realized how much of my old money mindset had been shaped by the environment I grew up in. For many, bills were synonymous with stress. Whether it was the water bill, the electric bill, the gas bill, or the phone bill, the message was always the same: Bills were a burden. Receiving one meant less money in the bank and more feelings of lack and tension.

That belief system, often passed down unconsciously, creates a cycle that feels endless — until you decide to break it. You can start shifting your relationship with money by paying close attention to how you feel when you receive a bill, when you pay it, and after you release money to fulfill a financial obligation. Your emotions and thoughts in these moments are windows into your money mindset. Once you become aware, you can choose to rewrite the narrative and align with abundance. The cycle only continues if you let it.

Take a moment to notice how you talk and feel about gas prices, rising food costs, and the overall cost of living. Are you joining the collective narrative of fear, lack, and anger around inflation? Or are you standing firm in your Rich B$tch ability to generate abundance no matter what?

One story empowers you, while the other keeps you broke — not just in your wallet but in your mindset.

Paying bills, releasing money, and navigating financial obliga-tions are profound opportunities to master the flow of giving and receiving with love and gratitude. When you embrace this mindset, wealth flows more freely. Receiving and paying bills doesn't have to be a burden. Instead, it can be a rich, liberating experience.

These days, when I pay a bill, I feel grateful: grateful to release money, grateful for what it provided, and most importantly, grateful for my ability to trust myself to create more. The energetic standard I've set is this: *I am safe to release my money, and I trust and celebrate its ever-flowing presence in my life.* This is the Rich B$tch energy I hold for myself — and for you.

Yes, it takes consistent work and awareness to embody this fully. Even after becoming debt-free and growing my business to its first six figures, I noticed familiar thought patterns creeping in — hesitation around investing money, or unease when checking my bank account — even when I had plenty.

Financial freedom isn't a final destination, it's a daily practice, rooted in awareness, gratitude, and consistent Rich B$tch energy.

I had to reprogram myself to feel safe and abundant when spending money, trusting it would return to me multiplied. I had to disinvest my energy from past fears and old narratives, focusing instead on the future I desired, not the one I feared or had grown accustomed to.

This is the work. It's daily work. Sometimes it's a moment-to-moment commitment until one day, you're no longer *thinking* about becoming your future self, you *are* her. That's the shift from "becoming" to "being."

Until that day comes, ask yourself: How committed am I?

A Rich B$tch who becomes the energetic match to wealth pays her bills with ease and gratitude. She feels centered in safety, faith, and abundance when checking her bank account, and she trusts that every dollar she releases will return to her multiplied.

$$$

Rich B$tch Homework: Take Control of Your Finances

1. **LIST YOUR OUTSTANDING BILLS**

   Begin by creating a list of any outstanding or past-due bills you currently have. As you write them down, pay attention to how you feel. If feelings of anxiety or stress arise, pause and consciously shift your energy. Close your eyes for five minutes and invite in feelings of gratitude, trust, and ease. Visualize the experience of paying your bills with complete peace, imagining a reality where you have an overflow of money readily available to meet all your obligations.

2. **CREATE A PLAN OF ACTION**

   Develop a plan to address your outstanding bills, but make it non-rigid and stressless. Set a *wishful completion date*, something that feels light and empowering rather than heavy or punitive. This process isn't about punishment, it's about reclaiming your power. By taking aligned action, you're choosing to heal your money wounds, write a new story of empowerment, and become the energetic match to wealth. If you're unsure where to begin, ask for assistance. Reach out to creditors or account managers and inquire about payment plans or support options. You might be surprised by how willing they are to work with you when you communicate with clarity and honesty.

3. **PRACTICE GRATITUDE WHILE RELEASING MONEY**

   Each time you pay a bill, intentionally practice gratitude. For example: "I am deeply grateful to live in a home where I can rest, recharge, and spend time with loved ones. I honor my home and its ability to take care of me by investing in it through my mortgage and insurance payments. I trust that every dollar I release returns to me multiplied.

The Universe always provides for me in perfect timing." By shifting your perspective, you transform paying bills into an abundant, aligned act of trust and gratitude, one that reinforces your connection to wealth and security.

Financial freedom isn't a final destination, it's a daily practice, rooted in awareness, gratitude, and consistent Rich B$tch energy.

CHAPTER
TWELVE

CHAPTER 12: MONEY TRIGGERS

Money is a potent force — it triggers fear, envy, desire, judgment, hope, inspiration, and generosity. Your money triggers directly reflect your current level of wealth consciousness. It's a mirror showing where you've evolved and where your growth lies.

I quickly learned from the online coaching space that money celebrations and conversations are incredibly triggering for some women.

Celebrating financial success in this space perfectly illustrates the duality of being a source of inspiration for some and a target of resentment or judgment for others.

Here's a snapshot of the types of responses I've received online after holding conversations about, or celebrating, money:

"You're giving me so much hope that I, too, can get out of debt!"

"OMG, thank you! This is so inspiring!"

"I'm so turned off by women who share how much money they're making."

"If you aren't transparent about what you're making, you're lying."

"I won't hire a coach who *isn't* sharing what she's making."

"I won't hire a coach who *does* share what she's making."

"I'm so sick of coaches bragging, rubbing their money wins in everyone's faces while the world suffers."

Here's the reality: **There will always be suffering in the world.** That's duality. But being broke does nothing to ease that suffering. Financial freedom, however, can make a difference. If I were still living paycheck to paycheck, I wouldn't have been able to donate the amounts I've given in recent years. **Wealth creates the *capacity* to contribute meaningfully.**

But no matter how you approach money conversations, it's often a lose-lose situation if those around you aren't evolving their relationship with it. You're damned if you do, and you're damned if you don't. Why? Because money, like love, sex, and power, is still considered taboo, filthy, and shameful for women. And just like love, sex, and power, money is something many women deeply desire — because it represents freedom. But when a woman in lack sees another woman thriving in abundance, it's triggering. It highlights what feels out of reach, stirring envy and judgment where inspiration could exist.

If we want to change this dynamic, we must begin to rewrite our narratives around money, and not just for ourselves but for the generations of women who come after us.

Your money triggers are a spotlight on your wealth consciousness level, revealing how far you've come in healing your money wounds and where there's still work to do. Instead of resisting these reactions, use them as opportunities for growth.

When someone else's wealth triggers you, pause and ask yourself: What can I gain, learn, or heal from this experience? Your triggers aren't here to punish you, they're here to teach you and show you what's possible when you choose to transform your mindset.

Imagine for a moment that you're in a relationship with someone who, though their insecurities aren't personal to you, is deeply ashamed and afraid to show you off. Despite the fact that you're an absolute catch — radiant, extraordinary, and everything they could ever want — they lack the inner healing to hold you in your full brilliance.

Their fear isn't about you, it's about them. They're consumed by what others might think. At social gatherings, they avoid talking about you, terrified of judgment. They hesitate to celebrate how incredible you are, worried someone single might feel offended. To protect themselves from their own discomfort, they keep you hidden, tiptoeing around their social circles and stifling your connection.

This relationship is trapped — boxed in by fear, insecurity, and limited expression. For them, this dynamic might feel safe and secure, but for you, it's suffocating. You're not meant to be hidden. You're meant to be celebrated, admired, and held in the highest light.

Now ask yourself: If this wouldn't feel acceptable in love, why would it feel acceptable in any other area of my life? You deserve to live boldly, without fear of judgment, and to honor the fullness of who you are. Anything less isn't security, it's limitation.

Scenarios like this one might feel all too familiar, but let's be honest: the mere thought of being in a relationship like that should make you cringe. In a stifled relationship like this, you'd feel less than, unappreciated, insignificant, and unworthy. You certainly wouldn't feel cherished, valued, or special, would you?

But for most people, their relationship with money mirrors this exact dynamic. They tiptoe around it, feeling uncomfortable talking about it. Money is treated as a hush-hush topic, cloaked in secrecy and shame. Celebrating the freedom and opportunities it provides? Forget it — it doesn't feel safe.

And yet they desperately want more of it. They dream of abundance, overflow, and liberation, but they're trapped in a relationship with money that's based on avoidance, fear, and silence.

So, how can you attract more of something you're unwilling to honor, celebrate, or even acknowledge? It's time to rewrite the story — to move from hiding to celebration, from shame to empowerment, and from fear to liberation.

Just like a fire can't keep burning if you smother the flames and deprive it of oxygen, your bank account won't grow if you're too afraid to breathe life into it. Wealth needs energy, attention, and intention to thrive — it's not something you can hide from or tiptoe around.

If you're pursuing wealth, which is really the energy of freedom and relief, you're going to be judged. People will have opinions simply because you desire abundance or a luxurious life. To some, wanting more will automatically mean you're shallow, incapable of enjoying life's simple pleasures, indifferent to the struggles of others, or just a terrible person altogether.

But let's set the record straight: *Abundance and simplicity can coexist.* Loving the finer things in life doesn't mean you can't savor the simple things. Personally? I crave a good PB&J just as much as a perfectly cooked steak dinner. I can lose myself in the magic of camping under the stars and feel equally at home indulging in room service at a swanky hotel.

Desiring wealth and enjoying luxury doesn't make you selfish or shallow, it makes you human. You're allowed to want more, to embrace comfort, and to live a life that lights you up while still holding space for gratitude and simplicity. Abundance is expansive — it allows for all of it.

Somewhere along the way, the desire to have it all was labeled "bad" and dismissed as superficial. But let's be real: that couldn't be further from the truth. Unfortunately, many people buy into these judgments, giving them power and creating a reality filled with shame and discomfort around wanting more.

But it doesn't have to be this way.

Let's choose to have it all. You're not here to live for others, follow their rules, or conform to their beliefs. I refuse to let someone else's lack of healing or limited wealth consciousness impact mine, and you shouldn't either. We're here to live bold, expansive, abundant lives. So, why settle? Let's stop placing unnecessary limitations on what's possible and fully step into the big, beautiful life we're meant to create.

If we can normalize lack (and let's face it, the world has done that with ease), then we can certainly normalize success — without the shame or judgment that so often follows when we choose to celebrate it.

Let's talk about the duality of money and material possessions: the *damned if you do, damned if you don't* energy that often arises, where judgment and inspiration exist side by side.

In May 2021, I shared a story online about purchasing my first Louis Vuitton handbag. The responses were wildly mixed. For some, my story was a source of inspiration, hope, and celebration — proof that they, too, could create abundance and achieve their dreams. For others, it triggered shame, disgust, and judgment, as though my success was somehow offensive.

Even though I was completely transparent in sharing my experience, my story ignited a lot of emotions that day. It was a reminder of how deeply money, and what it represents, can stir people's wounds. The duality is real, but it's also a reflection of where we're at collectively.

The truth? Your success is allowed to exist unapologetically, and your celebrations don't need anyone else's permission. Normalize success. Celebrate it boldly. It's time to rewrite the narrative.

Here's what I shared:

I opened up about how uncomfortable I felt the first time I walked into the Louis Vuitton store. I was sweating — caught in a mix of excitement and unworthiness. I couldn't shake the nagging thought, *I don't belong here.*

I shared how I had to self-regulate before making the purchase, even though I had more than enough money to buy the handbag. My business had already hit six figures that year, but my stepping into this level of abundance still felt unfamiliar.

I also talked about how unaccustomed I was to spending several thousand dollars on a single item. It wasn't just a purchase, it was a new level of energy to hold and embody, and that kind of expansion takes adjustment.

It was a raw, transparent moment about stepping into a higher frequency of abundance, and it's one so many people can relate to but rarely talk about.

Despite voluntarily laying all of this out in my post — the emotions, the self-regulation, and the growth — some women couldn't see past the symbol of the designer bag. To them, the handbag became the focal point, and my story was labeled as tacky and boastful.

"This isn't wealth consciousness. It's poverty consciousness," one woman declared.

"While we're happy you dropped money on accessories because you can and it felt good, someone else sees that handbag as a mortgage payment," another said.

And there it was — duality striking again.

Is it any wonder that so many people desire to make and receive more money, yet struggle to attract wealth into their lives? The judgment, envy, and resistance tied to other people's success create energetic blocks that repel abundance instead of magnetizing it.

It is *never* your responsibility to dim your light just because someone else is triggered by your "too muchness." No matter how pure your intentions, no matter the obstacles you've overcome to get where you are today, some people will never see your heart or understand the depth of your journey. They'll reduce you to a snapshot of your current reality and project their own insecurities on you.

But that's *their* work to do, not yours.

It is not your job to feel guilty for loving money, desiring more, or spending it on things that bring you joy, lavish or otherwise. You are allowed to want, to celebrate, and to expand unapologetically.

In the name of self-love, sometimes the most powerful thing you can do is say, "F*ck off" and keep moving — respectfully, boldly, and with your head held high. Your light is not up for negotiation.

In your pursuit of becoming the energetic match to wealth, you will have to embrace *both* sides of success. Loving money and celebrating abundance will always come with a flip side: judgment, misunderstanding, and projection. Duality is part of the game, and learning to hold space for it is the price of expansion.

It's also not your job to judge someone else's relationship with money, whether it's how they earn it, spend it, save it, or avoid it. The world is already overflowing with unconscious projection. Your role is to bless and release, stay in your lane, and honor the truth that everyone is on their unique journey. Whatever their path looks like, it's *theirs,* not yours.

When you find yourself judging someone for what they buy, wear, or how they handle money, take a moment to reflect. That judgment is a mirror, showing you where healing is still needed within yourself.

For me, the desire to transform my relationship with money was deeply personal. After my first divorce and my own financial struggles, I became acutely aware of how many women face similar challenges. I vowed to change my circumstances, and not just for myself, but to become a living example of what's possible for other women who are ready to do the same.

And now, I am.

In my unwavering stand to give every woman the opportunity to choose her Rich B$tch life, I had to face a hard truth. As I began having conversations about money and celebrating my financial wins, I had to get comfortable with being highly misunderstood and judged.

Women shamed me left and right for speaking openly about money, celebrating big wins, expressing my desire to see more wealth in the hands of women, and, most controversially, declaring that we can have it all. But I understand this isn't about me. Their judgments, shame, and criticisms are projections of fear, spoken from the level of wealth consciousness they're currently at. It's not personal unless you allow it to be.

Did that stop me? F*ck no. Instead, I've doubled down on my mission.

I will continue to advocate boldly for normalizing success, celebrating wealth, and putting abundance in the hands of every woman who desires it (from the inside out). Because when one woman rises, she gives permission for countless others to rise with her. And that's the legacy I'm here to create.

Judge me or join me — I'm not stopping.

And here's something to remember . . .

Money loves to be:

- Celebrated, not shamed.
- Seen, not hidden.
- Loved, not feared.
- Encouraged, not judged.

If you want your relationship with money to thrive, treat it the same way you'd nurture a connection with the perfect partner. Money desires (and requires) a fun-loving, open-flow relationship.

Approach it with respect, joy, and unwavering trust, then watch how it shows up for you.

A Rich B$tch does *not* dim her light or tiptoe around her desires, accomplishments, or joy for anyone. She refuses to shrink, and she certainly doesn't hold back when it's time to celebrate her wins. Why? Because the world needs you to shine. Your brilliance is an example of possibility — a reminder that others can rise too.

Yes, your light may trigger some people, and that's perfectly okay. In fact, it's to be expected. But never forget that your light will inspire so many more, and *that* is what truly matters.

Money in the hands of women who are here to make an impact, disrupt the status quo, and rewrite the narrative of how women live is exactly what this world needs. The more money we consciously create, the more lives we can change for the highest good.

Isn't that f*cking fantastic?

$$$

Rich B$tch Homework: Celebrate Your Wins

Today, give yourself permission to publicly celebrate an achievement, milestone, breakthrough, or desire around wealth. Whether you go live on social media or post a story, let yourself be seen in the light of celebration. Share from your heart center.

When you share, be vulnerable, transparent, and unapologetically confident. Practice shining your light instead of dimming it. And if you encounter the flip side — trolls, judgment, or negativity — use it as an opportunity to practice feeling safe in your power. Send them love, bless and release, and keep moving forward like the Rich B$tch you are. Share with your post: "The Universe loves to surprise and delight me. I receive abundance with gratitude and ease."

Don't forget to tag me on Instagram **@kyerakacey** so I can celebrate you too!

If a wealthy woman triggers you, check your program-ming — because she's proof that financial freedom isn't just for men in suits.

CHAPTER
THIRTEEN

RICH
B$TCH MONEY GOALS

CHAPTER 13: RICH B$TCH LOTTERY

An affirmation without the B in B$tch — belief — behind it will always remain empty, unable to materialize into reality. Belief is the fuel that transforms words into action, energy, and results.

One afternoon in 2021, I was leaving the mall after an unplanned (but oh-so-satisfying) shopping spree when my phone buzzed with a message. A woman wanted to sign up for one of my private mentorship packages.

I couldn't help but laugh as I read it. Why? Because, first of all, the timing was classic — money out, money in. That's just how it flows when you trust it. Second, I lived by my favorite mantra: "The more I play, the more money I make." That little affirmation was more than words, it was my lifestyle. The more fun I had in my business and everyday life, the more the Universe showed up to play along, dropping paid opportunities and surprise deposits into my bank account like confetti at a party.

One thing that has remained constant as I've earned and spent money in ways I once only dreamed of is gratitude. The feeling, expression, and daily practice of gratitude have been pivotal in generating more wealth and opportunities. It's not that I'm surprised anymore by what I create or how I create it, because I fully expect to remain an energetic match for wealth as the conscious creator of my reality.

What continues to amaze me, however, is the sheer joy and wonder I feel with every abundant experience. Each one feels as exhilarating and fresh as the very first, and for that, I am endlessly grateful.

Gratitude is the gateway that expands our capacity to receive.

The more I chose to live as my future Rich B$tch self — taking aligned actions and fully embodying that unapologetic Rich B$tch energy — the more money I naturally attracted. My affirmation, "The more I play, the more money I make," wasn't something I repeated to convince myself of its truth. It was (and is) a belief, a deep, unshakable knowing that I carry. Time and time again, the Universe delivers proof of its validity.

Case in point: The day I indulged in a truly fun shopping spree, my business had an $18K day in sales. Coincidence? Hardly. I was moving in the frequencies of gratitude, liberation, and play, which primed me to receive.

Now, let me be clear: wealth, living a rich life, and even the concept of "play" look different for everyone. What feels expansive and joyful to one person might not resonate with another, and that's perfectly okay. You get to define what those terms mean for you, and here's the catch: To become an energetic match to wealth, you must let go of judgment and shame, especially toward how others choose to enjoy or spend their money. And not because it's polite, but because judgment and shame operate on a frequency that blocks abundance. Let's face it, judgment isn't the Rich B$tch vibe. The Rich B$tch vibe is freedom — honoring everyone's choices, including your own.

I want to share something with you that helped me create the experience of becoming an energetic match to wealth, something simple yet transformative that you can try for yourself.

In my early twenties, I created a game called "I Won the Lottery," which I would play after finishing my nine-to-five. Like all powerful practices, its brilliance was in its simplicity and the intention behind it.

Here's how it worked: After work, I would walk to the convenience store a mile down the street from my apartment and purchase a Cash for Life lottery ticket. The grand prize? Four thousand dollars a week for life.

At the time, I was earning around two thousand dollars a month and juggling debt. Yet, during that walk, none of it mattered. I would silence my phone, clear my mind of the day's chaos, and enter a state of pure presence. To the rest of the world, I was in airplane mode. This wasn't just a ritual but a practice of creating from a clean, energetic slate, stepping fully into the frequency of wealth and abundance.

As I walked, I immersed myself in mental rehearsal, imagining a new reality far removed from the office job that drained me and kept me stuck living paycheck to paycheck. In my mind, I was already wealthy. I envisioned myself investing, spending, and donating the winnings with ease. The only rule? I wasn't allowed to think about anything but winning.

I painted the experience with vivid, emotional detail. Often, tears of relief would well up as I imagined holding the quarter I'd use to scratch the ticket and reveal my prize. I saw myself clutching the winning ticket, my heart racing with excitement, as I called my family to share the news. I pictured us celebrating over an extravagant dinner that I paid for effortlessly.

In those moments of playing "I Won the Lottery," I wasn't just pretending, I was embodying the energy of a rich woman. Like a child whose imagination runs so wild she believes she's a real-life superhero, in those moments of playing my game, I was a rich woman.

You might be questioning my sanity at this point. But if you really think about it, playing the game "I Won the Lottery" is no different from the woman who closes her eyes and envisions her wedding day: every detail of her walk down the aisle, the way her partner looks at her, and the joy of her happily ever after.

It's the same as the athlete who sees herself crossing the finish line before the race even begins, feeling every muscle firing with precision, holding her breath steady, and hearing the deafening roar of the crowd celebrating her victory. Or the speaker who mentally rehearses her big moment in front of an audience, feeling the rhythm of her words, imagining the pauses filled with anticipation, enjoying the laughter after a perfectly delivered joke, and hearing the resounding applause as she closes with a triumphant "job well done."

The common thread? Imagination paired with belief creates reality. These moments of vivid rehearsal are more than daydreams, they're acts of creation, training the mind and body to align with a future that's already written in the energy of their certainty.

Let's stick with the wedding day visualization as it's so universally relatable. Some women can tell you exactly what their dream wedding looks like, down to the finest details. They know the style of the dress they'll wear, the venue where they'll say "I do," the shade of their bridesmaids' dresses, the song that will play during the ceremony, and even the intricate design of their wedding cake — all before they're engaged or even in a relationship.

Why? Because they're already becoming the energetic match to their dream wedding. Through this vivid mental rehearsal, they're stepping into the emotions, the joy, the excitement, and the love they'd feel on that day. They're energetically aligning with the outcome they wish to create, rehearsing it as if it's already theirs.

This is the fastest path to manifestation. But it's not passive. It requires the action and embodiment of everything the letters in RICH B$TCH stand for. **Manifestation happens when belief meets intention and inspired action, creating the perfect formula for dreams to materialize.**

To become the energetic match to your desires, you have to take personal **r**esponsibility, move with **i**ntegrity, have **c**ourageous **c**onversations, **h**eal for the highest good, **b**elieve in your ability and worthiness to receive that which you want, **i**nvest the time (and potentially money) in creating it, **t**rust in your ability to be the energetic match to your desires and **t**rust your intuitive guidance along the way, **c**onsciously **c**reate based on desire not fear, and lastly, remain **h**eart-centered in your pursuit.

Here's the challenge most people face, and it might be what you're struggling with too: Most people believe they can't feel happy or grateful until their desires manifest into their reality. This mindset is a trap and one of the biggest reasons vision boards often fail. Let me explain.

Imagine you desire wealth. You create a vision board with images of money raining from the sky and a private jet. For a moment, you feel a spark of excitement as you look at it, but then you return to feeling broke, worried, or frustrated. Your mind and body are now in opposition — your thoughts are projecting abundance, but your emotions are anchored in lack. That conflict creates a feedback loop, keeping you stuck in the same reality on repeat.

It's like someone who can't feel grateful until they land a new client, sign the contract, or see the payment hit their account. Relying on external circumstances to dictate your emotional state creates a never-ending cycle of chasing validation. This approach is unsustainable, and it's the exact opposite of how manifestation works.

True manifestation starts within. It's about aligning your thoughts, emotions, and energy to the reality you desire before you see any physical evidence of it. That's when the magic happens.

This limited way of thinking — the belief that "I can't feel what I want until I have what I want" — creates separation, keeps desires at arm's length, and delays their arrival. Why? Because it keeps you locked in the energy of lack. When this unconscious pattern runs the show, even if someone achieves wealth (or whatever they desire), they often discover an unsettling truth: Money didn't fix what they thought was missing. All it did was amplify who they already were, exposing the void that was there all along.

The key to keeping the vision of your desires alive lies in feeling elevated emotions *ahead* of receiving them. The more consistently you align with these feelings, the more energy works to collapse time and shorten the distance between creation and manifestation. That's when things start to happen with ease. And isn't that far more impressive? To create wealth from a state of flow rather than forcing it?

Let's break it down with an example.

Imagine you're a week away from hopping on a plane to Las Vegas for a bachelorette party. In the days leading up to the trip, as you plan, pack, and chat excitedly with your girlfriends, you're already altered. Your thoughts, feelings, and emotions are heightened, purely from the anticipation of what's to come. That elevated state was generated by thought alone.

Still skeptical? Close your eyes and imagine biting into a lemon. Just the thought will cause your body to produce more saliva in anticipation. This is the power of the mind: Thought alone creates a physical and emotional response.

At any moment, your Vegas trip could fall through. Plans could change. But you're not focusing on worst-case scenarios because you *believe* it's happening. There's no doubt in your mind — you're already energetically there.

Now, imagine bringing that same level of certainty, excitement, and anticipation to the following:

- Wealth and abundance flowing into your life
- Attracting soul-aligned clients
- Weekly spa services
- A beautiful home renovation
- Steamy, connected moments with your soulmate
- A private chef preparing your meals
- A vacation house on the water

- Girls' trips that light your soul on fire
- A private jet waiting to take you anywhere
- A weekly cleaning service for your sanctuary
- Deep, rich friendships with like-minded women

Or whatever your personal dreams might be.

Imagine living in that energy, where doubt doesn't exist, and the arrival of your manifestations feels as inevitable as that plane ride to Vegas. Your thoughts, emotions, and actions would radically shift. You'd step into a completely new reality created by belief alone.

Manifestation isn't magic, it's a tool. It's a tool for creating potential and living a life that's rich in experiences, connections, and joy.

After countless walks to the store and playing the game "I Won the Lottery," my winning ticket finally arrived. But here's the plot twist! It didn't come in the form of a scratch-off. Instead, it came through my coaching business, an outcome far greater than anything my human mind could have imagined. Why? Because I didn't limit the *how*.

Let me say it again: To become the energetic match for your desires, you must mentally rehearse the outcome you want, feel the elevated emotions of already having it, and embrace those feelings *now*, in the present moment. This requires unwavering belief in both the manifestation and your worthiness to receive it, alignment from your heart center, and continuous gratitude for what's on its way.

$$$

Rich B$tch Homework: Dream Big

1. Buy a lottery ticket that feels fun to you and play the game "I Won the Lottery."
2. If imagining wealth for yourself feels challenging, focus on someone you love — a family member or friend. Picture how you'd contribute to their life with an overflow of cash. Imagine their joy and how it would feel to give from a place of abundance.
3. Dream big, let your imagination run wild, and most importantly, have fun!

The more I play, the more money I make.

CHAPTER FOURTEEN

RICH
B$TCH MONEY GOALS

CHAPTER 14: RECEIVING MONEY

Two kinds of people in the world receive money: those who trust the process of its arrival with all their heart and accept it with ease, and those who don't.

Let me start today with a powerful example of what it looks like to trust completely in the timing and process of receiving money.

In 2022, I reached out to a talented artist to commission a custom piece. A day later, she replied with excitement, letting me know she'd be available to begin the project the following month. She also mentioned she'd take care of my payment at that time.

I paused. *That's odd. She doesn't want a deposit to hold my spot? What if I change my mind? Isn't she worried she might lose the sale?*

Those thoughts surprised me. I had already evolved my own business model to operate in the same energy of trust she embodied. Yet after years of living in fear around money, it wasn't shocking that a scarcity-based thought would sneak back in. Weeds — those old, limiting beliefs that no longer serve us — can always grow back. That's why routine maintenance, through awareness and alignment, is essential.

I told her I'd wait to hear back and was excited to start. In the meantime, I watched her social media and noticed how relaxed and happy she seemed, effortlessly living her life and pursuing her passions.

A week passed, then another. Three weeks went by before she finally sent me the invoice and told me she was ready to begin. I paid promptly, but I couldn't stop thinking about her calm confidence during that time — the way she trusted completely in receiving money without urgency or attachment. She was an example of being in heart-centered alignment.

It was a crucial element missing in my business mentorship — not just the first time I hired a coach, but even the second and third. Only one ever talked about the energy of trust and alignment when it came to receiving money. No one discussed the importance of who we're giving our time and energy to, especially when it comes to our clients. The focus was always on making, growing, and sustaining money. But no one stopped to ask, "Who are you actually exchanging with?" Let me be clear: It matters. It matters more than anything.

For instance, most online coaches and entrepreneurs are taught to prioritize handling price objections and collecting money immediately after a potential client says yes to working together. Whether it's a full payment or a deposit, the emphasis is on securing the money and signing the contract right then and there.

The reasoning is simple: Without an upfront financial investment, there's a higher risk the client will back out. The longer the delay, the more likely they are to second-guess their decision. An exchange of money is framed as not only a commitment but also the glue that binds the agreement.

This way of thinking and operating creates an energy of stress and urgency around money, leaving little to no room for trust or personal power to lay the foundation for a strong client relationship. Instead, it functions on a frequency of convincing (desperation), "I need you" (lack of belief), and "I don't trust you to follow through, so pay me now before you change your mind." While it may seem well-intentioned, it's deeply flawed.

When we operate this way, we not only attract less-than-ideal clients but also function from a fear-based frequency, declaring through our actions, if not our words, that we don't trust money can come to us with ease or believe in others' power to make aligned decisions and follow through on their commitments.

This mindset is one reason why so many online coaches burn out or find themselves surrounded by demanding, misaligned clients. Imagine treating every sales call or potential client like a child who can't be trusted to make a sound decision without pressure. It's not sustainable, it's not empowering, and it's certainly not the energy of ease or abundance.

This approach focuses solely on the transaction, not the heart-centered alignment. It overlooks the energy of who you're saying yes to and what you're inviting into your business and your life. It's not just about making the sale, it's about ensuring that the exchange is rooted in integrity and resonance, because the energy of your clients will always ripple back into your own.

Wealth with ease can absolutely become your reality, whether it's working with dream clients, receiving money through your dream job, or building the life you desire. But the frequency in which you move will dictate the reality you're cocreating with the Universe.

When you don't believe you can receive money with ease, you'll find yourself stuck in the exhausting business of convincing people. You'll operate from a place of low self-worth, pouring unnecessary energy into closing sales or, worse, spinning in a constant loop of "figuring out" where your next client or paycheck is coming from. It's an outdated, stressful, and completely unsustainable way of doing business. True abundance requires trust, alignment, and belief in your power to attract wealth without force or struggle.

Let me give you another example of receiving money with ease and how staying aligned with the frequency of your highest truth always yields the greatest results.

One day, I received a message from a woman I'd never met before, asking how she could book a reading with me. I shared the link to schedule her session and make payment based on my availability. A few moments later, she messaged again, saying my price was higher than she'd expected and asking if I offered any discounts.

Pause here for a moment, because this is where so many people lower their standards, dismiss their boundaries, and abandon their highest truth. They settle, thinking "something" is better than nothing, rooted in a lack of trust that the Universe can and will provide the full, aligned, ten-out-of-ten experience.

Her response to my pricing didn't faze me. I wasn't disappointed, worried about "losing a sale," or questioning the value of my rates. Why? Because it's not our job to convince anyone of our worth, our work, or the evolution of our business. Just as we choose our standards and alignment, others have the free will to choose their reality and what feels right for them.

Someone will always charge more, and someone will always charge less. It's not good or bad — it just *is*.

$$$

Rich B$tch Energetic Business Standards:

- We don't chase people.
- We don't make price exceptions out of fear or lack.
- We don't convince anyone.
- We trust in others' power to make aligned, free choices.
- We create consciously with clients who are self-led, excited about the exchange, and energetically aligned — not stressed or operating from scarcity.

So, here's how I responded: I kindly told the woman that I didn't have any specials or discounts available (the price is the price), but I could point her toward a group where she could post what she was looking for and specify her price range. I assured her she'd find plenty of aligned options and wished her well. She thanked me, and I went about my day.

To my surprise, not long after, she messaged me again, excited to say she had decided to book a reading with me. After our session, she expressed deep gratitude for the insights she received, and later, she sent me a heartfelt testimonial — completely unsolicited.

This is the power of staying in alignment with your truth, your standards, and your trust in the process. When you honor yourself, you call in clients who honor you too.

$$$

SIDENOTE: People often ask me how I handle price objections. The answer is simple: I don't. That's an energetic standard I hold.

$$$

The clients I attract are already aligned — they know they want to work with me, whether they've been following me for years or just discovered me yesterday. I'm happy to lovingly answer questions about my offers, but I will never convince someone how to spend their money. Everyone is capable, empowered, and responsible for deciding their next best steps without being pushed or coerced.

Your energetic standards create your reality.

There is an infinite number of ways to receive money in your life. You can receive it through force, manipulation, struggle, lack, compromise, or fear. You can stay stuck collecting a paycheck from a job you despise, feeling undervalued and unfulfilled.

Or you can set a new standard for yourself. You can raise the bar.

Living and embodying the Rich B$tch principles means receiving money from a place of alignment with your greatest truth, for the highest good of all, without compromise. From that frequency, wealth doesn't just arrive, it surprises and delights.

It's important to recognize that your ability to receive money is directly connected to how openly and graciously you receive in your everyday life — both the big and small moments.

Think about your automatic response when someone compliments you. Do you accept it fully, or do you downplay, invalidate, shut it down, or dismiss it altogether?

How do you receive yourself when you look in the mirror or stand naked with a partner? Do you immediately zoom in on your flaws and the ways you don't measure up, or do you honor your body with gratitude for all it allows you to do each day?

What about when someone offers to buy you dinner? Do you graciously say thank you and allow it, or do you insist it's unnecessary and decline?

When someone offers to help you, do you feel guilty for accepting or worry about being a burden? Or do you embrace the support with gratitude and say yes with ease?

These small moments reveal how open you are to receiving, and they directly impact your relationship with money. Your ability to receive expands your heart and sends a powerful signal to the Universe, affirming your energetic standard and your openness to being surprised and delighted by life. Beyond that, receiving is a gift not only to you but also to the person offering their love, gratitude, or support. Giving and receiving are both expressions of abundance, creating a flow that benefits everyone involved.

You'll know this energetic standard is fully anchored and embodied when your natural state of being effortlessly attracts support, money, and pleasure. It's not forced, it's magnetized. It flows because you've become the frequency of receiving.

Here's an example of receiving abundance in a way that often goes unnoticed: One summer in Austin, Texas, I was having dinner with my mentor at a stunning, upscale seafood and steak restaurant.

The atmosphere was perfect: mouthwatering appetizers, endless laughter, and that rare, beautiful feeling of being fully present in the moment.

As we were waiting for the main course, our waiter came over with steak knives. But mid-motion, as he was placing them on the table, he suddenly paused before picking up one of the knives and saying, "I'm going to replace this for you—it's not up to my standards."

My mentor and I looked at each other and smiled before laughing, completely charmed by his care and attention to detail. Could we have told him not to worry about it? Of course. But why would we? Instead, we embraced the moment and allowed ourselves to fully receive this thoughtful act of abundance. And here's the truth: It was never just about the knife. It was about saying yes to life's flow of good things. Whether it's a flawless steak knife, a heartfelt compliment, or a game-changing opportunity, the magic happens when you allow yourself to receive it fully with gratitude and without resistance.

Abundance isn't just about big checks or grand gestures. It's in the small, everyday moments that remind you to lean in, say yes, and let the Universe delight you.

Let's talk about setting your energetic standards—your boundaries, deal breakers, and nonnegotiables—around receiving money.

Whether you're self-employed or working for someone else, you are the one who sets the tone. You claim what you're available for and what you refuse to tolerate. This could mean saying no to opportunities that don't align with your values or reevaluating situations you've agreed to if they're creating energy leaks.

Here's an example of how one of my clients powerfully claimed her energetic standard:

I run a live group mentorship program called MASTERY. During one of our coaching calls, a client shared that she'd been approached about a potential job opportunity. However, the woman wanting to hire her was being difficult and creating unnecessary friction. Most people would take the money, convincing themselves that a paycheck is better than walking away.

But not in my world. A Rich B$tch chooses alignment, love, and unwavering standards — no exceptions.

Recognizing the disconnect and lack of ease in communication with this potential client, my client decided to prioritize her standards over the paycheck. She politely declined the opportunity, choosing alignment and trust over the short-term gain of money.

What happened next? She made space for higher-level opportunities and aligned abundance to flow her way. That's the power of maintaining your standards. By pulling the weeds — those misaligned situations and energy leaks — you create space for magic to enter your life and business.

$$\$\$\$$$

Rich B$tch Homework: Up Your Standards

1. **PRACTICE RECEIVING WITH GRATITUDE**
   - Say yes when someone offers to help or do something for you.
   - Say thank you when you receive a compliment or kind gesture.
   - Let yourself feel comfortable being served, supported, loved, and cared for.

2. TRACK YOUR ABUNDANCE

- Start writing down every act of abundance you receive, big or small. It could be finding a penny on the ground, receiving a smile from a stranger, or a friend offering to buy you coffee. I did this once while traveling, writing down everything I received—and the more I noticed and celebrated, the more abundance I attracted. Small or large, it all counts.

A Rich B$tch knows the Universe is her sugar daddy, so she graciously receives every gift, compliment, and blessing — big or small — because she knows receiving is the key to even more abundance.

CHAPTER
FIFTEEN

RICH
B$TCH MONEY GOALS

CHAPTER 15: THE DUALITY OF ABUNDANCE

Every day, you filter your experience of life through one of two lenses: abundance or lack.

One afternoon, I was napping when my doorbell rang, waking me up. I checked the security cameras on my phone to see my fourteen-year-old nephew standing on my front porch with two of his friends. Since my schedule was clear for the rest of the day, I decided to turn their unannounced visit into an impromptu outing. I drove them to Mochi Dough, a local spot known for its mouthwatering Japanese donuts.

We placed our order on the touchscreen — one dozen donuts and three Boba teas — and as I checked out, one of his friends caught a glimpse of the total. With disbelief, he blurted out, "Fifty-five dollars for donuts? What a rip-off!"

His reaction stuck with me.

As we drove home, I couldn't help but think about the programming already ingrained in this boy, a middle schooler, around money. His automatic response turned an experience of abundance — a spontaneous outing, delicious treats, and fun — into one of lack.

It wasn't just about the price, it was a reflection of a mindset, one that could potentially shape his relationship with money for years to come.

This moment wasn't just a casual trip for donuts, it was a reminder of how early we start filtering life through abundance or lack, and how important it is to choose which lens we live through.

A middle schooler doesn't independently conclude that fifty-five dollars for donuts and drinks is a rip-off. Whether you agree with his statement isn't the point. What's striking is his *programming*.

Notice how he turned an experience of abundance — receiving not one, not two, but three donuts (each a flavor of his choice) and a drink he didn't even have to pay for — into an experience of lack by attaching the cost to the idea of it being a rip-off.

You can predict the trajectory of his relationship with money based on what he's been told, what he's witnessed, or what he's absorbed from his environment. His beliefs are reflections of the people and experiences surrounding him.

As you step into becoming the energetic match to wealth, chances are you'll uncover similar programming within yourself. As your old self falls away, you may begin to see that somewhere along your life's journey, a financial experience or interaction reflected back to you a belief you attached to the idea that *abundance creates lack*. From this perception, you may have unknowingly adopted a subconscious belief about money — one that has kept true abundance, or its limitlessness, at arm's length. This belief may have influenced how you've shown up in life, perhaps with caution, reservation, or even disgust when it came to money.

And that's the real work here:

To identify, unravel, and release those stories so you can reprogram yourself to live, give, and receive from a place of wealth consciousness, not lack.

As an example, some of the most common beliefs I've encountered in my coaching practice that reflect the pattern of "abundance creates lack" sound like this:

- *Even if I make a lot of money (abundance), I'll owe a significant portion of it for taxes (lack).*

- *I have 500 followers (abundance — hello, imagine 500 people in a room!). But Claire has way more. My 500 isn't good enough (lack).*
- *If I become rich (abundance), I won't be able to trust people or their agendas (lack).*
- *If I'm wealthy or love material things (abundance), people will think I'm less spiritual (lack).*
- *If I have a life rich with experiences and wealth (abundance), I'll attract jealousy and resentment (lack).*
- *Celebrating my success (abundance) will make others gossip or feel bad (lack).*

Do you see how abundance and lack often coexist within the same unconscious space of thought?

Here's a fun story to illustrate what's possible when you shift your energy and choose to look for abundance instead of lack:

In summer 2021, I was flying out of Detroit Metro Airport en route to Marco Island. I'd been up since 4:45 a.m., ready to manifest my perfect beach day — bikini on, piña colada in hand, toes in the sand — and all before lunchtime.

But life had other plans.

At security, the agent noticed that the last name on my license didn't match the one on my ticket. Apparently, when my husband (at the time) booked the flights, he accidentally used his last name for both of us (despite the fact that I'd never changed my last name when we got married).

"I can't let you through," the agent said flatly. "But she can." He pointed to the Delta ticket counter.

I rushed over, explaining the mix-up and emphasizing how little time we had before the flight departed.

The ticket agent listened sympathetically but shook her head. "I can't fix this without proper documentation," she said. "The only option is to book an entirely new flight, but it won't be for the one you were originally on. And honestly, I'm not sure I can get you out today."

Cue frustration.

My inner voice was quick to chime in: *Kyera, don't go there. Don't spiral.*

This was one of those moments when all the self-regulation and Rich B$tch work I'd been doing *really* mattered — when staying aligned was *hard.* So, instead of succumbing to the growing frustration, I paused. I took a breath and reminded myself: *This is a game. Play it.* Because when you choose abundance over lack — even in the most inconvenient, challenging moments — the Universe conspires to meet you there.

What happened next? Let's just say the Universe wasn't done surprising me.

It would have been easy (almost too easy) to let my ego take the wheel. To own the frustration, wallow in my emotions, and play the victim. But I stopped myself and asked: *What would a Rich B$tch do?*

I stepped away from the ticket counter, closed my eyes, and started taking deep breaths. Yes, I was in the middle of a busy airport, and no, I didn't care who was watching. As I inhaled and exhaled, I repeated my mantra: *This experience is happening for me, and something great will come out of it.* I worked on opening my heart and generating feelings of gratitude. I wasn't about to let this situation hijack my energy — I was determined to master the moment and shift into a higher frequency.

When I felt calm and aligned, I returned to the counter. And that's when the magic began.

The ticket agent greeted me with excitement and said, "Good news! I found a flight with a noon departure, and there are two open seats, side by side."

Did it mean waiting an extra five hours at the airport? Yes. But I was overjoyed to know we'd still be leaving that day.

Mastering the moment had shifted everything. Instead of feeling rushed, panicked, or resentful about the delay, I chose abundance over lack. I spent the morning leisurely enjoying breakfast at the airport's National Coney Island, shopping for a few things I'd forgotten to pack, and relaxing before our flight.

The abundance didn't stop there.

When we finally arrived at the resort, something extraordinary happened. As we were checking in, the woman at the front desk, unprompted, decided to upgrade our entire stay. We were moved to the adults-only side of the resort (a feature I didn't even know existed) where we received upgraded amenities, exclusive dining, access to a private rooftop pool, a private beach, and complimentary breakfast every morning.

Our room? Beyond stunning. Completely updated, it sat on the top floor with breathtaking ocean views from the balcony. My heart was overjoyed, and all I could think was: *I created this.* Had I stayed stuck in anger and frustration at the airport, there's no way this upgrade would have unfolded. But because I chose to shift my energy, I became an energetic match for the abundance I ultimately received.

The lesson? **Your internal state creates your external reality.** *Master the moment, and the Universe will deliver.*

At the airport, it would have been easy to view an abundance of time — five extra hours before takeoff — as *lack* because it meant less time on the beach. It would have been predictable to let the delay dictate my mood and pull me into frustration.

But a Rich B$tch does not let external circumstances disconnect her from the internal, elevated emotions she is committed to maintaining. A Rich B$tch refuses to let inconveniences, opinions, or triggers cut her off from the abundance she's creating or the abundance she is *worthy* of receiving.

This reminds me of the woman who commented on my post about purchasing my first luxury handbag in comparison to being a mortgage payment for someone else.

It is another prime example of the "abundance creates lack" mindset. Her lens of lack could have had a ripple effect on me. I could have allowed her words to trigger shame around my celebration of success and abundance. I could have let it disconnect me from my joy. But I didn't. Why? Because I *choose* to see the abundance in my life, not the lack.

Someone else being triggered by your healing, success, or celebrations is *not* your work to do. It's theirs. And as a Rich B$tch, you don't carry the weight of someone else's unhealed beliefs. Your work is to keep your focus on the abundance you're creating, knowing that it is your birthright to receive it. You can celebrate your life without guilt, shame, or apology. Because when you live unapologetically in your light, you create space for others to rise into theirs.

Your job is simple yet profound: to live life as *abundantly* as possible and to lead by example, showing the world how to become the energetic match to wealth. This means prioritizing the management of your energy at all times — cultivating elevated emotions, finding abundance in the here and now, and embracing the duality of life with grace.

Abundance is not just something you chase, it's a frequency you embody.

The truth is, we are only ever separate from abundance when we *choose* to magnetize lack. Every thought, belief, and emotion either pulls us closer to or pushes us further away from the flow of wealth and prosperity.

Your work is to choose abundance over and over again, knowing that it's not a destination, it's a state of being — available to you right here, right now.

$$$

SIDENOTE: Insight without action makes no difference. You can have all the knowledge in the world, but if you don't apply it, nothing changes.

$$$

It's so easy to stay upset, to let negativity take root, and to justify reacting from a place that's not rooted in love. But catching yourself in those moments — when your emotions are pulling you away from your power — is critical to becoming the energetic match to wealth.

Negative emotions aren't the enemy. You're human. You will experience them. This work isn't about avoiding them but about rewiring yourself with habits and responses aligned with the Rich B$tch principles, habits that feel so natural they replace the old patterns that have kept your life status quo.

I've attended countless events and watched people receive transformational information — insights that could alter the trajectory of their lives. But when it comes time to take action, they fall back into old programming. Their lives don't change because they don't *apply* what they've learned.

So, let me say this again: It matters *the most* when it's the hardest for you to embody your Rich B$tch energy. That's when transformation happens. That's when you break through the limits of your past. That's when you create a new standard for your future.

You've got this.

$$$

Rich B$tch Homework: Focus on Abundance

1. **REFLECT ON "ABUNDANCE CREATING LACK"**
   - Identify areas where wealth or abundance in your life has led you to feel lack. For example: Have you made more money but felt more pressure? Have you celebrated a win but feared judgment?
   - Ask yourself: How can I shift my perspective to recognize the abundance present and express gratitude instead of focusing on lack?

2. **EXAMINE FEAR AND SELF-EXPRESSION**
   - Where are you holding back from sharing your success or your desires for more out of fear?
   - Write down what you're afraid will happen if you show up unapologetically in your truth and success.

3. **MASTER FRUSTRATION**

   Think about a recent moment of frustration that disconnected you from abundance. How could you have responded differently to remain in alignment with the Rich B$tch energy? What will you commit to doing the next time frustration arises?

4. **EMBODY YOUR RICH B$TCH SELF**
   - How does your Rich B$tch self unapologetically celebrate her success and use it as an example of what's possible?
   - Create a plan or practice for sharing your wins in a way that feels authentic, inspiring, and aligned with your highest self.

Remember, this isn't just journaling homework, it's action homework. Write it down, then put it into practice. You're creating a new energetic standard for yourself, and it starts right here.

The moments when it's the hardest to align your energy with the Rich B$tch principles? *Those* are the moments that define you.

CHAPTER
SIXTEEN

RICH
B$TCH MONEY GOALS

CHAPTER 16: BREAKING GENERATIONAL PATTERNS

Transforming your relationship with money demands relentless courage to shatter generational patterns, bold leadership to carve new paths, and unapologetic ownership of the truth: Becoming the energetic match to wealth is entirely on you.

Money is one of the most critical factors shaping the quality of our lives. Yet it's among the most misunderstood, judged, shamed, mishandled, and taboo topics. Most of us were taught that money is essential for survival, but we weren't taught how to generate money in ways that align with our soul's desires, allow us to thrive, and bring freedom and peace of mind.

Instead, we were raised with mindsets steeped in lack. We were programmed to make just enough to get by, to rely on others for financial security, and to tolerate joyless work because we believed we had no other choice. The prevailing belief for generations has been: Find a job. Stick with it no matter how much you hate it. Work until you're lucky enough to retire — if you even can.

WHERE WAS THE TALK OF PURPOSE? OF HEART-CENTERED LIVING?

The focus wasn't on desires or fulfillment but on survival. Work was practical — something you endured because you had to pay to live.

Let's dive deep and look closer at where it all begins: our earliest memories of money.

Our brainwave patterns are slow and highly receptive from birth to age six. During this time, we operate almost entirely from the subconscious mind, the part that absorbs without question because we haven't yet developed the analytical skills to challenge what we see or hear.

At this stage, we accept, believe, and model what we're taught by those around us. Parents, guardians, siblings, teachers, neighbors, celebrities, cartoon characters — anyone in a position of influence becomes our blueprint for truth.

We don't question it. We can't. We're living on autopilot, focused on surviving, growing, and being cared for, all based on the abilities, beliefs, and patterns of those responsible for us. Mirror neurons shape our foundational behaviors, wiring us to mimic what we see. The people we spend the most time with, usually our parents, become our models for how to think, feel, and act. And unless they break the generational patterns passed down to them, their habits, beliefs, and fears around money become the default programming you inherited.

Here's a simple example of mirror neurons: Imagine a parent feeding a child. The parent moves the spoon like an airplane, opens their mouth wide, and makes an "ah" sound to encourage the child to eat. What does the child do? They mimic the parent, opening their mouth in response.

It's not just eating. Mirror neurons influence our facial expressions, body language, and reactions to the world around us. As children, we learn how to respond to life by observing how our parents react to external stimuli, including money.

Now, let's layer in another factor: **generational trauma.** Events like war, economic depression, military service, immigration struggles, and societal instability create deeply rooted fears and beliefs that get passed down, often unconsciously. If your family lived through such challenges, the way they handled money — scarcity, fear, survival — was likely shaped by those experiences and handed down to you.

Think about it.

Did you grow up watching your parents come home from a grueling nine-to-five, exhausted from a job that drained them and paid far less than they deserved? Did you see them stress over bills, groceries, or rent, only to pour a glass of wine or crack open a beer to numb the reality of doing it again the next day? Sounds f*cked, right? That's the polar opposite of Rich B$tch energy.

And the language you heard around money? Probably more of the same:

- "Money doesn't grow on trees."
- "A penny saved is a penny earned."
- "We can't afford that."
- "I'm not paying to heat the outside! Close the door!"

Maybe your family shopped at discount stores or relied on hand-me-downs. Maybe you were told to put things back on the shelf at the grocery store or were pressured to get a job as soon as you were legally able, with the expectation that you'd contribute to the household.

If lack was the dominant narrative in your childhood, you've likely inherited that pattern. Maybe you tolerate a joyless job or complain about the cost of living, repeating what you saw growing up.

Here's the wake-up call:

Unless you actively reprogram your thoughts and behaviors around money, you're operating on autopilot, replaying the beliefs ingrained in you from your environment.

Your money story isn't yours. It's someone else's — a hand-me-down narrative passed through generations. And unless you break the cycle, you're likely passing it on to the next.

But here's the good news: **You're the one who can change everything.**

The fact that you're reading this right now is proof. You're the one daring enough to break the cycle. And you're ready (whether you think so or not) to rewrite your money story and create a reality that's yours, not someone else's outdated version of survival.

You're the one.

Become the Rich B$tch you were born to be.

Being a Rich B$tch isn't just about making money, it's about who you become in the process:

- The **ceiling-breaker** who shatters limitations.
- The **healer** who mends generational wounds.
- The **intuitive leader** who forges new paths.
- The **unapologetic dreamer** who claims her desires.

You're not just fighting for your own financial freedom, you're breaking years of inherited programming. It's not easy, but it's worth it. Because when you heal, you don't just heal for yourself. Your light raises the collective energy, showing others what's possible.

When people see your success, they think, *If she can do it, so can I.*

This is how you lead: by living boldly, unapologetically, and as proof that wealth isn't just about money. It's about joy, love, alignment, and purpose.

Let me share a glimpse of my life before I stepped into the Rich B$tch I am today.

Before I broke free from mediocrity (a.k.a. settling for just enough to cover the bills with barely anything left over), I worked at a law firm as a legal assistant for a criminal defense and family law attorney. Let me tell you that it was *not* because I wanted to be there, and it sure as hell wasn't my life's purpose.

$$$

SIDENOTE: If practicing law is your calling, more power to you! It's a badass profession, and my business attorney is living proof — she's a fierce, wave-making Rich B$tch in her own right. But for me? It was a far cry from the life I was meant to lead.

$$$

One Friday afternoon, I was sitting at my desk on a call with a client when my boss walked over, handed me my paycheck, and whispered, "Don't cash this until next week." Then he hurried out of the office before I could say a word.

The f*cking audacity.

And this wasn't the first time either. I was living paycheck to paycheck with nothing saved, and my rent was due. Being told to hold off on depositing my *earnings* was beyond stressful, but you know what was worse? Depending on someone else for my financial security.

The following week, my boss's wife rolled up to the office in a brand-new white Escalade, so shiny it looked like it had just been delivered straight from a car commercial. Meanwhile, my coworkers and I sat at our desks, clutching paychecks we'd been explicitly told *not to cash.* The absurdity was almost comical — there she was, flaunting luxury without a care in the world, while the rest of us were silently calculating how many days we had before rent checks bounced.

While everyone else was busy complaining, I had a f*cking epiphany.

It wasn't my boss who had the audacity, it was me — for ever believing that someone else was responsible for making my dreams come true. At that moment, it hit me: it wasn't my boss's problem to make me wealthy. It wasn't his responsibility to ensure I was financially free. That was *my job.*

That moment woke me the hell up. I realized that if I wanted financial freedom, I couldn't rely on anyone else to provide it. And if the way I was making money wasn't aligned with my desires, gifts, or purpose, I would never experience true wealth.

Let me say this loud and clear: **You're here to become the energetic match to wealth and create more money in your life, but money in the bank isn't where true wealth is found.**

You could have millions and still feel bankrupt inside.

True wealth is overflow — joy, love, gratitude, alignment, bliss, and purpose. It's about living a life that energizes you, spending your time in ways that feel meaningful, and creating a reality that lights you up from the inside out.

At twenty-four, I realized that becoming a Rich B$tch was entirely up to me. No more waiting for permission, no more excuses — I committed fully to my calling as an entrepreneur. Fresh out of a state-licensed hypnotherapy school in Michigan, with specialized training to work with cancer patients, I leveraged my credentials to advertise in *Psychology Today*. Then, I found the perfect office space, signed the lease, and started serving clients on weekends and after my nine-to-five. That single step wasn't just the launch of my business, it was the foundation of a brand-new life.

I know firsthand how following your intuition and chasing your dreams can feel impossible and downright terrifying. I wasn't just nervous, I was investing $400 a month in office space, every extra penny I had after bills, with no guarantee of clients walking through the door. And when my first client finally booked a session, fear hit me hard — who was going to take a twenty-four-year-old seriously?

The moment she sat down, I felt the weight of her hesitation and heard the unspoken question lingering in the air: How old is this woman? My deepest fear materialized before me. But instead of retreating, I met it with unwavering presence, leaning into my psychic gifts. I surrendered to intuition, allowing divine wisdom to flow through me, offering her exactly what her soul needed, even beyond the confines of a traditional hypnotherapy session. This became my sacred ritual: attuning to energy, forging deep trust, and creating a space where every client felt safe enough to fully open up.

Maybe you've been there too, questioning your worth, your voice, your offerings. That voice of doubt? Impostor Syndrome ... she's the biggest b*tch in the room, and you'll have to square off with her just like I did.

Because deep down, I *knew* I was meant to help people — and chances are, so are you. When you trust your soul's calling, break the generational cycles that have kept others stuck, and take the leap despite the fear, the Universe responds. It mirrors back confirmation, alignment, and unstoppable momentum. My success wasn't dictated by age, credentials, or self-doubt — it was fueled by my belief (the B in B$tch) in my purpose. And as I showed up fully, not only did clients keep booking but referrals started pouring in.

And that's how you start: by choosing to stop settling, start aligning with your Rich B$tch future, and begin taking the first step toward the life you're here to create.

The Universe doesn't test your faith; it responds to it.

You're reading this because you're ready to break free from inherited beliefs and rewrite your money story.

You can never fail at your purpose as it's already etched into the fabric of your destiny, written in the stars. Trusting your intuition might feel terrifying, but that fear is the doorway to your greatest growth. Walk through it.

When you trust yourself and step into your highest timeline, the Universe will rise to meet you. You're the one to break generational patterns. Now, it's time to act like it.

Rich B$tch Homework: Examine Your Money Beliefs

1. What unhealthy money patterns from your upbringing are you still carrying? Reflect on your parents' relationship with money and how it shaped your beliefs.

2. What's your earliest memory of money, and how does it make you feel?

3. How is your current relationship with money? What do you struggle with?

4. Identify your limiting money beliefs. Examples:
   - *I never have enough.*
   - *Rich people are bad.*
   - *I don't deserve nice things.*

5. What new, empowered money beliefs do you want to adopt and pass on to the next generation?

You're the author of your wealth story — so ditch the struggle plot and write yourself a damn masterpiece!

RICH B$TCH TRUTH

CHAPTER
SEVENTEEN

CHAPTER 17: CREATING YOUR RICH B$TCH SELF

Every lesson in this book is a key ingredient in the ultimate recipe I like to call "wealth." Together, they create the perfect alchemy for abundance, success, and unapologetic prosperity.

Sometimes, when baking, we realize we're missing an ingredient. So, we improvise, substitute, or skip it entirely. Sure, the recipe might turn out okay, but it won't be great. Sometimes we can get away with it, and sometimes we can't.

Certain ingredients, however, are nonnegotiable. They can make or break your success in baking — or creating. **This lesson is one of those critical ingredients.** It's the foundation, the glue, and everything in between. Without it, you might as well close this book and walk away.

In 2016, I faced what many married women would call their worst nightmare: I discovered my first husband was having an affair with his coworker. As you can imagine (or maybe even relate to), I was shattered. Grief, heartbreak, rage, despair, and confusion engulfed me. My sense of self-worth crumbled beneath the weight of it all.

It felt like I was living the Tower card in a Tarot deck. For those unfamiliar, this card depicts a tall, seemingly solid structure being struck by lightning — its foundation shattering and everything violently crashing down. It's the ultimate symbol of upheaval and destruction, and that's exactly what my life felt like: everything I'd built, everything I believed in, reduced to rubble in an instant.

And yet, in the midst of that devastation, I learned the most important lesson of all, one that became the foundation for rebuilding not just my life but the wealth, joy, and power I stand in today.

$$$

SIDENOTE: If you're experiencing a "Tower card" moment, let me remind you of its hidden gift. Destruction always carries its counterpart — creation. While everything around you may feel like it's crumbling, burning to the ground, and slipping through your fingers, a clearing is happening. Space is being made for something greater, something aligned with your highest potential.

This breakdown is not the end but the preparation for a new beginning. A fresh timeline is forming, one that's designed for the highest good of you and everyone connected to your journey.

Yes, it hurts. Yes, it's messy. But I invite you to trust in the process. Trust in the clearing because something extraordinary is on its way to you. The ashes of this moment will be the soil in which your greatest transformation grows.

$$$

Through all the chaos and destruction, I didn't just lose my marriage, I lost myself. My identity had been so entangled with him that when it was over, I didn't know who I was without him.

If you've been through this kind of heartbreak, you understand. You share dreams and hopes with someone, like we did. We had an entire future mapped out, a history that felt irreplaceable. It was everything I had been depending on, everything I was looking forward to.

We shared parts of ourselves no one else had seen. We were vulnerable in ways that felt transformative, filling in the gaps left by the lives we had before each other. We created moments so profound, so unique, that even through the pain, they lingered. Some things can't just be erased.

But in the blink of an eye, it was all gone. My life suddenly felt meaningless.

One afternoon, I sat on my bedroom floor, crying so hard I couldn't breathe. In that moment of hopelessness, a single question surfaced: Who am I without him?

That question would change everything.

The woman you see today — Kyera Kacey, the Rich B$tch CEO — didn't appear overnight. She didn't emerge from the ashes by chance. She was consciously created, intentionally willed into existence. She required grit, courage, and a commitment to rebuild. And believe me, she took a lot of hard work.

When my book *She Without He* was first born as a thought, it came from that very moment. Sitting on that floor, crying out to the void, I realized I was at a crossroads. That question, "Who am I without him?" wasn't just a cry for clarity, it was the spark that ignited my alignment with my higher calling.

It was the moment my true self began to rise.

Remember, the first step is always awareness.

When I went through the loss of my first marriage, I had a harsh realization — one that so many women experience: I had no f*cking clue who I was. My identity had become wrapped up in being part of a "we." A "we" that made decisions together, moved as a unit, and defined so much of my existence.

Even before that relationship, I'd been living in old programming, unconsciously surviving the circumstances life threw at me — relationships, work, family, and social interactions. I wasn't designing my life, I was reacting to it.

As I began the process of uncovering my authentic self, I had another revelation: If I felt this way, so many other women must feel it too.

Most women don't truly know who they are. They don't know what they deeply desire, how to use their voice powerfully, or what their purpose is beyond the narratives they've been handed. Narratives that demand they be:

- Caring
- Soft
- Kind
- Unobtrusive
- Quiet
- Giving
- Easygoing
- Flexible
- Accommodating
- A follower

Most women have never taken the time, or been encouraged, to ask themselves who they are *outside* the roles they've been assigned or the boxes they've been put in. Many don't realize they can define themselves, create their own rules, and intentionally build a life aligned with who they want to be.

If this resonates with you, hear this: **You have a choice.**

You have the power to create the Rich B$tch version of yourself — the woman you've always wanted to be.

You can decide what you're available for.

During that time, I also had a sobering realization about money: I wasn't financially equipped to stand on my own. Like so many women, I hadn't been taught how to create and sustain financial independence. So, I made a promise to myself that afternoon: **I vowed never to find myself in a position where my financial security depended on anyone else.**

I promised to dig myself out of that dark hole, create financial freedom for myself, and teach others how to do the same. But to do that, I had to make some changes. I had to become selective with my time, energy, and focus. I had to set new energetic standards for who and what had access to me.

I started asking myself a simple but profound question: "Is this loving to me?"

And then, I committed to finding — and following — the answer.

I became crystal clear about where I was willing to place my attention, who I was giving it to, and why. Simply put, I established boundaries.

Most women are conditioned to wrap their identities and purposes in titles like *mom, wife, sister, girlfriend,* or any of the many roles tied to caregiving and relationships. While there's nothing inherently wrong with identifying with these titles or embracing these roles, the issue arises when our entire sense of self-worth, purpose, and meaning is tied solely to them.

Think about it: What happens if one of those roles is lost?

If, God forbid, we lose a spouse or a child, our sense of identity can be devastated. Without that external role, many of us are left wondering who we are because we've built our self-worth around being something *for* someone else or attached our purpose to something external rather than cultivating a deep connection to who we are within.

Your soul's purpose — who you came here to experience yourself as — comes from *within.* It's not tied to any title or role. It can never be lost, and no one can take it away.

Independent of titles like *mom, wife,* or *girlfriend,* you have a purpose within you, a calling that has always been there. It doesn't depend on external validation or permission. It's yours, waiting for you to become conscious of it and answer it.

$$$

A NOTE TO MOMS: To every mom reading this, I want to be clear: I see you. Raising children is a full-time, hands-on-deck, 24/7/365 responsibility. It's superhero work.

When my sister passed away unexpectedly just days before Christmas in 2021, my role as godmother to her twelve-year-old son gave me a greater understanding of the essential developmental role parents play in raising their children. I have nothing but immense respect for you.

So, I am not downplaying, dismissing, or devaluing the significance of motherhood. I'm not saying being a mom isn't your purpose or that it's not deeply meaningful. I *am* saying that you are more than *just* that role — and that I believe we have more than one life purpose.

$$$

My intention is for you to become fully aware of your innate worth, independent of external titles, and to equip yourself financially so you can care for yourself, no matter what life throws your way. When you have the financial means to support yourself, you are no longer reacting to life, you are creating it. You have options, freedom, and the ability to make choices from a place of empowerment. More money doesn't just mean more "stuff." It means more *freedom*. It means less stress during hard times and more opportunities to live life on your terms — when you want, how you want, and where you want.

Because you, my love, are so much more than a title. You are a force.

The next questions for me were these: Was I going to unconsciously let infidelity, debt, and heartbreak define who I was for the rest of my life? Would I take on the role of victim and continue relying on others for support, validation, and purpose? Would I keep making choices that gave my power away?

Or was I going to take responsibility? Heal, move forward, create my future Rich B$tch self, claim my divine power, align with my calling, and define a new happily ever after?

The answers? You already know.

When I joined an online support group for women going through divorce, I started noticing a pattern. As women shared their stories, a theme began to emerge: victimization.

Let me pause and say this: I am a fierce advocate for seeking help when you need it. There's immense courage in being vulnerable and asking for support, especially when you are struggling to function in your daily life. Trustworthy programs and groups can be life-affirming, empowering, and beautiful reminders that you are not alone in your experience.

However, not all support groups operate from a place of healing and empowerment. In my experience with this particular divorce group, it was anything *but* supportive. The room was filled with women who, five, ten, twenty, or even thirty years later, were still holding themselves and their exes hostage to a moment in time (the past). They were stuck. Rarely did I see women who had moved on, thrived, evolved, or reclaimed their joy.

Once I saw this pattern, I made a vow: **I will not be one of them.**

Following the train wreck that was my divorce, I knew all too well how to be a victim. Negative thoughts and behaviors were on autopilot. But if I was going to change my life and finances, I needed to learn to be something *other than* a victim.

I needed to learn how to be a wealthy, liberated woman.

So do you.

To bring your Rich B$tch self into existence, you must *consciously* create her. You need to know her inside and out, like the color of your eyes.

Who is she? What are her boundaries? What are her deal breakers? How does she walk, talk, and carry herself? What does she wear? How does she behave in relationships? How much does she earn, and how does she earn it?

Know her every move. Know her every desire. Know her feelings.

For example:

- If your Rich B$tch self walks like Beyoncé at the 2013 Super Bowl halftime show, you need to embody fierce confidence.
- If your Rich B$tch self wants to be as wealthy and influential as Kim Kardashian (love her or hate her, she's built an empire), you must feel empowered, magnetic, and significant.
- If your Rich B$tch self is attracting "the one," you must exude self-love, heal past traumas, and trust wholeheartedly.
- If your Rich B$tch self wants to make seven figures, you must feel gratitude for that wealth *before* it's in your bank account.

Act as if it's already done.

Creating the Rich B$tch version of yourself requires a clean slate. You can't drag your lack and limitations into abundance — they're incompatible. This means letting go of the stories, experiences, and habits that no longer align with liberation and love.

I could've spent the rest of my life telling myself I couldn't trust men because of my ex's infidelity. I could've stayed angry, bitter, and closed-hearted, sabotaging future relationships. I could've blamed my financial struggles on him or my upbringing.

Would I have been justified? Sure. But I would've been *powerless.*

**There's no power in victimhood.
There's no power in blaming and complaining.**

So, I made a choice: I let it all go. I burned the book of my old story and wrote a new one.

There's a version of you living a wildly different life, one filled with abundance, joy, and ease.

- She's safe with money, undeniably worthy of receiving it, and joyful when releasing it back into the Universe.
- She attracts wealth, love, and opportunities in the most effortless ways.
- She's living in financial overflow and is deeply in love with her life.

She's waiting for you to claim her.

Becoming a Rich B$tch requires letting go of old identities and stepping into the frequency of abundance. It takes work, consistency, and accountability — but trust me, it's worth it!

My life today? I created it. I'm not here because of luck. I'm here because I made bold, expansive choices and let go of moments and stories that no longer served me.

**To change your life,
you have to change yourself.**

No one can do this work for you, but let me remind you of one thing: **You are absolutely worthy of it.**

$$$

Rich B$tch Homework: Create Who You Want to Be

1. **IDENTIFY YOUR ROLE MODELS**

   Write down the top five people you admire. Ask yourself: What about them inspires me? What qualities do they have that I want to bring out in myself? You will find that you're attracted to others who exude qualities you want to bring out in yourself.

2. CREATE YOUR RICH B$TCH SELF

Grab a journal and bring her to life. Who is the highest, most powerful version of yourself you can imagine? Pair each desire with a feeling. Be bold. Go deep. Don't hold back.

3. CHALLENGE YOUR LIMITS

Notice where you feel resistance or hear negative thoughts. Catch them, ask if they're loving, and reframe them into something positive and freeing.

4. PAIR DESIRES WITH FEELINGS

- *I desire to work from anywhere in the world. → This makes me feel liberated, happy, and adventurous.*
- *I desire six-figure months. → This makes me feel relieved and excited.*
- *I desire aligned clients who cherish our time together. → This makes me feel grateful, inspired, and motivated.*
- *I desire to work 10 a.m.–2 p.m., Monday through Thursday. → This makes me feel rested, aligned, and joyful.*

RICH B$TCH TRUTH

Becoming your Rich B$tch self won't happen overnight, and that's okay. Real change takes time, effort, and energy. You didn't become who you are now in a day, and your transformation will require consistency.

You've got this. The life you want is waiting for you to claim it.

CHAPTER
EIGHTEEN

RICH
B$TCH MONEY GOALS

CHAPTER 18: RICH B$TCH ENVIRONMENT

The environment of a Rich B$tch is a direct reflection of who she is and what she's creating. It exudes alignment, clarity, and abundance. Her space is intentionally designed to support her vision, with room readily available for the arrival of her manifestations.

While it's true that who we are isn't defined by our material possessions, let's get real: Everything around us is energy, vibrating at a specific frequency, and that energy absolutely influences us.

You know what I'm talking about. How often have you heard someone say, "OMG, these crazy energies" during a full moon or blamed Mercury retrograde for everything from lost emails to spilling coffee on their white shirt? Maybe you've even said it yourself. (No shame — but girl, the planets aren't to blame!)

Everything is energy, and energy affects EVERYTHING.

That's why it's time to take a good, hard look at your space and ask yourself the million-dollar question: *Does this belong in my future?*

Be honest. If it's not aligning with the fierce, abundant, Rich B$tch you're becoming, why are you holding on to it? You don't need that old sweater with holes in it or that chipped coffee mug "just in case." You're leveling up, and your environment should reflect that.

I learned this lesson the hard way when I stumbled upon silver eye glitter in my makeup drawer — the same one I'd bought from Hot Topic in middle school.

Let me just say: absolutely not.

First, nobody wants pink eye. Second, my Rich B$tch environment has no room for twenty-year-old makeup clinging to my past. That had to go — immediately.

When our energy expands and we evolve, it's crucial to lovingly release what no longer aligns with who we're becoming. Holding on to things from the past keeps us stuck, as if one foot is rooted in who we used to be, while the other is awkwardly pointed toward the future. This creates resistance, slowing down the arrival of what we truly desire.

A Rich B$tch commits to her future with both feet firmly planted in alignment. She intentionally clears the space for her manifestations to arrive, and they flow to her faster because she's fully available for them.

Creating something new means *making space* for it to show up. No exceptions.

Let me ask you this: If you were single and dreaming of finding *the one,* would you keep photos of you and your ex plastered all over your home? Absolutely not. Imagine bringing a hot date home and having to explain *those* pictures — cringe! If you're manifesting a new relationship, your space needs to scream "I'm ready for love!" not "I'm still hung up on my ex."

Now, think about those clothes from eighth grade. Can you imagine rocking them today? Yeah, no. You outgrew those years ago. When they didn't fit anymore, they got tossed, donated, or handed down to make space for something new, something that actually fit you.

Holding on to things (whether it's old belongings, outdated relationships, or stagnant situations) that you've outgrown slows down the arrival of what you *really* want. You can wish for wealth, love, and abundance all day long, but if your environment screams *lack* — if it's cluttered with stuff you don't use, need, or even like —

you're sending mixed signals to the Universe. How can you receive anything new when there's no space for it?

I had my own wake-up call when I found that glittery makeup lurking in my bathroom. (Seriously, what was I thinking?!) Mortified, I headed to my closet and found high school clothes still hanging around too. High School! I couldn't even remember the last time I'd worn them.

That's when I decided it was time to "Marie Kondo" my life.

If you don't know who Marie Kondo is, let me fill you in. She's a world-famous tidying expert (yes, that's a real thing!). Her method is life-changing and super simple: instead of asking, "What should I get rid of?" you ask, "What do I truly want to keep?"

Hold each item in your hands and ask yourself: *Does this spark joy?* If the answer is yes, it stays. If it's a no (or even a *meh*), it goes.

This isn't just about decluttering your physical space, it's about creating an environment that screams "I'm ready for my next level!" It's about clearing the old so your new manifestations have a place to land. When you let go of what no longer serves you, you're telling the Universe: "I'm ready. Bring it on."

While Marie Kondo suggests asking, "Does this spark joy?" I like to take it up a notch. My standard is: "Does this make me feel like a Rich B$tch?" If it doesn't align with that energy, it's out — simple as that.

So, when I decided to tackle my closet and dresser drawers, I quickly realized I was going to need reinforcements. I ran downstairs to grab some industrial-sized garbage bags because it was time for a major purge.

Let me tell you, there were *plenty* of things that didn't make the cut. Not only did they not spark joy, but they also actively sparked lack, reminding me of a version of myself I had lovingly worked hard to outgrow.

As I started tossing items, something interesting happened. I came across several pieces of clothing that still had the tags on them. They were beautiful, high-quality, and expensive — items I genuinely loved but had never worn. Why? Because of the same limiting mindset that kept me preserving "nice" purses in my closet while rotating through cheap, junky ones. I didn't want to ruin the nice things, so I avoided using them altogether. Meanwhile, I kept settling for what I didn't care about, telling myself I was being "practical," when in reality, I was operating from lack.

That moment served as a pivotal turning point.

Here I was, hoarding things I loved, waiting for some *special occasion* to use them yet constantly settling for less in my day-to-day life. How could I claim to be stepping into my Rich B$tch energy if I wasn't even allowing myself to *live* like one?

This process wasn't just about clearing out clothes or purses. I was stepping into alignment with who I was becoming and making space for a life that fully reflects that. Because a Rich B$tch doesn't wait for permission to enjoy what she has, she lives her life unapologetically, in abundance, every single day. And from that moment on, so did I.

This was the moment I uncovered a limiting belief I had been clinging to for years: *If I wear something expensive and it gets ruined, I'll no longer have something nice. Better to save it for a special occasion, or not wear it at all, so I can hold on to it.*

Let's unpack that for a second. The mindset behind this belief is rooted in lack: *If I use or wear something I love, something I'm not accustomed to having, and it gets damaged, I won't be able to replace it.*

Sound familiar? Think about that beautiful candle you bought but never lit because it felt too precious to use, or that fine china collecting dust in the cabinet, reserved for "special occasions."

What if, instead of waiting, you lit the candle today, enjoyed your fine china for an everyday meal, and celebrated life as it's happening? What if you embraced joy, pleasure, and abundance *now* instead of endlessly deferring it?

When you cling to things out of fear — fear of damage, fear of loss, fear of scarcity — you're sending a clear message to the Universe: "I don't believe I can have more. I don't trust abundance."

That realization hit me hard. I noticed this pattern everywhere, even with my purses, as I've said. When I started buying designer bags, I initially clung to my old, inexpensive ones "just in case." I rationalized that I'd need them for certain situations, like going to the movies with my nephew and hauling a ton of snacks, which inevitably ended up at the bottom of my bag. Keeping the cheap ones was my way of "protecting" the expensive ones.

Those old bags weren't just clutter, though, they were symbols of my scarcity mindset. By keeping them, I was telling myself, "You're not ready for this upgrade. You're not fully committed to abundance."

So, I got rid of them. All of them. And with that, I made a new commitment to myself: "Use it anyway."

Now, when I go to the movies, my large designer purse is stuffed with all the snacks my nephew can carry. If chocolate gets spilled inside? Who cares. I know I can replace it if I need to, but more importantly, I know it's just *not that serious.* Life is meant to be lived.

This shift wasn't just about my purses; I was stepping into the energy of my future self and practicing abundance daily. By letting go of items that no longer bring you joy or resonate with who you're becoming, you create space for abundance to flow into the *here and now.* Your future self isn't waiting to live her best life, she's doing it today. So, stop taking yourself too seriously, have fun, and use the damn candle!

It's time to cut ties with everything you've outgrown, figuratively and literally. Trust that by releasing what no longer serves you, you're making space for something far better than you can even imagine.

Think of it like a relationship you know it's time to leave. You don't need to stress about replacements or obsess over how and when upgrades will show up. They *will* come as a natural response to the aligned Rich B$tch moves you're making.

Right now, your priority is simple: Clear the stagnant energy, make space, and prepare your environment to welcome your manifestations. By focusing on becoming the energetic match to wealth, and creating a physical and energetic space that reflects your Rich B$tch self, you're sending a powerful signal to the Universe: "I'm ready. Bring it." And trust me, it will.

$$$

Rich B$tch Homework: Make Space

This exercise is one of my absolute favorites — it's fun, liberating, and deeply empowering. And trust me, every Rich B$tch who's ever done this agrees that the sense of lightness and clarity you feel afterward is unmatched.

It's so inspiring to witness women create space for their future desires, so if you're called to share your purge, tag me on Instagram **@kyerakacey** and use **#richbitchmoneygoals**. I'd love to celebrate this moment with you!

HERE'S HOW TO GET STARTED:

- Pour yourself a glass of wine or a cup of your favorite tea.
- Order a pizza or a treat you love.
- Put on your favorite playlist and grab your sage to clear the energy as you go.

- Block out your schedule so you can dive into this task uninterrupted.

Now, let's get down to business — it's time to *Rich B$tch your home!* Make sure you have garbage bags or boxes for donations.

You can start anywhere that feels right, but here's your ultimate checklist:

1. **CLOSET**

   Go through clothes, shoes, handbags, and accessories. Anything that no longer makes you feel like your Rich B$tch self has got to go.

2. **YOUR MAIN PURSE**

   Clean it out! Yes, even that forgotten gum wrapper from three years ago.

3. **MAKEUP AND BRUSHES**

   If it's old, expired, or unused, toss it.

4. **BOOKS, JOURNALS, NOTEBOOKS**

   It's easy to hold on to these because of the emotional investment, but ask yourself: *When was the last time I actually used this?* I once purged an entire box of journals and two boxes of books, and the feeling of freedom was incredible.

5. **BEDDING AND TOWELS**

   If they're frayed, torn, or just don't spark joy, it's time for an upgrade.

6. **MISCELLANEOUS JUNK**

   That one junk drawer? You know the one. Clear it out.

7. **YOUR CAR**

   Take a look — you'll be surprised how many things have accumulated that need to go.

8. **ATTIC AND/OR GARAGE**

   If you store things here, it's time to take inventory and let go of what no longer serves you.

9. **OFFICE SPACE**

   Don't underestimate the power of a clutter-free workspace to support your abundance mindset.

> If your environment isn't giving Rich B$tch energy, it's giving problems — and we don't do those. Upgrade the vibe, raise the standards, and evict anything (or anyone) that doesn't match your next-level wealth frequency.

CHAPTER NINETEEN

RICH
B$TCH MONEY GOALS

CHAPTER 19: RICH B$TCH SISTERHOOD

A Rich B$tch defines sisterhood not by the size of someone's bank account but by the depth of their love, integrity, laughter, and unwavering support. Her sisterhood is heart-centered, built on trust, and aligned with her highest values.

Change is inevitable. As you grow, your life will transform — your friends will shift, your relationships will evolve, and sometimes you'll face tough decisions to honor your expansion.

Now is the time to take a hard look at the unhealthy, toxic relationships in your life. The ones that lack balance, drain your energy, and take more than they give. It's time to decide: Will you continue to tolerate these connections, or will you choose to release them and reclaim your power?

Sometimes relationships evolve with us as we grow and expand — that's the dream, the best-case scenario we all hope for. But when they stay stagnant while you rise, the energetic match dissolves. At that point, change often looks like moving beyond the relationship.

Maybe that person was exactly what you needed at a certain point in time, teaching you a valuable soul lesson (and vice versa). But if they're not investing in their growth as you are, it might be time to accept that the relationship has run its course. It's time to say goodbye and honor your evolution.

This decision isn't easy — it's complex and deeply personal, especially when it involves someone you've loved for years or even family. Many people feel trapped by guilt or a sense of obligation, staying in unloving relationships that no longer serve them because of karmic soul ties or a distorted sense of loyalty.

But when you choose to stay in relationships (personal or professional) that don't honor you, you send a clear signal to the Universe that *this* is your standard. You're saying you are willing to accept whatever those relationships offer, whether it's unkindness, apathy, emotional unavailability, self-abandonment, unhealthy behavior, or even a bandage for loneliness.

You deserve better. And it's up to you to demand better.

The Universe only gives you what you believe you're worthy of receiving. If you think you're only good enough for a friends-with-benefits situation, that's exactly what you'll attract. If you believe you must undercharge or compromise your fees to keep clients, you'll find yourself surrounded by people who confirm that reality.

Raising your standards, choosing yourself in the name of love, and honoring your highest truth are the ultimate initiations into becoming an energetic match for wealth in every area of your life. More often than not, that's your next-level "strategy."

Wealthy people understand the power of social influence. They treat their network with the same precision and care as a thriving company manages its top employees — because success isn't personal, it's a potential they're laser-focused on creating, sustaining, and growing.

They know the culture they live in, the environments they immerse themselves in, and the people they surround themselves with directly shape their life, health, and business. That's why they don't waste time taking action to realign when something feels off.

This is also why they invest — sometimes hundreds of thousands of dollars — into private mentorships, live events, programs, and masterminds. They understand that to expand quickly, they need to sit at the table with high achievers who teach, inspire, and activate them.

Your standards define your reality.
Raise them, then watch your life transform.

If you want to collapse time and achieve faster results, align yourself with those who have already paved the way. Success leaves clues, and proximity to greatness accelerates your path to it.

Surround yourself with people who embody integrity and high-consciousness leadership — those who are out in the world creating and engaging in extraordinary things. Simply being in their presence invites expansion. Their drive, focus, and high-level energy inspire you to reach for higher potential. Their vibration doesn't just motivate, it *pulls* you upward, attracting you to a more elevated way of being.

Every piece of information you consume, whether it's a podcast, a conversation with a friend, a TV show, or even your own thoughts, is either raising or lowering your vibration. Every choice contributes to what you're an energetic match for, shaping the reality you're creating.

Here's a truth you can't ignore: Where your time and attention go, your energy flows — and your reality follows.

Let me share a story that highlights the power of holding your energy and values at the highest level. This pivotal moment in my business shows how critical it is to align yourself with integrity, and not just for your own growth but also for the opportunity it gives others to rise.

We are all interconnected, and our choices create ripple effects. When you lead with alignment, you invite others to expand, embrace love, and rise to their highest potential, for the greatest good of all.

At the start of my business, I hired an employee who wasn't aligned, but I didn't see it right away. Over time, it became clear: instead of feeling supported on the back end of my business, I felt like I was taking on even more work. This misalignment was a massive, ongoing energy drain, and it became a frequent topic of conversation with my mentor. It was also evident that our mindsets around money were worlds apart. No matter how much I wanted this to work, it was very evident that it *wasn't* working.

The solution? My next initiation into higher levels of success, both internally and externally, required me to realign my business by releasing what wasn't working. Letting this employee go was undeniably for the highest good, but that didn't make it easy. As an employer, letting someone go comes with the territory, but it's never comfortable (unless you're Kevin O'Leary from *Shark Tank*). Still, I knew I had to trust the process.

Sometimes the most loving thing you can do,
for yourself and others, is to let go.

When we have the courage to face discomfort, to make the tough but necessary decisions, and to reset the frequency of our lives and businesses, immediate relief follows. Alignment always brings clarity, peace, and forward momentum.

This was one of the most powerful lessons in creating success: **Release what no longer serves you, and trust that it's clearing space for something greater.**

If it's aligned with your highest truth,
it's in love.

It's no accident that just months after fully aligning my business, I hit my first six-figure cash month.

Aligned support isn't just helpful, it's a nonnegotiable. It's a vital key to unlocking true wealth and abundance. When everything aligns, success flows effortlessly.

I no longer waste time catching people up to speed. My current team is flying *with* me. They embody Rich B$tch principles and are fully aligned with the greater vision. They cocreate alongside me and do the behind-the-scenes work that keeps our frequency high.

Your team should make your life easier, not more complicated. Their beliefs must align with your company's mission and be fueled by excitement for what's possible. You deserve high-level support from people who innovate, deeply care, and invest in their own growth.

That's the f*cking Rich B$tch standard.

We also trust our intuition when it signals that something, or someone, is off. These standards are what build and sustain your Rich B$tch sisterhood.

Social influence is a force — it will either empower you or derail your growth. It's time to stop appeasing others at the expense of your well-being and success. Raise your standards, hold your boundaries, and watch your life transform.

You're not just the average of the five people with whom you spend the most time, you're the sum of *everyone* you allow into your space. This even includes people you don't personally know but whose energy, influence, or opinions you engage with.

In your pursuit of becoming an energetic match to wealth, your transformation will inevitably trigger people. But it will also open powerful portals, offering you the chance to evolve by choice.

Making space for your next level doesn't just happen in your closet. If you're truly committed to your transformation, you'll need to declutter your professional and social circles too. Yes, this process can look messy. It will almost certainly feel uncomfortable. But that's the price of growth. So, keep shining bright, keep making Rich B$tch moves, and let your light blaze a trail for your highest self to step into becoming.

Toxic relationships are some of the most money-draining energy leaks you'll ever encounter. If removing someone from your life feels aligned and loving for you, trust that it's also aligned and loving for them. **Highest truth. Highest love. Highest good for all.**

Like everything in life, your choices come with both a payoff and a cost. If you want to be a Rich B$tch, you must learn how to release the anchors holding you back — without guilt, without hesitation, and without looking back. And yes, sometimes, this even includes clients.

After the sudden death of my sister, a private client who had been with me for over a year told me flat-out, "You've changed, and I don't like it. I miss the old Kyera."

Turns out, she wasn't just telling me this. She had also been having these conversations with other clients in my world, openly discussing how "Kyera's changed." Of course, she conveniently omitted the full truth.

What she really missed about the "old Kyera" was the version of me that lacked boundaries and structure, especially around payments. She missed the Kyera who tolerated her late payments without accountability. But that version of me wasn't serving anyone. The "old Kyera" was enabling unhealthy money habits, creating energetic leaks in my business, and staying silent instead of calling clients forward into their growth.

**You don't step into your Rich B$tch power
by staying silent. You step into it by owning your worth
and demanding alignment in every area of your life.**

My client who "missed the old Kyera" had grown comfortable with habits that didn't align: making late payments, offering little to no communication about it, and relying on my tolerance to enable her behavior. So, when I implemented boundaries and structure in my business (for the highest good of all), she wasn't happy.

But here's the reality:

I implemented boundaries. *Kyera's changed.*
I raised my standards. *Kyera's changed.*

I stopped tolerating a lack of communication. *Kyera's changed.*
I filtered every decision through the lens of "for the highest good of all." *Kyera's changed.*
I sealed energetic leaks in my business. *Kyera's changed.*

Was it true? Had I changed?

F*ck yes, I had!

And I'm damn proud of it. Growth requires change, and change requires unwavering commitment to your worth.

I realized that some actions in my business clashed with my values, and for the highest good of all, I realigned my business to reflect those values. In doing so, I became a wiser, more intentional CEO.

It became clear that my lack of boundaries and hesitancy to call clients forward wasn't kindness, it was avoidance. I was dodging the discomfort of hurting people's feelings at the expense of my own well-being. By people-pleasing, I was enabling the very unhealthy money patterns my clients were desperate to outgrow.

So, I stepped up. I became a stronger leader. **And that single act was a service to everyone.**

As I aligned my business, the clients who couldn't accept my new boundaries chose to leave. And you know what? That's okay. Sometimes people evolve with you. Sometimes they don't. When the Universe starts cleaning house and removing what no longer serves you, your job isn't to resist, it's to release.

**Let go, and trust in what's coming.
It's always more extraordinary.**

Expiration dates aren't just for the food in your fridge. Some of you are clinging to expired relationships and wondering why you're sick, drained, uninspired, and out of balance.

For the clients who were projecting negativity and stirring discord, I extended an invitation to have a powerful, transparent conversation. As part of a year-long mastermind I was leading, this was their chance to step into their next level of leadership — an opportunity to rise with higher consciousness and expand.

They declined.

And that's their choice. I made mine: alignment, integrity, and leadership for the highest good of all.

As they left, they created space — a vacuum for new, aligned individuals with higher consciousness to arrive. The group's energy grew stronger, more united, and more inspired. I was deeply grateful for the expansion this shift brought to my life and business.

Being a Rich B$tch demands fierce self-love. Self-love isn't selfish, it's a gift to everyone you interact with, even if it triggers them.

Becoming the energetic match to wealth is about evolving in every aspect of your life, not just your finances. When you become the kind of woman who aligns her life, business, and relationships to the frequency of abundance, for the highest good of all, you step into a higher responsibility. You're called to create space for others to expand. And as you clear that space, you develop the confidence and strength to face challenges that require your leadership and personal power.

What kind of challenges, you ask?

- **Can you hold the weight and discomfort of expansion** as your Rich B$tch muscles tear and stretch, knowing they will grow back stronger? Or will you drop the weight because it feels too heavy to carry consistently?

- **Can you model what a self-regulated Rich B$tch does,** meeting challenges with integrity, self-love, and the highest good in mind?

- **Can you accept that not everyone will like you?** Will you handle the energy and emotions projected onto you as you evolve, staying rooted in love and aligned action?

- **Can you embrace being a mirror?** Will you allow others to see in you the qualities they desire or fear within themselves, sparking opportunities for their growth and self-reflection?

- **Will you take responsibility** for the areas in your life that aren't contributing to your success or the success of others?

- **Can you recognize where you've enabled unhealthy habits in others** and take bold action to end that cycle?

- **Will you act, even if it means cutting ties** with people you've outgrown or those who no longer align with who you're becoming?

**Remember this: Who you
spend time with matters — a lot.**

Your standards, or lack of them, are constantly communicating to the Universe what you believe you're worthy of receiving. Raise your standards, and the Universe will rise to meet you.

So, let go and create alignment.

Saying goodbye to people you love or have a long history with isn't easy — even when it's clear they've become unhealthy for you. I've walked this path of letting go more times than I can count.

**Becoming the energetic match to wealth isn't
about ease, it's about living in unwavering truth.**

It's about being brutally honest with yourself: Who and what are you consistently choosing? What are you giving your time and energy to that drains you rather than contributes to your Rich B$tch future? Once you get clear, you can begin plugging those leaks and attracting from a place of true soul alignment.

But let's get real: being a Rich B$tch isn't all courageous conversations and big decisions. It's also about sharing belly-aching laughter, having ridiculous fun, and surrounding yourself with people who know how to bring the *high vibes*.

Need proof? Let me share a moment of *peak* Rich B$tch sisterhood.

It was the last day of my 2023 retreat in Ireland (also my birthday), and one of my incredible clients decided to surprise me with — wait for it — a male dancer. Yes, you read that right. Because if you're going to celebrate, you might as well go all out, right?

So, there I was in the presidential suite of a five-star luxury hotel when this guy shows up and casually transforms into a construction worker (because apparently, that's what the Rich B$tch sisterhood ordered). Then, as "She Knows" by Ne-Yo starts blasting, he struts over, leads me to a chair in the middle of the suite, and kicks off a performance we'll never forget.

I wasn't exactly planning on seeing a naked man that night — or being hoisted into a chair that sounded like it was auditioning for its own demolition derby as it creaked while I was bounced up and down — but hey, life's full of surprises. I was just happy he didn't drop me!

We laughed so hard that I'm pretty sure we burned off every calorie from all the sticky toffee pudding and other desserts we devoured during that retreat. But here's my favorite part: Our Rich B$tch frequency didn't just manifest *any* dancer, we attracted a respectful one. In between his moves, he kept pausing to check in with me, saying, "Are you okay?"

"Sir, I'm being serenaded by Ne-Yo and a construction fantasy — you think I'm *not okay*?"

That's the magic of the Rich B$tch sisterhood: love, high vibes, and endless laughter — even when it comes with a side of choreography and costume changes ordered by your clients.

$$$

Rich B$tch Homework: Build Your Rich B$tch Sisterhood

Take a hard look at the relationships in your life.

- Are your friends, team members, and frequent connections people who lift you higher — or have you outgrown them?
- Have the courageous conversations you need to release anyone no longer aligned with your vision, making space for more bliss and alignment in your life.

If you don't yet have your dream circle of high-vibe Rich B$tches, start by creating a desire list:

- What qualities do you want in the people you surround yourself with?
- How do you spend time together?
- What kinds of conversations do you have?
- How do these relationships make you feel?

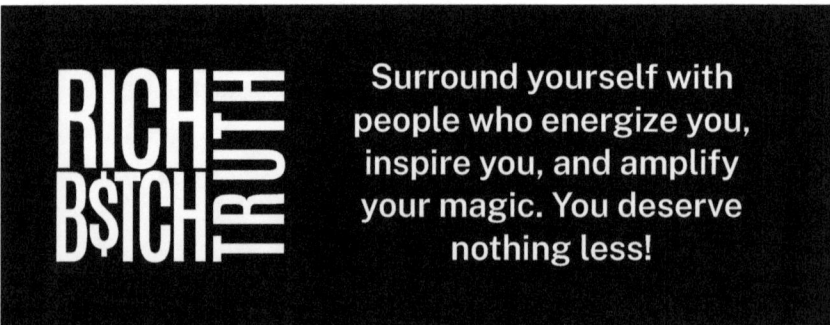

RICH B$TCH TRUTH

Surround yourself with people who energize you, inspire you, and amplify your magic. You deserve nothing less!

CHAPTER
TWENTY

RICH
B$TCH MONEY GOALS

CHAPTER 20: ABC: ALWAYS BE CONVINCED

A Rich B$tch is unwavering in her conviction of who she is. She lives fully aligned and connected to the ultimate power source — the one within her. Her self-belief is her foundation, and her inner light fuels everything she creates.

In business, we're often told that the golden rule in sales is ABC: Always Be Closing. For most, this idea is paired with the belief that success requires outworking the competition and tirelessly convincing clients to invest.

I disagree. Why? Because the foundation of every sale isn't in effort, it's in belief. You can't close a sale if you don't believe you can.

The truth is, competition only exists in one place: your mind.

This reminds me of a client's experience that perfectly illustrates this concept. In 1997, he was invited to teach at the largest post-graduate university in the United States. Among the instructors, there were sixteen men, all close in age and with nearly identical training. On the surface, they seemed evenly matched.

Yet there was one glaring difference: their annual salaries ranged dramatically — from $80,000 to $1,000,000.

What set the $1,000,000 earner apart wasn't his credentials or effort. It was his mindset, his belief in his worth, and his ability to connect with his inner power. Success in business isn't about grinding harder or outpacing others, it's about aligning with your value, owning your worth, and stepping into the energy of *certainty*. That's the real secret to creating extraordinary results.

When my client discovered the drastic difference in salaries, he couldn't help but ask one of the men in charge, "Why is it that we have sixteen instructors, all doing the same work, yet everyone is making something different?"

The answer to that question holds a powerful truth about worth, belief, and abundance.

The man who embodied the power of belief in his worth and his ability to create success didn't just make waves, he created a tidal wave in the Universe. His financial success wasn't born from grinding himself into the ground, hustling nonstop, trying to prove his value, or outworking the competition.

It was created through belief.

He believed in wealth. He believed in his worth. Most importantly, he moved into the *feeling* of wealth, embodying it so deeply that it became his reality. Because of this unwavering certainty, he confidently asked for what he believed he was worth — and the Universe delivered.

Believing you're worthy of receiving $1,000,000, paired with the belief that you can *create* millions of dollars, makes you an energetic match for wealth. It's not just a mindset, it's an embodiment. When you see wealth through this lens, the game changes. Sales is no longer about Always Be Closing. It becomes Always Be Convinced.

First, sell yourself. Convince yourself of your worthiness and your ability to create $1,000,000 in your business. When you believe it, you align with it. And when you align with it, the results are inevitable.

If you're not sold on *who you are,* what you offer, and what you bring to the table, how the hell do you expect anyone else to be?

If you're not convinced you can create anything your heart desires, you'll settle for mediocrity and less. If you're not convinced you can create an abundant, fulfilling life, you won't bother investing the time, energy, or belief into becoming the energetic match to wealth. Instead, you'll think, *What's the point? It won't happen anyway.*

But let me tell you: *Wrong.*

"ABC" isn't just Always Be Closing, it's Always Be Convinced — convinced of your worth, convinced of your power, convinced that if it can happen for her, it can happen for *you.*

You get to desire and have *this.* And you get to desire and have *that.*

It's not an either/or game — it's *this AND that.* You get to live the life of your dreams. Now convince yourself of it, because that's where it all begins.

This takes me back to the early days of my career, creating coaching packages for women navigating divorce. At the time, I was still stepping into my role as the CEO of my business and learning how to become the energetic match to wealth. My mentor advised me to start by conducting market research to determine my pricing. Like many new entrepreneurs, I followed the guidance and researched what others in my field were charging.

We're often told that the key to pricing is to compare and compete — find out what others are charging and position yourself somewhere in the "sweet spot." Not too high, not too low. The logic is to make yourself attractive and "reasonably priced" for potential clients.

If I could stand in front of every person who's ever received that advice and throw up a giant STOP sign, I absolutely would!

That said, I'm grateful for the experience. The Universe was teaching me something invaluable, and I was listening. Had I not gone through the process of conducting market research, I wouldn't have learned this critical lesson, a lesson that has helped me scale my business with greater ease, build confidence in my intuition, and lead from innovation, not imitation.

Here's what happened:

While conducting market research, I came across a woman in my field who wasn't just a private consultant, she was also a published author and a globally respected psychotherapist who had appeared on NBC's *The Today Show* and *Oprah Radio*.

I was floored when I discovered she charged her clients *less* than I was charging mine.

Wait, what the f*ck? I was completely confused. I felt the disconnect immediately. Something didn't add up, and it forced me to rethink everything I'd been told about pricing and the way we determine our worth in business.

This exact moment revealed a fundamental truth to me, and here's the lesson the Universe was preparing to deliver: Taking someone else's life and business decisions — their work, their choices, their pricing — and using them as the measuring stick for our own potential and possibilities is, for lack of a better word, f*cked.

Comparing experiences, credentials, or paths and using that information as your guiding light doesn't just limit you, it distorts your vision and keeps you playing small. Your worth, your business, and your potential have nothing to do with someone else's decisions.

Had I not already been fully sold on who I was, discovering her pricing could have been a massive mind f*ck. I might have questioned my value, dropped my prices, and moved completely out of alignment. Worse, I could've fallen into that all-too-common trap of asking myself, "Who am I to do this?"

But that didn't happen. Fear didn't even surface. Instead, I was liberated. A deeper truth and unwavering certainty landed for me that day.

It was a light-switch moment, one that could never be turned off — a *once you know, you can never not know* revelation. Let this be *your* moment. No matter who you are, where you come from, what credentials you do or don't have, or what your past looks like, *creating wealth has nothing, literally nothing, to do with anyone else.*

Stop looking to other people to determine your worth. Stop letting others dictate what you're deserving of, what your desires should be, what your packages or pricing should look like, or what path you "should" be on.

Your worth is not up for debate. Your path is your own. Claim it.

Stop comparing yourself.

Ultimately, I realized that the psychotherapist's pricing wasn't "bad," it wasn't "too low," and it wasn't "wrong." It was simply *her truth* and *her choice.* For all I know, creating a multi-million-dollar business might not even be her desire — or maybe she already has one. Maybe she doesn't care about building wealth in the way I do. Maybe she manifests her desires in completely different ways.

Not everyone prioritizes becoming the energetic match to wealth, and even if they do, their definition of wealth might look entirely different from yours.

And that's *her business.* It's not mine. And it's not yours.

When you make decisions based on what others are doing, you are significantly limiting yourself. Who you are, what you desire, and what you choose to be the energetic match for can only come from one place: *within you.* From your heart. From your intuition. From your truth.

Your path is yours to create. Honor it.

Stepping into your Rich B$tch energy and fully embodying your future self requires one thing above all: certainty. Certainty in who you are. Certainty in your worth. Certainty in your ability to become the energetic match to wealth.

But before you can move forward, you must clear what's blocking you.

Rich B$tch Homework: Clear Your Blocks

1. **LIST EVERY EXCUSE AND JUSTIFICATION BLOCKING YOU**

   Write down every limiting belief, excuse, or justification that's been holding you back from creating your desired wealth. These are the scripts you've either sold yourself on or were indoctrinated with by others. This exercise will help you identify what's keeping you stuck so you can begin recognizing these beliefs as outdated programming, not your truth.

   Examples of common limiting beliefs:
   - *I can't because I'm too old.*
   - *She's prettier / smarter / more experienced than me (competition).*
   - *My fifth-grade teacher called me stupid, so I'll never be smart enough to succeed.*
   - *I'll never be as good as her.*
   - *My family doesn't support me and expects me to fail.*

2. **REWRITE YOUR STORY WITH EMPOWERED TRUTHS**

   Now, take that list and rewrite each limiting belief into an empowered truth. These are the new, powerful scripts you'll sell yourself on and live by.

   Examples of empowered truths
   - *My age is my superpower — it means I bring experience, wisdom, and perspective.*
   - *There is no competition because no one can replicate my unique energy and gifts.*
   - *The opinions of others, past or present, do not define my intelligence or worth.*

- *I am in a league of my own, and my growth is my only focus.*
- *I'm surrounded by support, both seen and unseen, and my success inspires others to believe in what's possible.*

3. ANCHOR THESE NEW BELIEFS

Read your new truths daily. Write them on sticky notes, set them as affirmations, or revisit them when old programming tries to creep back in.

This exercise is about reclaiming your power, dismantling the stories that no longer serve you, and replacing them with ones that elevate you into your Rich B$tch future.

Your reality starts with the beliefs you choose to embody. Choose powerfully.

RICH B$TCH TRUTH

CHAPTER
TWENTY-ONE

RICH
B$TCH MONEY GOALS

CHAPTER 21: RICH B$TCH ALIGNMENT
Alignment Without Compromise = A Key Code to Success

True success isn't just about achieving goals, it's about doing so in a way that feels aligned with who you are at your core. Alignment without compromise is where your power lies. It's the secret sauce that ensures your journey to success is as fulfilling as the destination itself.

In summer 2023, I wrapped up a seven-week program called The Psychic Mentorship Academy. Throughout the program, I emphasized one powerful principle: the importance of going inward to seek answers. This practice allowed my clients to break free from the habitual conditioning of seeking validation, approval, or opinions from others — of looking outside themselves for truths that can only be found within.

This is a transformative practice. It calls forth your inner presence, leadership, and power. It helps you trust yourself as the divine channel you already are.

Yes, you have this ability too.

You possess an inner knowing, a direct channel to Source that's always available to you. It's there to support you, to guide your ascension, and to help you become the energetic match to wealth in this lifetime.

But let's get real for a second. There are situations, opportunities, or relationships in your life that you've said yes to — places where you compromised. Maybe consciously, maybe unconsciously. Deep down, your heart and soul knew those choices weren't aligned with your highest truth. You felt the dissonance, the internal tug-of-war as your spirit whispered, "This isn't it."

Alignment without compromise is the path forward. It requires listening to that inner knowing, honoring your truth, and choosing to step fully into your power. Every moment you honor what feels aligned, you create harmony within and magnetize abundance into your external world.

The question is: Are you ready to stop compromising and start trusting the divine wisdom within you? Because that's where the magic begins.

I've had countless moments in my life when I ignored my inner knowing, dismissed my intuition, overlooked divine guidance, or brushed off the clear signs from my body or the Universe. Each time, I paid the price.

When we don't honor what we know to be true, or when we dismiss the truth of our hearts, we create disorder in our lives. This dissonance is deeply felt in our bodies and inevitably reflected in our external reality. Why? Because our external world mirrors our internal field: our frequency, thoughts, feelings, and beliefs.

On my journey to becoming the energetic match to wealth, bringing alignment into every area of my life, and refusing to compromise, was not optional. It was *essential.* It became part of the foundation for my success, and I can confidently tell you that it's been just as pivotal for others.

I've had the privilege of working with some extraordinary self-made millionaires. Every time, I would ask them, "What's one thing that has greatly supported you in generating a multiple seven-figure business?"

Their answers have been strikingly consistent, and the wisdom they've shared always points back to one core truth: **Success doesn't start with strategy — it starts with alignment.**

Though their responses carried layers of wisdom, they could all be distilled into one powerful word: **alignment.** Authentically aligning every aspect of your life and business with your truth and desires is the single greatest strategy you can implement to become the energetic match to wealth. When you are in alignment, you experience a deep connection to yourself and your purpose. From that space, resistance fades, and flow takes over.

When you're vibrating at the frequency of your desires, they naturally begin moving toward you. Alignment is a magnet for manifestation — it's not forced, manipulated, or controlled. It's a natural pull.

While alignment may seem obvious in the pursuit of wealth, common sense isn't always common practice. The reality for most people, especially new entrepreneurs, is that alignment isn't at the forefront of their strategy. Instead, they create from fear — fear of failure, fear of judgment, fear of not meeting expectations — or they focus on what they *think* their clients want, often at the expense of their own desires and vision.

When you create from this space, compromises are made, boundaries are crossed, and misalignment becomes the norm. It creates resistance and chaos, making it nearly impossible to build the life or business you deeply want.

Alignment isn't just a strategy, it's the foundation. Without it, you're building on shaky ground. With it, you're unstoppable.

The same principles of alignment apply to relationships. Most people aren't actively pursuing relationships that align with their highest truth. Instead, they find themselves entangled in relationships that cater to a wounded part of themselves, reinforce a false belief, or satisfy outdated conditioning.

But here's the hard truth: A relationship out of alignment with your highest truth only perpetuates the experience of lack in your life. Go within and reflect — you already know this to be true.

When you make decisions from a place of prioritizing others over yourself or compromising your integrity to avoid discomfort, you step out of the Rich B$tch energy. And when you're not living in alignment, it stifles you, in your energy, your creativity, and your ability to manifest.

Sooner or later, the misalignment becomes impossible to ignore. The breakdown in your life grows so significant that you're forced to confront the energetic leaks draining you and make a choice: either create alignment where it's missing or continue to struggle.

It's that simple.

To illustrate, let's keep with the theme of money and take, for example, Tiffany.

Tiffany was a client of mine who, when we first began working together, was stuck in a cycle of fear-based decisions. She was taking coaching calls late into the evening, convinced that if she didn't accommodate those working nine-to-five jobs, she'd lose clients and leave money on the table.

Her fear created a belief that her potential clients were only available for late-night sessions. So, she made herself available, even though she *hated* taking calls after 5 p.m. And because she tolerated it, people booked those late-night slots.

But remember: You get what you tolerate.

What Tiffany failed to realize at the time was that you are always aligned with something — energy and frequency demand it. The real question is: *What are you in alignment with?*

- Is it fear or love?
- Lack or abundance?
- Self-hatred or self-love?
- Self-abandonment or belief in self?
- Purpose and desire, or the expectations and demands of others?

Tiffany was aligned with fear and self-abandonment. She prioritized what she *thought* others needed over what she truly desired. And it's no surprise that she struggled — her sales were inconsistent, her energy was drained, and the abundance she craved felt out of reach.

The lesson? Alignment is everything. When you create from fear, scarcity, or a need to please, your results will reflect that misalignment. But when you operate from love, purpose, and self-belief, you step into your power, and that's when you activate your Rich B$tch era.

The key is to choose alignment that serves *you,* not what fear tells you to settle for.

Every entrepreneur I know started their journey with a grand vision: to make an impact, generate wealth from purpose, and live life on their terms. In other words, to create *freedom.* Yet I've watched so many online business owners unknowingly build their businesses on shaky foundations. Why? Because they don't fully trust that they can create abundance without sacrifice.

They do things they don't enjoy. They make themselves overly available to clients during hours they'd rather spend with their family. They push, hustle, and struggle, only to burn out and then wonder why their sales are inconsistent and their joy is missing.

If you want to align your life to become the energetic match to wealth, you have to confront the areas of your current reality that are rooted in lack.

In Tiffany's case, she was experiencing lack on multiple levels:

- **Lack of joy in her business** — she resented taking late-night calls.
- **Lack of trust** in her ability to succeed with boundaries.
- **Lack of belief** that she didn't have to compromise to succeed.

- **Lack of meaningful time** spent with herself and her loved ones.

And here's the kicker: When you align with lack in one area, it often spills into others. It's no wonder Tiffany was also experiencing a lack of money — her business model was a reflection of the energy she was operating from.

Alignment isn't just a nice idea, it's the foundation of everything you're building. If you want wealth, you have to align with joy, trust, and self-belief. When you create from that space, you transform your experience of attracting and making money.

Integrity and alignment are nonnegotiable when it comes to money and success. I see this issue often in the coaching industry, and it's one of the reasons so many online coaches struggle to make money.

For example, if you're a coach claiming to stand for freedom but you don't actually *feel* free, and your actions aren't in the frequency of freedom, there's a misalignment. That dissonance creates an energetic block that keeps abundance at arm's length because it's not aligned to *say* something you're not actively *being* for yourself first. Embodiment is everything.

Imagine a relationship coach trying to sell programs while privately stuck in a toxic relationship. The energy behind that offering is misaligned. The lack of integrity would show up in her frequency, creating resistance instead of attraction. And as you can see, that approach isn't sustainable — not for her clients, her business, or herself.

Your alignment — how you embody your values and truth — creates the foundation for wealth. It's not just about what you say, it's about who you *are* and how you show up every single day. Without integrity and alignment, the flow of abundance will always feel like a struggle.

When Tiffany finally chose to lead with her highest truth, everything shifted. She brought alignment into her business by changing her hours of availability and trusting that the right clients would find her regardless of her schedule. And guess what? Her business didn't slow down, it picked up.

The best part? That alignment created a ripple effect, positively influencing every area of her life.

Now, if you're thinking, *Kyera, it can't be that easy,* you're absolutely right. It's not easy — because if it were, more people would be living vibrant, fulfilled lives filled with health, wealth, and success.

Tiffany's transformation wasn't just about changing her availability or stopping the offers that drained her. We took it deeper. Together, we evolved her marketing and messaging and aligned every aspect of her business to her unique energetic blueprint.

One size does *not* fit all.

What worked for Tiffany may look completely different for you. The key is to make changes from the inside out — rooted in your truth, not someone else's formula. That's when success flows naturally.

The result? Tiffany felt fully aligned, free, happy, energized, and creative — a perfect *ten out of ten.*

That's the Rich B$tch vibe, and it positioned her to become the energetic match to wealth. When you align your life and business to your truth, success doesn't just show up, it *soars.*

Why is creating alignment so difficult?

Because it's not about the external adjustments, it's about the *internal* shifts required to allow alignment in the first place. It's easy to move things around on the outside, but the real challenge lies in maintaining the frequency necessary to sustain those changes.

To create true alignment, you'll need to demonstrate qualities like:

- Courage
- Self-love
- Belief in yourself
- Confidence and leadership
- Firm, fierce, and loving boundaries
- The ability to express your voice, speak your truth, and communicate clearly
- Worthiness
- Acceptance
- Forgiveness
- Trust

Take this example: Maybe you've been working for years without a raise, and you're quietly (or not so quietly) resentful about it.

Let's say alignment for you would mean getting paid more, but you're afraid to ask your boss for a salary increase. The internal work in this case might include:

- Feeling worthy of receiving more money.
- Building confidence to speak your truth.
- Demonstrating leadership by taking action to shift your external experience.

And if you muster the courage to ask for that raise and get denied, alignment doesn't stop there. If your intuition is nudging you toward more meaningful and aligned work elsewhere, the next layer of internal work will show up. You'll need to:

- Trust yourself and your worth.
- Walk forward with courage and profound self-love to pursue your highest timeline.

Alignment isn't a "filler word," and it's certainly not fluff. It's the foundation for becoming the energetic match to wealth. Alignment isn't just an idea, it's a *requirement*.

Rich B$tch Homework: Reconnect with Your Inner Truth

1. STOP COMPROMISING

- Find a quiet place where you can sit alone without distractions.
- Close your eyes and take several deep, intentional breaths, allowing your body to relax and your mind to settle.
- Ask your heart: *Where have I dismissed what I know to be true? Where have I justified making compromises in my life?*
- Be open to what comes up — no judgment, just awareness.

The purpose of this exercise is to reconnect with your inner truth, to stop ignoring the wisdom within you, and to reclaim the power you've given away through compromises.

By creating space for presence and listening to your heart, you strengthen your trust in what you already know to be true and begin the process of calling back your power.

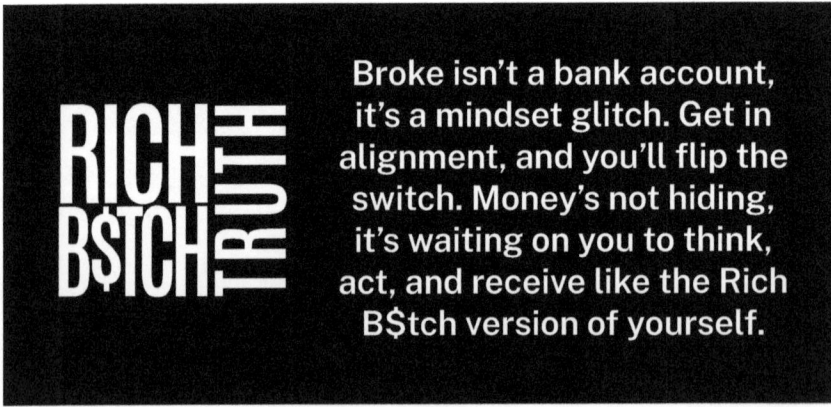

RICH B$TCH TRUTH

Broke isn't a bank account, it's a mindset glitch. Get in alignment, and you'll flip the switch. Money's not hiding, it's waiting on you to think, act, and receive like the Rich B$tch version of yourself.

CHAPTER
TWENTY-TWO

RICH
B$TCH MONEY GOALS

CHAPTER 22: RICH B$TCH PLEASURE

Pleasure is the elixir of creation, the force that fuels our boldest visions, our most magnetic presence, and the unapologetic expression of our highest Rich B$tch self as we step into the journey of becoming the energetic match to wealth.

When I talk about pleasure in this chapter, I'm not referring to fleeting indulgences like your favorite donut or a scalp massage at the spa. I'm talking about the electric force of an orgasm — the kind that awakens, expands, and transforms. Accessing a ten-out-of-ten experience of pleasure, both within ourselves and in our intimate partnerships, is not only essential, it's our birthright.

A few months after leaving my marriage, I boarded a flight to Mexico bound for Tulum, where I would finally meet seventeen extraordinary women in person — a sisterhood forged through a year of deep masterminding online.

Ironically, it was the very program I had invested five figures in, only to lie on the intake form, too afraid to face the truth because I knew that speaking it would mean being held accountable to it.

It was the third and final question on the form that stopped me in my tracks: Most importantly, in exactly one year from today, what would have had to change both personally and professionally for you to feel like this had been a life-altering experience?

I knew the answer instantly, and it had nothing to do with money. *If things don't change with my husband, I need to leave my marriage.*

But like most people when faced with an uncomfortable truth, especially the possible unraveling of a marriage, I was terrified. So, I lied. I made it about money because chasing numbers was easier to hide behind than facing heartache and the absence of pleasure in my marriage.

I want to hit my first six-figure month, I wrote instead. A true statement, but not the truth that would change everything. Because real transformation isn't in the numbers, it's in the liberation that comes from admitting what's misaligned and then having the courage to do something about it without delay. And money alone can't buy that.

Instead of bringing Rich B$tch energy to an opportunity for more, I hid behind "Basic" B$tch answers — because I was still choosing fear over aligning with the truth.

But don't get me wrong, you can make money being out of alignment. I did. And I made a lot. Hell, I hit my first six-figure month in that mastermind. But in the Rich B$tch community, we know that making money and being *wealthy* are two very different things.

And despite my financial success, pleasure was nowhere to be found in my marriage, not even close. My sex life was giving what we in the Rich B$tch community call DPE: Dry Pussy Energy. Because no amount of money can compensate for a relationship that drains your vitality instead of igniting it.

I had mastered the art of making money but abandoned the art of receiving, feeling, and being deeply fulfilled. As women, we forget that the portal between our legs doesn't just birth life, it births energy, creativity, and power.

There's a reason the clitoris, unlike any other organ, exists solely for pleasure, with 8,000 nerve endings designed for bliss. Ancient traditions have long recognized female pleasure as a gateway to cosmic creation. In Sanskrit teachings, Shakti is the divine feminine force, the essence of universal creation, and orgasm is a sacred activation of this energy.

Tantric traditions describe orgasm as the ignition of Kundalini — the serpent energy coiled at the base of the spine — rising to expand consciousness and awaken divine connection. This surge isn't just physical, it's a metaphysical catalyst, elevating vibrational frequency and amplifying creative potential. Many believe orgasmic energy is one of the most potent forces of manifestation, aligning desire with the quantum field of infinite possibility.

As my business continued to grow, so did the undeniable pressure of the glass ceiling above me. But it wasn't revenue, systems, or strategy holding me back, it was a void of pleasure. The very thing I had been denying myself.

Pleasure isn't a luxury, it's the elixir of the feminine — the key to her deepest healing, wildest expansion, and most unapologetic rise. It's what fuels a Rich B$tch life. To suppress pleasure — in our bodies, our relationships, or our work — is to cut off the very force that magnetizes abundance, love, and power into our lives.

Healing the feminine means reclaiming this truth: A Rich B$tch knows that her ability to receive pleasure is directly linked to her ability to receive wealth. (Not money . . . *wealth.*) When we stop denying ourselves, the Universe stops denying us too.

On the first morning of our girls' trip, as the sun rose, I walked to the ocean and perched on a rock overlooking the crashing waves. The salty air kissed my skin as I stripped off my top in a moment of pure surrender and sank into meditation — unguarded, unburdened, utterly free.

When I was done, I stood, unhurried and unapologetic, and walked back to my room, breasts bare, greeting the other women as they made their way to breakfast.

And there it was . . . the collision of liberation and pleasure.

Not just in the sun warming my exposed skin or the stark contrast to Michigan's snowstorm back home, but in the freedom to exist exactly as I am without seeking permission. To walk topless without shame, without fear, without shrinking under the weight of someone else's discomfort.

I had left a marriage where this kind of expression was unacceptable, yet I was raised to see bodies as just that: bodies. Not something to be hidden, not something to be sexualized, not something to be ashamed of. I've never been one to cover up or conform to modesty, and in my previous marriage, my self-expression was a constant source of conflict until I couldn't f*cking take it anymore.

What was I doing in a marriage where he needed me to be someone I wasn't? No one else could answer that or change it but me. I wanted to be adored for the woman I am, not diminished for it.

I remember doing a photoshoot wearing a white blouse with nothing underneath, my breasts largely exposed. I loved the image so much that I used it in a graphic to promote my program The Unreasonable Woman, yet I hid it from my husband, knowing he wouldn't celebrate it or tell me how sexy I looked. Instead, he'd lecture me on how unprofessional and unacceptable it was.

Eventually, I couldn't ignore the contradiction: an *unreasonable* woman playing *reasonable* in her marriage. I might have been making a lot of money, but I wasn't a fully turned-on woman until I stood for having it all — without compromise, without apology, without dimming my fire. I, like most women do, had forgotten the magnetism and sheer power that ignites when pleasure is at the forefront of our lives.

But here, in this moment, wrapped in the energy of sisterhood and the magic of Tulum, I was fully seen — by myself, for myself. *And that liberation was the catalyst to making pleasure in my life a nonnegotiable.*

Liberation is contagious, and when one woman sets herself free, she gives others permission to do the same. By the end of the trip, more women shed their inhibitions, joining me in being topless or fully naked. We were celebrating the beauty of bodies instead of hiding them, instead of feeling ashamed.

Oh, and that glass ceiling I had been hitting? Pleasure didn't just crack it — it shattered it.

The six-figure month ceiling became a *multiple* six-figure celebration the following year, but the real shift wasn't just in numbers or hiring a team (a new level of support and receiving), it was in *me*. That leap didn't come from strategy alone; it came after months of deep, unrestrained pleasure. Because eventually, I found myself in the presence of a man who didn't just meet me there, he *expanded* me. He unlocked a level of turn-on I never knew existed, one that rippled through every inch of my mind and body. He gave me something I had never fully received before: unconditional love, emotional safety, and the kind of toe-curling pleasure that makes the hair on the back of your neck stand up. The wild woman in me wasn't just accepted, she was unleashed, celebrated, and set free.

I realized this was a woman's natural state — deeply turned on, fully expressed, and undeniably aroused in every aspect of life. Anything less was conditioning, suppression, and a betrayal of self.

For once in my life, my body was worshipped. Every inch, every curve. At thirty-six, I built a lingerie collection for the first time, reveling in the power of a woman fully turned on by her own existence. I was desired and devoured, whether draped in lace for a night out or curled up in baggy sweatpants, ugly crying over a movie, stuffing my face with pizza and ice cream. My rage, my emotions, my bigness, my softness, my body, my heart, my mission, my quirks — nothing was too much. He didn't ask me to shrink, and he never asked me to change. He wanted more, not less.

And pleasure in the bedroom? Let's just say I'd faked my fair share of orgasms throughout my life — so many, in fact, I'd worked my way through the entire menu. Appetizer, main course, dessert... I had faked my way through every round at one point or another. Until I finally understood: *Pleasure and wealth are the same energy.*

When I stopped performing and started fully receiving, *everything* changed.

Pleasurable, mind-blowing sex and being a Rich B$tch are undeniably linked because both require you to own your desires, take up space, and receive without apology. A woman who feels sexy, who knows her worth in and out of the bedroom, radiates a confidence that magnetizes everything — money, opportunities, admiration, devotion.

And let's not forget that when a woman orgasms, she glows... literally. Her body floods with feel-good hormones, reducing stress, improving sleep, and even making her skin more radiant. That post-orgasmic energy isn't just physical, it's an aura, a magnetism that makes people stop and take notice.

When you prioritize your pleasure, you activate your feminine power, and that energy doesn't just stay in the sheets, it spills into how you walk, how you negotiate, how you attract wealth, and how the world responds to you. Sexy, confident women don't chase, they draw everything in.

On the flip side, when you fake pleasure, whether in the bedroom, in relationships, or in business, you send a message to your subconscious that your authentic needs and desires don't matter. This creates a pattern of self-abandonment, where you prioritize external validation over inner truth. Wealth flows to those who are fully in their power, not to those who diminish their own needs to keep others comfortable.

Faking pleasure teaches you to settle. It normalizes "good enough" instead of fully satisfied. This mindset doesn't just stay in the bedroom, it bleeds into your business, your pricing, your relationships, and your money habits. When you normalize lackluster experiences, you subconsciously lower your standards in all areas of life, including wealth creation.

Wealth is an extension of receptivity, your ability to receive abundance, pleasure, and support without guilt or resistance. A Rich B$tch knows that if she struggles to receive pleasure (even from herself), she'll struggle to receive money, opportunities, and success with full ease. Suppressing pleasure tightens your energy, making you contracted instead of open to the limitless abundance that's meant for you.

Rich B$tch Reminder:
Pleasure = Power = Wealth

A Rich B$tch doesn't just make money, she magnetizes *wealth*. And wealth isn't just numbers in a bank account, it's the full-body, soul-deep experience of receiving pleasure without guilt, shrinking, or self-denial.

When you suppress pleasure — whether in the bedroom, in your business, or in life — you suppress abundance. When you fake it, you settle. And a Rich B$tch doesn't settle — she claims it all!

$$\$\$\$$$

Rich B$tch Homework: Turned-On Woman, Turned-On Wealth

Pleasure isn't a luxury — it's your power source. If you're blocking pleasure, you're blocking wealth. Time to rewire that.

1. **RICH B$TCH TRUTH CHECK**

   If you were given my intake form, what truth would you be scared to admit? Write it down. No fluff, no filter. Now ask yourself: What would it cost me to ignore this truth for another year?

2. PLEASURE AUDIT: WHERE ARE YOU FAKING IT?

- In business? (Saying yes when you want to say no, under-charging, overworking?)
- In relationships? (Hiding parts of yourself, dimming your desires, settling for "good enough," faking orgasms?)
- In your body? (Rushing through self-care, avoiding pleasure, feeling disconnected?) Write down what needs to shift. Then shift it.

The moment you stop performing
and start fully *receiving*,
the Universe stops holding back.
So lean in. Open up. Take up space.
Pleasure is the key, and *you*
are the lock. Turn it.

CHAPTER
TWENTY-THREE

CHAPTER 23: LUXURY IS IN THE EYE OF THE BEHOLDER

Luxury is deeply personal. It's not defined by the price tag but by the richness of the experiences that bring joy, meaning, and connection to your life.

For some, luxury isn't about material possessions or extravagant displays, it's the peace of living in a modest cottage on a quiet lake, surrounded by nature's stillness. It's the simple joy of sipping fresh coffee on the front porch at sunrise, the warm embrace of suburbia, and the beauty in the ordinary.

Luxury might be attending a local symphony orchestra's performance, feeling the music resonate in your soul, or the thrill of a fun road trip with friends, exploring local wineries and creating unforgettable memories. For others, it's found in the happiness and fulfillment of watching their kids surpass milestones, grow into their own unique selves, and step into the world with pride and purpose.

For some, luxury is all about *feeling significant* — stepping into a life that exudes prestige, comfort, and indulgence.

It's the breathtaking view from a multi-million-dollar high-rise, where the city's hustle and bustle buzzes far below as you sip champagne from your private balcony. It's lounging in bed on a lazy Sunday morning, draped in silky robes, with room service delivering your favorite decadent breakfast right to your door.

Luxury might be the electric thrill of sitting close enough to feel the energy of performers in ground-floor seating at a massive concert, where thousands of fans amplify the experience around you. It's the indulgent pampering of an exclusive day spa, where every detail is designed to make you feel cared for and radiant.

And let's not forget the added comfort and prestige of first-class travel, where spacious accommodations and exceptional service make the journey just as exciting as the destination.

This is luxury: feeling significant, celebrated, and deeply connected to a life of elevated experiences. Whatever makes you feel like the main character in your story, embrace it unapologetically — it's yours to claim.

Luxury, in its material form, is an *experience*, not a price tag. Whether it's the excitement of driving a Porsche 911, the timeless elegance of a Chanel handbag, the thrill of a weekend glamping trip, or the joy of scoring a rare thrift shop find, luxury is all about how it *makes you feel.*

It might be a girls' night out filled with laughter, fancy shoes that make you feel unstoppable, or the indulgence of dining at a cozy restaurant. It could be the bliss of slipping into comfortable jeans that fit *just right* or savoring a gourmet ice cream cone on a hot summer day, the sweetness melting in perfect harmony with the moment.

Luxury isn't about how much it costs, it's about the energy it brings into your life. It's the way it lights you up, makes you feel alive, and adds a layer of joy, beauty, or connection to your day. It's not about *what* it is, it's about *how it makes you feel.*

**Luxury, like beauty,
lives in the eye of the beholder.**

When I lead retreats in Ireland, my clients and I stay at a five-star luxury resort, and it's nothing short of breathtaking. Everything is perfection, from the exquisite food to the elegant amenities, the stunning rooms, the panoramic views, the serene energy, the meticulous attention to detail, the genuine care from the hotel staff, and its prime location.

But my friend would completely disagree, and that's okay. For her, luxury in Ireland means staying at an Airbnb. She values the privacy and comfort of having her own space, which brings her a deeper sense of joy and fulfillment.

That's the beauty of luxury — it's entirely personal.

Now, think about your version of luxury. If you could snap your fingers and instantly bring something new into your life, what would it be? Maybe it's something for yourself, or perhaps it's something you'd do for someone else.

Would you buy a dream home or a sparkling diamond ring for your engagement finger? Maybe an unlimited shopping spree or enough money to purchase land and open the dog rescue you've been dreaming about?

Perhaps you'd pay off your parents' mortgage or take your family on a once-in-a-lifetime vacation. Maybe you've been fantasizing about owning a horse and learning to ride, buying a boat to host summer parties on the lake, or paying off your own and your friends' student loans. Or perhaps it's a brand-new car to call your own.

It doesn't matter what your desire is, it only matters that it lights you up.

And here's the key: For any of this to happen, you must become the energetic match to receive it. Align with the frequency of abundance, joy, and possibility, and watch your dreams start moving toward you. Luxury, in whatever form it takes, is yours to claim.

I'm about to share how I became the energetic match for my dream car, a vehicle I deemed the epitome of luxury. What I say will either inspire you to realize you can create this for yourself or have you questioning my Rich B$tch sanity. Either way, one thing is undeniable: what I do *works*. If it works for me, it can work for you. The only question is, are you ready to claim it?

Let me take you back to my teenage years and my first car — a used 1996 forest-green Nissan Maxima that cost $2,200. While I was grateful for the freedom it provided, let's be real: it was far from luxurious and definitely not what I envisioned in my Rich B$tch future.

Picture this: You're driving down the freeway and you suddenly watch your spoiler fly off in the rearview mirror. Or you're cruising around with a hole in the driver-side floor big enough to fit your foot through.

It wasn't glamorous, but like many teens I knew, that's just how it was. We took what we could get and made it work. But even then, I knew that someday I'd be rolling through life in something that truly reflected the vision I had for my future.

Like most people, I spent my younger years living in a "one day" reality.

One day, I won't drive a car that's falling apart.

One day, I'll have fancy leather seats.

One day, I won't feel stressed about paying for an oil change or replacing all four tires at once.

One day, I'll have all the upgrades I want.

One day . . .

Does this sound familiar?

Any car I leased back then was done in the energy of lack. Every dealership visit was filled with worry. I'd sit there with a knot in my stomach, stressing over what the monthly payment would turn out to be. I'd calculate the cost of insurance and strip away any extras, no matter how much I wanted them, just to keep the payment as low as humanly possible. The entire experience of car shopping wasn't exciting or joyful, it was *stressful*. It was survival mode, not abundance.

But when you operate from lack, you create more lack. Inner work pays the biggest checks.

A Rich B$tch doesn't live in "one day."
She swaps it for "Day One." Because the moment
you decide to stop waiting and start creating
is the moment your life begins to shift.

After investing in my first mentor and surrounding myself with successful entrepreneurs — observing them, receiving inspiration, and soaking up their insight — I felt a spark of possibility ignite within me. I began to entertain the idea that I, too, could make enough money to own a car that once felt completely out of reach. Even though I wasn't there yet financially, I knew one thing for sure: I could begin the process of becoming the energetic match to wealth *right then*.

With heartfelt passion and consistent effort, I committed to collapsing the time it would take to make that dream a reality.

Much like the "I Won the Lottery" game I used to play, I started my "Day One" by envisioning myself driving a new car. I embraced the elevated emotions ahead of the experience, feeling the joy, excitement, and freedom as if it was already mine. And this wasn't just visualization, it was a powerful act of stepping into the frequency of what I desired, making it inevitable.

I stopped getting into my car feeling blah, or ungrateful. Instead, I made a conscious decision to role play. Every time I got behind the wheel, I told myself, "This is the last car I'll ever lease in the frequency of lack."

I began driving with intention.

As odd as it may sound — because, let's face it, adults tend to outgrow daydreaming — I started imagining myself stepping into a luxurious car, feeling proud and elevated. Gone were the days of mundane energy and autopilot routines. I transformed my daily drives into moments of alignment, visualizing myself in the kind of vehicle that matched the version of me I was stepping into becoming.

Every time I sat in the driver's seat, I allowed myself to feel the elevated emotions of pride, excitement, and luxury. I wasn't just visualizing, I was *feeling*. And in that powerful intersection of thought and emotion, I became the energetic match for my future car.

Even traffic jams became opportunities. I'd observe the cars around me, noting what I loved and what didn't resonate. Over time, I became crystal clear on what I wanted. I made a list of my top choices, infusing it with intention and trust that it was already on its way.

That's how I turned an ordinary experience into a manifestation practice. It wasn't about where I was in that moment, it was about where I was going. When we shift our mindset from seeing our desires as distant dreams to knowing they're *in process* — already happening — we begin to alter our reality and the world around us.

To take my manifestation practice to the next level, I started touring dealerships like Porsche, Audi, Mercedes, BMW, and Land Rover. Each visit became a masterclass in embodying the energy of *belonging*.

As I walked through the showrooms and slid into the driver's seats, I practiced feeling like I belonged there — as though this was my usual routine, and I knew exactly what I was doing. Like I'd done this a thousand times before. This step was *crucial* because if you're test-driving a car you don't feel worthy of driving, working in a job you don't feel adequate for, or viewing homes you don't believe you deserve, that energy will create blocks in your manifestations. You can't attract what you feel unworthy of receiving.

As my business grew, so did my alignment with wealth. I kept practicing, refining, and embodying the energetic match to abundance. It wasn't long before my daily drives in my car no longer required me to imagine they were anything else. I was ready to upgrade.

One day, I was test-driving an Infinity QX80. The white leather interior caught my eye, and as the salesman enthusiastically explained all the bells and whistles of this top-of-the-line, fully loaded model, I listened politely. But in that moment, I had a clear vision of what I *would* be driving — and it wasn't the car I was sitting in.

That vision was my inner knowing, guiding me to something bigger, something even more aligned with my Rich B$tch energy.

The QX80 just wasn't it. I knew it as we pulled back into the dealership. The salesman, still eager to close the deal, kept talking, rattling off features and trying to convince me it was the perfect car. "You know," I said, interrupting him mid-sentence because I knew with absolute certainty I wasn't buying the car, "It's just not big enough."

His demeanor shifted instantly. Annoyed, he snapped back with a sharp tone, "Well, we can't always have it all."

I stood up, looked him straight in the eyes, and without hesitation, replied, "Maybe you can't, but I can." Then I walked out — unshaken, unapologetic, and fully aligned with the energy of knowing I *would* have it all.

I didn't say this out of arrogance. I said it because no one — not a car salesman, not society, not anyone — gets to define my limits. No one tells me what I can or can't do, create, or have. That power belongs to me and me alone.

I'm also not available for projections. While he might not believe in his ability to consciously create the reality he wants, *I know* I can. And *I know you can too.* To step into the life you desire, you must make a bold trade: exchange the belief of "I can't" (which serves no one, especially not you) for "F*ck yes, I can."

This shift is some of the most challenging and transformative personal work you'll ever do because no one can do it for you. It requires rewiring years of programming and doubt, often in the face of others projecting their fears and limitations onto you.

Here's the secret: Their programming doesn't have to be yours. Their doubts, disbelief, and small-mindedness have nothing to do with you unless you let them.

This work is about holding the belief that you can do something, have something, and become someone, even when the world says otherwise. It's about becoming so rooted in your truth and potential that no one can shake your vision. That's how you reclaim your power. That's how you create the life you've been dreaming of.

I left that dealership with clarity and confidence, and shortly after, I ordered a 2022 black Cadillac Escalade — fully loaded with every unnecessary add-on I desired.

This was the *complete opposite* of what my former self would have done years ago when lack was the driving force behind every decision. Back then, I would've stripped away anything "extra" to ensure the lowest possible payment, choosing practicality over desire every time.

But this time, nothing about my decision was practical, and that's precisely why it was aligned. My ego tried to chime in, reminding me I didn't "need" a luxury SUV. But my higher self knew better. Life isn't about *need*. Life is about creating and defining luxury on your terms. It's about becoming the energetic match for your desires — not because you have to, but simply because you *can*.

When you understand this truth, everything shifts. You no longer feel the need to justify your decisions to anyone, not even yourself. When you step into your power and live from alignment, desire becomes reason enough.

It took eight months for my car to be built, but then the text finally came: "Your 2022 Cadillac Escalade is ready to be picked up."

I cried the entire way to the dealership. I was overwhelmed with gratitude for what I had created—the journey I'd taken, the challenges I'd overcome, and the woman I had become to make this moment possible.

But I also cried out of sadness. I thought back to the day I told my sister I'd ordered the car. We'd made plans to celebrate its arrival together, but we never got to. That's the duality of life—sometimes the celebration of a milestone is met with the ache of loss for something or someone no longer here to celebrate with you.

Getting back to the story, though—here's where it gets magical. My favorite part of this experience was the synchronicities. If you're present, open, and aware, signs from the Universe are *everywhere*. They're there to guide you, affirm your journey, and remind you that you're exactly where you're meant to be.

This moment was no exception. Let me share what happened next.

As I was getting ready to leave the dealership and take my new Escalade home, the woman helping me turned to me with a warm smile and said, "It's always fun being able to get a car like this to someone like you. So many times, people come in ungrateful. When someone like you comes in, and it's your first time getting a car like this, the excitement is quite special. Also, I looked at your date of birth. Good for you. Go get 'em, girl."

Her words landed in a way that went beyond the surface. I smiled, fully receiving her compliment, understanding exactly what she meant. In that moment, I also felt my sister's love and presence so deeply that it took my breath away.

Behind her message of "good for you" was an acknowledgment of the rarity of this milestone. It's not common for a thirty-four-year-old woman to lease a $96,000 car, let alone without a cosigner. But here's what I know for sure: It doesn't have to *stay* uncommon.

It can become *every day* for women of any age to get what they want, how they want it, and when they want it. Your desires don't have to be practical. They don't even have to be labeled as "luxurious" by anyone else. Remember, luxury isn't about the price you pay, it's about the way it makes you feel.

Luxury is *relative to you*. It's about honoring what lights you up, what calls to your heart, and what aligns with your soul's desires. It's about saying yes to yourself and bringing into existence the things that matter to *you*—because you can.

You never have to explain or defend your desires to anyone.

Let's make your new normal *having it all*—and owning it unapologetically.

You get to create and live the life you want, free of guilt, shame, or struggle. Abundance is your birthright, and it's time to claim it with confidence, joy, and ease.

$$\$$\$$\$$$

Rich B$tch Homework: Create Your Dream

1. **DEFINE YOUR LUXURY**

   What does *luxury* mean to you? Take a moment to reflect and write it down. Is it peace of mind, upgraded surroundings, indulgent experiences, or something else?

2. IDENTIFY YOUR UPGRADE

What part of your life do you desire to upgrade? Dream big. Play with the possibility of a new reality where you *get to have it all* — no guilt, shame, or struggle attached. If the voice in your head starts telling you it's not possible, let it fall on deaf ears.

3. PRACTICE ACTING "AS IF"'

Choose one of your desires that currently feels out of reach. Maybe it's flying first class, buying your dream home, owning that perfect car, or taking the trip you've been longing for.

- Start to act "as if."
- Visualize yourself experiencing it: walking through the first-class cabin, sitting in the driver's seat, or waking up in your dream home.
- Let yourself *feel* the elevated emotions of having it now.

When I decided to start flying first class, I did exactly this. I claimed the desire and began to embody it energetically before it became my reality. At the airport, I'd rise when they called first-class boarding and imagine myself walking onto the plane and taking my seat. Every time I walked past first-class seating, I visualized stowing my carry-on and settling in. I felt it ahead of the experience. And now? I *only* fly first class.

4. DREAM BIG

Think about something you desire but feel is currently out of reach. What's *the dream*?

Before I knew the Escalade was my ultimate dream car, I considered a Tahoe or Denali. Why? Because they felt *more feasible.* But when I realized I was thinking that way, I knew I had to break patterns of lack and fully claim the truth that I don't have to settle. And neither do you.

So, what's your dream? Write it down. Own it. Claim it. And start stepping into the frequency of it today.

CHAPTER
TWENTY-FOUR

RICH
B$TCH
MONEY GOALS

CHAPTER 24: THE THREE-MILLION-DOLLAR SCAM

Money in the bank isn't wealth, it's just money in the bank. Wealth is a state of mind, an embodiment of wholeness that exists independently of anyone or anything outside of you.

In April 2021, my checking account balance showed $83,309.58.

At the time, it was the most money I'd ever had sitting in my account, and let me tell you, I felt *rich*. More than that, I felt proud. Accomplished. Grateful. Relaxed.

This wasn't just about the number on the screen, it was about what that number *meant* to me: the energy I'd cultivated, the obstacles I'd overcome, and the alignment I'd stepped into to get there.

It's moments like this that remind us that wealth isn't a dollar amount, it's a *state of being*. I felt like I could finally breathe.

But that sense of ease was short-lived.

When a former coach I trusted wholeheartedly presented me with an investment opportunity requiring $80,000 to participate, I quickly discovered I wasn't as "rich" as I thought.

The idea of reducing my bank account balance to just $3,309.58 — an amount that wouldn't even cover my monthly expenses — sent my heart racing. A wave of unease swept over me, and with it came a feeling I knew all too well.

That feeling was *fear*. Fear of not having enough. Fear of losing what I'd worked so hard to build. Fear of slipping backward instead of moving forward. Even with $83,309.58 in my account, fear showed up, uninvited but familiar, like an old acquaintance I had hoped to leave behind. It was a stark reminder that wealth isn't just about numbers, it's about our relationship with those numbers and the energy we allow them to hold in our life.

I quickly realized that having money in the bank was ultimately meaningless if my sense of safety, happiness, and wealth depended entirely on something external.

It made me question:

- Am I truly rich if I make money but feel unsafe letting it go or being without it?
- If my feelings of security are tied to how much money I do or don't have, am I truly secure?

I wanted more than a number in my bank account. I wanted to *embody* richness and safety, independent of any external circumstance. I wanted an experience of wealth that didn't hinge on the reflection of a specific balance in my checking account.

Then came the uncomfortable yet freeing question: *What's the worst that could happen?*

The answer? The worst-case scenario was that the entire investment was a scam. I'd never see that $80,000 again, and I'd end up right back in debt. No big deal, right? *(Cue sarcastic laugh.)*

But here's what I knew deep down: I'd been in debt before, and I pulled myself out. If I'd done it once, I could do it again. That embodied knowledge gave me the courage to make the decision. It wasn't about *trusting the investment opportunity.* It was about *trusting myself* to navigate whatever outcome unfolded. Because true wealth is not just about what you have, it's about who you *are* when circumstances change.

At this point, you're probably thinking I'm either the bravest b$tch you know or a complete idiot.

Here's how the deal was presented: I would invest $80,000 upfront (which I did) and, in return, receive $8,888 the following month (which I did *not*). This payout was supposed to repeat every month for nine months. Then, at the end of the term, I'd receive 200 percent interest on my original investment — an additional $160,000, on top of my $80,000.

Not bad, right? Who wouldn't want to make $160,000 in just nine months by simply loaning out their money?

Now, here's where things get interesting. This investment made *zero logical sense* for me. My income at the time was unpredictable, and I knew that tying up $80,000 in something so risky could have left me financially vulnerable.

And yet, my intuition was clear. It whispered: *Jump. Trust. You're safe.* So, I leaped. Not because it was logical but because I trusted myself — and my ability to navigate whatever came next.

"F*ckkkkkk! All right, I'm in," I said to my previous coach.

My friends? They were officially concerned about my ability to make sound decisions.

But if I had always listened to the people in my life telling me *not* to do something, this book wouldn't exist. My retreats wouldn't exist either. Hell, my entire life as I know it wouldn't exist. I would rather be labeled *crazy,* take a leap, and fall flat on my face than sit on the sidelines and wonder, *What if?*

I said yes because I trusted my intuition, knowing that my higher self was guiding me toward something my logical mind couldn't yet understand.

For you, this might sound familiar — saying yes to things that others can't wrap their heads around. That feeling of leaning into desire or intuition, even when it defies logic.

Let me tell you something: That *yes* to your intuition, that *yes* to the illogical, is part of your superpower. You're either using your power or diminishing it. You were called to *Rich B$tch Money Goals* because there's a part of you that resonates with me. You're a dreamer. A rebel. A generational pattern breaker. You're *the one!*

You want more out of life because you know deep down that *more* is meant for you. And right now, you're in one of two places:

- You're a dreamer actively making your dreams come true, or
- You're a dreamer sitting on the sidelines, frustrated with yourself because you want to follow your gut, but something is holding you back.

And because I love you, let me tell you the truth: *That something holding you back . . . is you.*

I invested the $80,000. And you know what happened? In May 2021, the very next month, magic transpired in my business.

I generated my highest cash month at the time. Care to guess what it was?

Eighty. Thousand. Dollars.

The exact amount I had just invested.

Trust your intuition. It's not crazy — it's *magic.*

It gets better.

Not only did I generate my highest cash month of $80,000 the following month, but I did so *without trying.*

Here's what I mean: I didn't stress about how I was going to make that money back — which, let's be honest, would've been a totally normal reaction to investing such a significant amount. I wasn't calculating numbers or strategizing, thinking, *Shit, I just invested $80,000. How do I make that back ASAP?* Instead, I trusted my inner guidance, releasing offers that felt fun, exciting, and aligned. There was no rigid plan, no scrambling, no pressure to hit an $80,000 month. Just pure trust and an inner knowing that the money I released was coming back to me, easily and effortlessly.

That $80,000 investment didn't just reduce my account balance to $3,309.58, it stripped away every false sense of security I'd ever placed on money. It was terrifying, liberating, and transformative all at once.

When I first considered saying yes, I felt physically sick. The thought of releasing that money stirred up *intense emotions*. But the breakthrough was I realized I didn't want my feelings of safety or security to depend on something external.

**Money in the bank cannot be your
source of safety, happiness, or wealth.**

It's just paper, an imaginary value we've all agreed to place on it. True safety comes from within. And when it does, you *know*, deep in your bones, that it can never be taken from you.

Don't get me wrong, I know we all need money to live. I get that. But here's the bigger point:

- Are you truly rich if you make money but don't feel safe letting it go?
- If your feelings of security depend entirely on the money you do or don't have, are you actually secure?

Spirit has reminded me, over and over again, that life is a game meant to be *played, lived,* and *experienced* — not feared.

Think of it like this: If you've ever played a video game, you know you can't get to the next level without first mastering the one you're on. Every level presents a new challenge that forces you to grow before you can advance.

Money, and life, work the same way. The challenges you face are the exact lessons you need to grow into the person who's ready for the next level.

The question is: Are you ready to play?

Your assignment in this lifetime is growth, evolution, and liberation, especially from generational money patterns rooted in lack and limitations about what you believe you're capable of creating.

Money, in its essence, is both a challenge and an illusion. You're not here to hoard it. You're not here to fear it, shame it, or *need* it. You're here to *liberate* yourself, learning how to receive and release it freely.

For me, that $80,000 investment opportunity became a game — a chance to play with trust, surrender, and abundance. I played it. And I won.

- Release the money and learn to feel safe without it. *Mission accomplished.*
- Release the money and detach from how it circulates back to you. *Mission accomplished.*
- Release the money and trust in your ability to create more. *Mission accomplished.*

That $80,000 investment didn't just leave me with $3,309.58 in my bank account, it led to an $80,000 month in my business the following month and eventually crossing the million-dollar mark in my career. None of this would have been possible if I'd clung to the money, tied myself to its absence, or feared letting it go.

The truth is trust, surrender, and aligned action are wildly underrated.

Here's a question for you to consider: If you had $83,309.58 in your account, would you let it all go if your intuition told you to? How much do you trust yourself?

Now, you might be wondering: *What happened with the investment? Why didn't you receive your money back?*

Well, the worst-case scenario came true. Month after month, there were new "issues" causing delays, and I received *nothing*. Then, on July 1, 2022, the US Securities and Exchange Commission (SEC) charged the man behind the investment opportunity with operating a $3 million Ponzi scheme, defrauding at least thirty-one investors.

But despite the loss, I don't regret the decision. It wasn't about the money — it was about the liberation, the lessons, and the trust I built in myself. The experience taught me something priceless: When you let go, align with abundance, and trust yourself fully, the Universe responds.

The SEC's complaint alleged that from June 2020 through April 2021, the man, Todd, claimed that investor funds would be used to finance a real estate wholesale business and purchase medical products for resale by a company in India. Instead, Todd retained at least $1.75 million for himself, using approximately $1.05 million to pay existing investors "dividends" or "interest" payments, perpetuating the Ponzi scheme.

Will I ever see that $80,000 again? I don't know — and honestly, it doesn't matter. It never really did.

What I *do* know is that through my business, I generated far more than the amount I was supposed to get back from Todd's "interest payments." And in no way would that have been possible if I'd been consumed with stress, anger, or resentment over the delays.

That's one of my proudest accomplishments, and it's why I feel so liberated around money today. It's the freedom I want for you.

When I made the choice to invest, I knew there was risk involved. I had to be okay with the possibility of the worst-case scenario. Otherwise, I would've fallen into victimhood, leaking my energy into anger, blame, and resentment.

Did I want to invest $80,000 and never see it again? Of course not. But the power of choice lies in taking full responsibility — choosing freely and with awareness of the risks.

When the worst-case scenario happened, I had two choices:

- Stay stuck in bitterness, or
- Take full responsibility, get over it, move on, and create joy and abundance in my life anyway.

I chose freedom.

Maybe you've invested in a coach or program you felt was complete trash after you paid for it. Maybe you're still salty about it. I get it, and your feelings are valid. My questions to you, though, are these:

- Is what you're focusing on and feeling *serving* you?
- Is it loving to you?
- Is it aligned with the Rich B$tch you're creating?

Here's the hard truth: So many people make money in the pursuit of freedom, but once they have it, they obsess over controlling it. On the flip side, people will spend money on someone's services and then cling to the outcome, acting as if that person owes them their life.

Control, whether it's over money or outcomes, will always keep you in a loop of lack.

Freedom isn't just about *having* money, it's about your relationship with it — how you trust, release, and allow it to circulate with ease. That's the real Rich B$tch energy.

Money trauma keeps people locked in self-imposed prisons, guarding their finances so tightly that they stop truly living. They won't take the trip, go on the adventure, invest in the program, say yes to the remodel, or buy the handbag. They deny themselves the experiences that could elevate their lives, even though they've created more money. Instead, they continue to live behind bars, prisoners of their own fear.

Yes, you may want to accumulate wealth and leave behind a legacy, but the greater ambition, the one that truly matters, is this: to leave behind an example of *how* you lived your life, with or without money.

As you continue your journey to becoming the energetic match for wealth, remember this: *You will always be a match for the moves you make.* When you release freely, you create space to receive.

It's the law.

And if you're wondering? Yes, I'd do it all over again.

$$$

Rich B$tch Homework: Listen to Your Intuition

1. **SAY YES TO YOUR INTUITION**
   - Choose one thing your intuition has been guiding you toward but that you've been too afraid to act on.
   - *Do it.* Even if it terrifies you. Trust yourself, stop waiting for the "perfect" moment, and listen to your inner guidance.
   - As you take action, consciously transmute any fear into liberation. Fear is just energy — redirect it toward your freedom.

2. **JOURNAL PROMPT**

   What has your intuition told you to do that you haven't said yes to yet? Write it down, sit with it, and explore what's holding you back. Then, take one aligned step forward.

3. **DAILY MANTRA**

   Write this mantra down: *I am an energetic match for the moves that I make.*

   Place it somewhere you'll see it every day — on your mirror, beside your bed, or as the background on your phone. Repeat it in the morning when you wake up and at night before bed to anchor yourself in this truth and keep showing up for the life you're creating.

 *Courage will set you free. Bravery is the action that gets you there. You've got this. Trust your power.*

CHAPTER
TWENTY-FIVE

RICH
B$TCH MONEY GOALS

CHAPTER 25: COMFORT IS THE ENEMY OF PROGRESS

Once you've embraced the Rich B$tch principles, you can't un-know them. They're a new standard imprinted in your awareness. From this moment on, your experience of abundance — or lack — is entirely a choice.

Every day, you have the power to choose: Will you embody the identity of the woman you're becoming, the one who lives in alignment with abundance and possibility? Or will you stay tethered to old habits, self-doubt, and scarcity?

By now, you've either been taking inspired action and are well on your way to creating an overflow of Rich B$tch abundance, or you're bumping up against self-doubt and outdated programming. Maybe you're questioning whether this work will work for you.

The "work" works when *you* work it. The results aren't about possibility, they're about commitment. Choose who you want to be, and then show up as her, every single day.

If you're doubting yourself right now, let me lovingly remind you of something important: Every negative, hopeless, and fearful thought you've had, I've had too.

I was once the girl watching *The Secret* on repeat, desperately clinging to the hope that what worked for others could one day work for me. I was the girl who listened to Tony Robbins on my morning runs, trying to spark motivation because I so easily forgot that I was the creator of my own life.

I was once the girl who dreamed of the day I could walk into a grocery store and buy whatever I wanted without comparing prices, calculating totals, or putting food back on the shelf because I couldn't afford it.

I was the girl triggered by her bills, avoiding her bank account like it was a source of shame. I was the girl working a nine-to-five office job, completely out of alignment with my soul's purpose, clocking in for a paycheck that barely covered my survival.

I was the girl convinced that manifestation and becoming the energetic match to wealth worked for everyone else, but *not me.*

I was the girl who saw others celebrating financial success and couldn't help but ask, "Why not me? What am I doing wrong?"

I know what it feels like to doubt your path, to wonder if it's even possible for you. But I learned that the version of you who feels stuck is not your final form, it's just the chapter before the breakthrough. You can rewrite your story, just like I did. Keep going — you're closer than you think.

I was once the girl who was half committed, half not. Half in, half out. Waiting for change, but too afraid to go all in.

Until I did the work of becoming a Rich B$tch.

Becoming the energetic match to wealth and believing in your ability to create it is like pregnancy — you either are or you're not. There's no halfway.

This work takes tremendous effort, and I know firsthand the kind of energy it requires. It's not easy, but it's worth it. So, ask yourself: If not now, when?

One day? *Someday?*

What about *today?* What about right now? This is your moment, not "someday." It's time to decide who you're going to be and show up fully in that energy. Because waiting only delays the life you're meant to live.

Nothing about me — my life, my looks, my circumstances, my environment, my background, or anything else — makes it easier for me to create the life I've built compared to you. You may want to believe otherwise, but let's be honest: that's just a convenient way to justify your lack.

And here's the problem with that. Excuses keep your dreams at a distance and your manifestations delayed. Besides, **comparison is the thief of joy**. It's a distraction, not a solution.

Everything I've embodied and used to create my reality — courage, grit, intuition, leadership, authenticity, consistency, gratitude (whether for the smallest blessings or the biggest wins), trust, self-love, and aligned action — is available to you too.

But if you are going to step into your Rich B$tch era, you can't f*ck around with excuses anymore. That's the old you. A Rich B$tch has long since graduated from that mindset — or at the very least, she's made the commitment to evolve every single day.

The question isn't whether you can do this. The question is whether you're ready to stop holding yourself back and finally claim the life waiting for you.

If you're feeling discouraged because it seems challenging to feel grateful before getting what you want, if you're struggling to connect to the vision of your future or frustrated that your desires aren't manifesting fast enough, take a deep breath. Relax.

It's okay to feel this way, as it's part of the process. The key is to tune back into your desires. Remember, like any other skill, this takes practice, consistency, and time. With repetition, you'll improve, and eventually, it will feel effortless. In fact, you may even reach a point where your manifestations arrive so seamlessly that you barely notice. Why? Because you've been living in the frequency of your desires for so long that they've simply become your reality — the *new normal*.

Repetition is the mother of all skills, and consistency always wins.

Here's an example: In 2020, I worked with two private mentorship clients who had lost their connection to their desires. This isn't unusual — it happens. But because they stopped aligning with their vision, they also stopped making Rich B$tch moves. Their energy shifted, and the results followed.

This is why staying connected to your desires is nonnegotiable. When you embody the frequency of what you want, it's only a matter of time before the Universe delivers. Stay the course. Trust the process. And remember, every moment of consistency moves you closer to the life you're creating.

Both clients came to me with the same desire: to make their return on investment (ROI) back in the form of money.

One client had a single day of private mentorship left with me, and the other had seven days. Yet both said the same thing: "I know I won't make my ROI back by the end of our time together."

I stopped them right there. "Who said you won't make your ROI back?" I asked.

They did. They had already decided it wasn't possible and justified it with reasons rooted in past experiences: a sense of limited time (hello, time is just a mental construct), lack, and scarcity.

So, we went to work. Together, we dismantled every limiting belief, every excuse, and every old pattern keeping them stuck in the energy of "I can't." We left no stone unturned.

And guess what? They both received their ROI back before our mentorship ended — and then some.

One client even closed a $70,000 deal. Hello?!

In one moment, they were stuck in lack, trapped in negative beliefs. In the next, they stepped into abundance, creating results that exceeded their expectations. None of this would have been possible had they stayed in their old story. The shift happened because they chose to let go of their limitations and embrace a new frequency.

When I first ran Rich B$tch Money Goals as an online program before turning it into book format, I showed up live for twenty-one days straight to ensure participants could consistently practice the work. Why? Because transformation requires repetition, consistency, and a commitment to rewriting the old story.

This is the power of stepping out of lack and into possibility.

**When you shift your mindset,
you change your reality — fast.**

Each time I ran Rich B$tch Money Goals, the results spoke for themselves. Women celebrated their first four-figure months, their first five-figure months, and their biggest wins yet — making more money during the program than they had all year in their businesses.

There were stories of liberation, sold-out offers in twenty-four hours, aligned relationships, and transforming lives.

Simply put: *This work works.*

But what you do with this knowledge after reading this book and doing the work? That's entirely on you. Your success depends on your daily commitment to continue the work, embody the principles, and hold yourself to the energetic standards of a Rich B$tch.

**REMEMBER:
Insight without action changes nothing.**

In the process of becoming, you're not just creating a new way of living or showing up, you're dismantling every fear, limitation, belief, and behavior that has kept you captive.

Choosing this path, stepping into accelerated ascension, and creating your reality is not for the faint of heart. It's for those willing to commit fully and unapologetically.

Here's what's on you:

- **Remove the anchors.** Eliminate people from your life who weigh you down instead of lift you up.
- **Set boundaries.** Ask yourself, "Is this loving to me?" Then act accordingly.
- **Jump when you feel the nudge.** Say yes to desires and intuition, even when logic says otherwise.
- **Move out of your comfort zone.** When you feel the call, invest immediately. Fear delays; action creates.
- **Create and honor new energetic standards.** The Universe will test you. Stay grounded.
- **Lead with your heart.** Your heart is your true North — follow it.
- **Self-regulate.** When you lose connection to your vision, step back, breathe, and re-center in elevated emotions and the Rich B$tch principles.
- **Curate your circle.** Surround yourself with a sisterhood that supports your growth. The energy you entangle with matters.
- **Sit at the table with other Rich B$tches.** Be in rooms where extraordinary things are happening and create ripple effects worldwide.

If you missed the message, let me make it crystal clear: Creating your dream life is on you. Becoming the energetic match to wealth is on you. Doing this work is on you.

But here's the magic: The possibilities you can create from this place? They are endless.

Alternatively, there might be a part of you — the old self — that just doesn't want to leave, clinging on like a houseguest who's overstayed their welcome.

But guess what? **It's motherf*cking time, sister.** Bless and release your past!

In the process of becoming and unbecoming, there will be moments when you don't feel like showing up for your future. Thoughts will creep in, whispering things like *Taking one day off won't hurt* or *I'm tired; I'll do it tomorrow* or even *This isn't working. I need to try something else.*

But let's agree on one thing: you've let that limited story run your life long enough.

If I can do this, tell me why you can't. Better yet, be brutally honest with yourself about the excuses you're still clinging to. What's standing in your way? Plug those energetic leaks because they're draining the very life force you need to create your Rich B$tch reality.

The old version of you, the one who's accustomed to running the show, doesn't want to leave. It's like a toxic ex trying to worm their way back into your life. You've already learned that actions speak louder than words, and this is no different.

So, let me be clear: **Your actions will always speak louder than your words.**

Talk is cheap. Anyone can say they want a new life, more wealth, or to become a Rich B$tch. But how you *show up* every day, moment by moment, will determine whether that's your reality or just another empty promise you make to yourself.

It's time to get real. Plug the leaks. Show up. Take the action. Because how you move today will define the life you live tomorrow.

Building your Rich B$tch future is like building a home — every brick you lay matters. Each action, belief, and decision forms the foundation for the life you're creating.

I can't even count the number of times I questioned my ability to become the energetic match to wealth. From the depths of debt to where I stand today, doubt showed up often. Duality is part of the process. You will have those moments too, and your free will determines how you navigate them.

But it's not about avoiding doubt or moments of lack. What *does* matter is what you do next. It matters that you don't camp out in lack. It matters that you realign, self-regulate, and bring the Rich B$tch principles back into your life as many times as necessary.

Becoming the energetic match to wealth is about staying connected to the energy of abundance, to your vision, and to your future self. It's about alignment, unwavering belief in your worthiness, and the conviction that you *will* create the life you desire.

When you slip back into lack, it's like hanging up on a phone call: the connection to your future is lost. But the good news is that all you have to do is pick up the phone again. It's that simple — and sometimes that hard.

There's nothing "reasonable" about becoming a Rich B$tch. But we're not here for what's sensible or practical. We do this work because we *can*. Because once you know the Rich B$tch principles, you can't un-know them.

You get to have it all. Not because it's logical or easy, but because you're willing to create it. That's your power.

$$$

Rich B$tch Homework: Set Yourself Up for Success

This homework isn't tied to any specific day — it's a lifelong commitment. If you're daring enough to choose abundance and create from desire, this work becomes ongoing for the rest of your life.

You must be passionate enough to consistently pour your

attention and energy into building your Rich B$tch future until it becomes undeniable. Once you start seeing results, the feedback in your life will fuel you to keep going.

HERE'S HOW TO SET YOURSELF UP FOR SUCCESS:

1. **CREATE A ROUTINE**

   Dedicate time daily for the next week — or if you're feeling ambitious, the next month — to connect with your future self. Spend time creating, visualizing, and feeling the elevated emotions of your future vision ahead of the experience. This focused energy collapses time and accelerates your manifestations.

2. **ALIGN VALUES WITH ACTIONS**

   Reflect deeply: Do your actions align with your values? For example, if you say you value freedom but take no meaningful action to create that freedom in your life or business, there's a disconnect. Get honest with yourself, then realign.

3. **LET GO OF WHAT'S NOT ALIGNED**

   When you find yourself clinging to something or someone, ask, "Is this loving to me?" If it isn't, release it. This might mean letting go of material possessions, relationships, or beliefs that no longer serve your highest good.

4. **CELEBRATE YOURSELF**

   Take a moment today to celebrate your effort. You've worked to dismantle old patterns, create new routines, and stretch beyond your comfort zone, and that's incredible. You are f*cking amazing! If you want me to celebrate with you, tag me on Instagram **@kyerakacey** so I can cheer you on.

5. BE THE LIGHT

Remember, the world needs your light. Be an example of this work. Shine unapologetically and take up space — because your energy and your presence matter.

This is the work of a lifetime. Show up for it boldly, knowing you are worthy of every bit of abundance coming your way.

QUESTIONS

RICH
B$TCH MONEY GOALS

QUESTIONS SUBMITTED FROM WOMEN AROUND THE WORLD ON
"Becoming the Energetic Match to Wealth"

It's not time that will heal or transform your financial circumstances. It's your *fierce courage* to confront, feel, and accept everything you once avoided. It's your *commitment* to change and your *consistency* in showing up to do the Rich B$tch work — even when there's no immediate evidence that it's working.

That's the magic.

When I run Rich B$tch Money Goals as an online program, our final day is always a live Q&A. It's a favorite because it gets real and raw and is deeply transformative. To bring some of that energy here, I've collected the most common questions women have asked me during those sessions, plus my responses. Let's dive in!

$$$

1. How do you feel gratitude when you're struggling financially and feel like there's nothing to be grateful for because life is so hard?

You know how, when you're thinking about getting a new car, you suddenly start seeing it everywhere? That's not a coincidence, it's your brain, specifically your reticular activating system, homing in on what you've been focusing on.

Now, apply that same principle to money and abundance. When you're financially struggling and hyper-focused on lack, guess what you start seeing? More lack. Everywhere.

So, here's the solution: Start stacking.

Create a daily ritual, ideally in a journal, where you intentionally acknowledge everything that feels like abundance. Bring your full presence and gratitude to the act, no matter how small the win seems.

Stack everything:

- A penny you find on the sidewalk? Stack it.
- A stunning sunrise? Stack it.
- A great laugh with a friend, food in your belly, or a warm bed to sleep in? Stack it.
- That free coffee someone bought for you? Stack it.

Dr. Joe Dispenza has said several times that gratitude is the ultimate state of receivership. If you want to receive more, start feeling grateful for what's already here.

Now, if gratitude feels like a stretch (and sometimes it does when life is heavy), take the focus off yourself. Do something for someone else. Volunteer at a hospice, food pantry, or animal shelter. Buy a stranger coffee. Helping others is one of the fastest ways to shift your energy because we are wired to give.

Here's a story that changed my life:

During my first divorce, I was grieving, broke, and hopeless, running on a path while hoping I could somehow outrun my problems. My face was red and puffy from crying, and I was spiraling in my own pity party.

About a mile from home, I noticed an older man walking along the sidewalk, carrying a guitar in one hand and trying to roll a tire with the other. He looked exhausted.

Part of me hesitated. I was already a mess — what could I do for him? But my intuition nudged me, and I finally stopped and asked, "Are you okay?"

He explained that his car had a flat tire, and he was trying to get to the bus stop with a new one to replace it. Without even thinking,

I told him to follow me. Together, we walked to my house, loaded his tire and guitar into my car, and drove to his vehicle.

When we got there, he showed me step by step how to change a tire, something I had never done before. In that moment, the heaviness I had been carrying lifted. I wasn't focusing on *my* problems anymore. I was simply helping someone else, and it felt good.

When we finished, he gave me a heartfelt hug, and we went our separate ways. He called me his guardian angel that day, but the truth is, *he was mine.*

Here's the lesson:

If you're drowning in lack and can't find gratitude, give. Giving lifts your vibration, shifts your perspective, and reconnects you to the abundance that's already here. Gratitude always brings clarity, and clarity opens the door for more.

$$$

2. How do I stop thinking negatively, especially about debt or not having enough money?

Did you know that on average, we think over 60,000 thoughts every single day — and 90 percent of those thoughts are *the same ones we had the day before?*

If your default thoughts are negative, you're essentially running on autopilot, repeating the same doom-and-gloom narrative.

Being negative can become an addiction. Just like smoking or binge eating, your brain gets hooked on the pattern of those thoughts, and breaking free requires discipline. It's not comfortable. It's not fun. But it's necessary if you want to create lasting change.

I get it because I've been there.

I used to be consumed by negativity about my financial circumstances. I felt trapped in lack and fear. But there came a moment when I realized my thoughts weren't just describing my reality, they were *creating* it. My desire to break free and create financial freedom became stronger than my attachment to staying stuck.

So, I made a commitment to myself.

HERE'S HOW I DID IT:

1. **Write It Down**

   I wrote down everything I wanted to experience and how I would feel when it happened. Not "if" it happened — WHEN.

2. **Act As If**

   I started acting as though my success was inevitable. My thoughts, feelings, and actions began to align with the version of me who already had what I wanted.

3. **Immerse Yourself in New Energy**

   I flooded my mind with empowering information. Tony Robbins, Dr. Joe Dispenza, podcasts — anything that served my vision was on repeat. I listened while running, driving, cleaning, and even grocery shopping.

4. **Meditate Daily**

   I started meditating every day. At first, it felt hard. Change always does. But I stuck with it, even when it felt like I wasn't "good" at it.

5. **Move Energy through My Body**

   Whenever an old, fear-based thought surfaced, I didn't just let it linger. I breathed through it — ten deep breaths if that's all I could do. Sometimes I shook it off or even screamed to release the energy. Whatever my body needed, I honored it.

6. **Seek Mentorship**

   When I couldn't do it all on my own, I sought mentorship. Sometimes you need guidance and a supportive outside perspective to break through.

7. **Audit Your Circle**

    I became hyper-aware of the people I was spending time with. If they weren't growing, evolving, or supporting my vision, I distanced myself. It's too easy to stay stuck when your circle isn't aligned with where you're headed. Surround yourself with people who inspire, encourage, and hold you accountable.

This work isn't always pretty.

When you're rewiring old patterns, your mind and body may rage against you. Your nervous system might kick and scream, trying to pull you back into your comfort zone. But comfort zones don't create change.

Overcoming negativity requires consistent effort, self-regulation, and the courage to stay present even when it feels hard.

But you don't have to do it alone. Build your village. Seek out people and environments that reflect the growth you desire. This journey is challenging, but with the right tools and support, you can transform your reality.

Your thoughts create your future. Make them work for you, not against you.

$$\$\$\$$

3. Do I need to know where my trauma and money wounds originate from to heal and manifest faster?

No, you do **not** need to know where your money wounds, negative mindset, or money blocks come from to manifest quickly, overcome lack, or become an energetic match to wealth.

What's essential is that you recognize and become *aware* of these patterns when they arise, not that you analyze their origins.

One of the reasons I stopped offering past-life regression and hypnosis to clients is because going back to the source of a block wasn't helping them heal or create the change they truly wanted. Sure, it gave them insight, but insight without action is pointless.

What creates abundance isn't knowing the "why" behind your situation. It's focusing on *what you want* and the energy you need to embody to bring it into existence.

HERE'S THE HARD TRUTH:

The more you dig up your past and relive painful memories, the more you invite that outdated energy into your present reality. It keeps you tied to what you're trying to outgrow. If you want to create something new, you have to stop anchoring yourself to the old.

To manifest wealth, you need to align with the *feelings* of your future — the feelings of having your desires met. Your energy should focus on a desired intention, backed with the emotions of joy, gratitude, excitement, or whatever else turns you on.

Bringing the past into this process doesn't serve you. It only reinforces the old patterns you're trying to leave behind.

SO, WHAT SHOULD YOU DO INSTEAD?

1. **Focus your attention on what you want.**

   Stop giving energy to what went wrong or how you got here. Turn your focus toward the desires you're ready to manifest.

2. **Tune into what excites you to create.**

   Dream big. What would light you up? What makes you feel inspired?

3. **Visualize and feel it daily.**

   Close your eyes and imagine already having what you want. Feel the emotions of living in that reality. Hold that vibration.

4. **Have fun.**

   This process isn't about forcing outcomes — it's about play, curiosity, and creation.

Leave the old behind. Step into your future self, and trust that the energy you align with will bring your desires into reality.

$$$

4. I'm struggling with having faith that I am worthy of receiving. How do I change that?

Knowing you're worthy to receive is a muscle that takes *consistent work* to build. And here's the challenge: No one can build it for you. That's why this work is hard.

You can't pay someone to embody worthiness on your behalf, just like you can't pay someone to lift weights for you at the gym. But just like a personal trainer can guide you, push you, and help you flex muscles you didn't even know you had, you can put yourself in spaces and environments that reflect your highest truth — and encourage you to come home to that truth within yourself.

That's exactly why I created The Rich B$tch Experience.

LET'S GET REAL:

If you're struggling to feel worthy of receiving, chances are you're already aware of choices you're making that *aren't loving to you.* Those choices reinforce unworthiness.

Take a hard look at your intimate relationships and closest friendships. Are they healthy? Supportive? Loving? People who struggle with worthiness often find themselves in situations — romantic, platonic, or professional — that mirror their self-doubt and unworthiness back to them.

Only you know how these dynamics feel for you. Pay attention to the energy you're carrying and the energy you're surrounded by.

FAITH IN YOUR WORTH:

To have faith is to trust. When we doubt our worthiness, we

doubt our intuition, our abilities, and even the people who see our potential.

Here's a game-changer: Build faith in the frequency of *"because I'm alive."* Simply *being you* is enough. Your life matters. You are here for a reason.

I could tell you all day long how worthy you are, but my words won't land if your beliefs don't align with them. This is a battle of *you vs. you.* And it's the toughest one you'll ever fight.

SO, HOW DO YOU START? GO BACK TO THE B IN B$TCH: BELIEF.

A Rich B$tch believes in herself.

If you're unsure what that looks like, start by asking yourself:

- What am I doing that shows I *don't* believe in myself?
- What choices am I making that aren't loving to me?
- How am I speaking to myself? Is it kind?
- What am I tolerating that I know isn't aligned?
- Where am I allowing my boundaries to be disrespected?

REWRITE THE SCRIPT:

Once you recognize these patterns, start changing them:

- What can you do today that's loving to yourself?
- How can you speak to yourself in a way that reflects self-respect and belief?
- Where can you say *no* and reclaim your energy?
- What boundaries can you strengthen?
- How can you say *yes* to yourself today?

The biggest b$tch you're up against is that inner voice telling you you're not enough. It's time to shut her down.

Get to work. I believe in you. Now it's time for you to believe in yourself.

5. I'm struggling. How do I keep ging when I can't see results?

This is one of the hardest things people face when they begin Rich B$tch work. That's why the **B in B$tch stands for belief** — belief in yourself, in your worthiness, and in the truth that what you seek is already seeking you.

If this work were easy, *everyone* would do it. Everyone would be healed. Everyone would be rich. But it's not easy — it's bold, it's transformative, and it's for those willing to do what others won't.

By now, I hope you've started to see the possibilities for yourself. Maybe you've even caught glimpses of evidence in your life:

- The fact that you're here, reading this book, is one.
- Witnessing others achieve what you desire is another.

These are signs, proof that the Universe is already nudging you in the direction of your desires. Keep investing time in your manifestations and elevating your energy because *nothing changes until you change your energy.*

DOUBT IS NORMAL, BUT SO IS PROGRESS

I experienced doubt many times along my journey. Fear showed up often. But I stayed consistent in my vision, held on to faith, and took aligned action, even when I was scared or uncertain of the outcome.

- I honored my intuition over logic, even when it didn't "make sense."
- I self-regulated (and still do when needed).
- I reminded myself that *everything I wanted already existed as a potential in the quantum field.*

It's not about whether your desires exist — they do. The work is about becoming the energetic match to their arrival, which means facing and overcoming your self-imposed limitations.

It's hard, but it's not impossible.

WHAT CHANGED MY LIFE? INVESTING IN MYSELF.

One of the biggest game-changers for me was repeatedly investing in private mentorship. Let me be clear: Most investments stretched me beyond my comfort zone. It wasn't always easy, but I never let fear paralyze me. I always chose mentors who were aligned with my energy and vision and who challenged me to step into my next level of leadership.

Why? Because being around someone ahead of me in their journey, who understood how I wanted to create, made all the difference.

YOUR CIRCLE MATTERS

The people you surround yourself with will either empower you or hold you back. Period. Your circle either lifts you up and supports your vision or keeps you stuck in the same patterns. Take a look around and ask yourself:

- Are these people aligned with where I'm going?
- Do they reflect my highest truth?
- Do they challenge me to grow?

If not, it's time to upgrade.

INVEST IN YOURSELF. IT'S TIME.

Step into the frequency of belief. Stretch yourself. Surround yourself with people who inspire and challenge you to expand. Everything you want is waiting for you — it's your move.

$$$

6. How do I keep the momentum going?

You show up for yourself and honor your commitments despite your feelings. Integrity is paramount.

I couldn't even count how many times I wanted to give up throughout my journey. It's normal for that feeling to pop up. Quitting is normal. Not "feeling like it" is expected. Justifying not doing something is normal. Excuses are normal. It's normal to settle in life, but that is not the Rich B$tch way. We claim our desires, we move accordingly, and we transform. We get shit done!

One of the most widely known and used statements due to its absolute truth is "talk is cheap." Anyone can talk. Anyone can say they will do something, be someone, and create something. Not everyone can follow through and back their promise with aligned action. Who are you going to become?

How do you keep the momentum going? You show up for yourself because you said you would. You keep going even when it feels hard, and you keep going even when you doubt — you just keep going. As you do, you build confidence in yourself because you're breaking through barriers that used to stop you and showing up when you'd usually quit. You race past that finish line to an even more fantastic finish line you didn't even know was there. As you build confidence, your energy changes, and you'll notice that you believe in yourself more than you did the day before. This is where things start to get fun.

Also, surround yourself with doers. Put yourself in the energy of Rich B$tches, building momentum despite their challenges. It takes a village, and you'll want to ensure you're in the right one.

$$$

7. What is the best way to hold the frequency and trust yet still detach from the outcome when manifesting? If I am trying to manifest something, I want it to show up, but I have no control over when it will, and I sometimes get discouraged.

The best way to hold the frequency of your manifestations is to *maintain the vision.*

When you keep your vision alive, when you practice experiencing the feelings of already having what you desire, you naturally stay in alignment with its frequency. Why? Because where your attention goes, your energy flows. The more you occupy mental and emotional space with your dreams and the excitement of your creation, the easier it becomes to hold that frequency.

WHEN YOU LOSE CONNECTION, RECONNECT

Losing the frequency is like losing Wi-Fi — it happens. The solution? Reconnect.

Plug yourself back into the vision. Close your eyes, breathe, and imagine it as if it's already done. Refocus and elevate your emotions. Every time you do this, you drop another pebble into the water, sending ripples of energy out into the quantum field.

You might not see the ripples right away, but they're coming. Trust the process and tune back in.

MAKE MANIFESTATION PLAYFUL

Manifesting doesn't have to feel heavy or serious. In fact, *it shouldn't.* Stop overthinking. Get curious. Be loose, playful, and in flow.

I'll share an example:

The first large amount of money I manifested with this playful energy was $15,000. I asked myself, "What would be fun to create and tune into?" A $15,000 week felt exciting and light, so I started visualizing it multiple times a day for weeks.

Here's the key: I didn't stress about it or approach it with pressure or desperation. I was simply having fun, imagining the celebration and excitement as if it were already done.

And guess what? It *did* happen. But the craziest part? I didn't even notice it at first because I was so caught up in the feeling that it was already done. I had been celebrating it internally for weeks, so when it manifested, my reaction was calm. Why? Because the brain doesn't know the difference between a vividly imagined experience and an actual one.

THE TAKEAWAY: Keep your vision alive. Be consistent, playful, and joyful in your energy. Manifesting works best when you're having *fun.*

$$$

8. When I embody the feelings of abundance and allow ease, I can't even imagine having more than $5,000 in my bank account. If I've never had it, how do I know what it should feel like?

This work is all about the **C** in B$tch: **Conscious Creation.**

It's about intentionally designing what you desire to feel and experience as you align yourself with the energetic match to wealth.

Here's the fun part: *No one is telling you how to feel.* You're in the driver's seat, creating your reality based on your deepest desires.

So, let's start with a question: What do you want it to feel like?

BRING IT INTO EXISTENCE

To consciously create means to *bring something into existence.* Imagine you just won $2,000,000. How would you spend it? If someone said, "You'll only get the money if you tell me exactly what you'd do with it and how you'd feel," you'd figure it out really fast, wouldn't you?

The truth is, **confusion is an illusion.** If you're struggling to feel abundance or imagine having more than $5,000 in your account, it's because you've conditioned your body to feel lack more than you've practiced feeling abundance. Lack has become the automatic response, and breaking that pattern requires effort and intention.

STOP OVERTHINKING AND START DREAMING

Manifestation is supposed to be fun. You're overthinking something that's meant to spark joy and curiosity.

- What's something you've *always* wanted?
- How would it feel to have it?
- Picture that dream vacation. Where would you go? How would flying first class or in a private jet feel?
- What would you eat? Where would you stay?
- What's an experience you've longed for but haven't yet allowed yourself to have?

PLAY WITH POSSIBILITY

Allow yourself to be curious. Explore what it means to live in abundance. Give yourself permission to daydream without limits.

The more you practice stepping into these elevated feelings and visualizing your desires, the more you shift your state of being to match the energy of wealth and abundance.

This is where the magic happens.

So, keep practicing. Stay curious. And most importantly — have fun.

$$$

9. When bills and debts feel overwhelming, especially compared to your current income, how do you make empowered choices about what to do about them or trust in yourself and the Universe that it will all end up okay?

We make empowered choices when we are connected with our intuition.

Your intuition sees pathways that your logical mind cannot. It has been guiding you your entire life, moving you closer to your dreams. But here's why so many feel disconnected: most humans have spent years, if not lifetimes, dismissing their inner knowing, doubting their truth, and silencing the whisper of their soul. That's why confusion arises. Is it fear talking? Or is it intuition?

HERE'S THE TRUTH:

At your core, you are *not* confused. Your intuition is always there. It's not separate from you, it *is* you. It's your internal compass, your divine GPS, always calibrated to lead you toward your highest path. The question is: Are you willing to listen?

This is where the **T** in B$tch comes into play: **Trust.**

Empowered choices, especially in the face of fear, require profound trust. Trust that you can light a match in the darkness and illuminate your way. Trust that your intuition knows the steps forward, even when logic screams, "This makes no sense!"

One of the reasons I've created the results I have in my life and business is because I built a powerful relationship with my intuition.

I stopped waiting for certainty or guarantees. I started saying, "F*ck it," then jumped — even when I was terrified — because my intuition whispered, "This is your path."

And as I trusted myself, my life began to change. The more I leaped and landed, the stronger my trust became. With each win,

I trusted a little more. With each expansion, I honored my intuition more deeply.

Now, it's your turn.

Cultivate your connection with your intuition. Lean in. Start listening and trusting its guidance. Begin owning the magic you bring to the world — the gifts, the purpose, the medicine that only you possess.

If you're reading this, it's not a coincidence.

This is your sign to deepen your connection — with yourself, your inner knowing, your guides, and your intuitive gifts. You are a light warrior, and the work you're here to do in the world begins within you.

Start now. Trust the whisper. It's leading you somewhere extraordinary.

$$\$\$\$$$

10. I have manifested small things, like free coffee at work or a friend buying me lunch, but larger things rarely manifest for me. How do I manifest more?

You can say you want more money, then find a dollar stuck between your couch cushions and not even recognize that you just manifested what you asked for: *more.*

But we both know one dollar isn't your end game.

How would the Universe know that one dollar isn't the more you desire if you don't define it with clear intention?

How do you manifest "more"? You *define* it.

Clarity is everything. Be specific about what "more" looks like for you — more money, a specific job, a dream home, a soul-aligned partner. Define it with such precision that the Universe has a direct GPS coordinate to deliver your desires.

Once defined, pay attention to your desires daily. Energy flows where attention goes. This is why the I in B$tch stands for **Invest** — invest your time, energy, and resources into the creation of your desires.

You bring your manifestations to life by giving them your focus and energy.

This work goes beyond wishful thinking, it's about swapping out the old for the new:

- The thought of *lack* for the thought of *wealth*.
- The thought of *stress* for the thought of *ease*.
- The thought of *fear* for the thought of *possibility*.

Here's why this matters: **Ninety percent of the thoughts you think today are the same thoughts you thought yesterday.** If your old thoughts are rooted in lack, fear, or struggle, and you keep feeding them your energy, then nothing changes.

Manifestation is the work of *reconditioning your thoughts and feelings*.

New thoughts (such as "I have consistent six-figure months") create new feelings (like *relief, excitement,* and *gratitude*), and those feelings shift your frequency, making you an energetic match to what you desire.

If you aren't manifesting what you want, it's because your energy and attention are still invested in your old patterns of thought and feeling, keeping you tied to a reality of lack instead of one of abundance.

Want *more*? **Define it. Feel it. Invest in it.** Shift your energy toward what you desire, then watch how quickly your reality begins to transform.

$$$

11. My significant other has a negative money mindset and doesn't believe in the law of attraction or manifestation. How do you maintain a high vibe and become the energetic match to wealth when your partner is negative and judges the way that you spend money?

Brave question — I love it. Let's dive in.

First, remember this: As a Rich B$tch, **your energy and feelings are your responsibility.** Period. No matter what's happening around you, your environment doesn't dictate your mood or energy. That doesn't mean it's easy — far from it — but this work isn't about bypassing challenges, it's about facing them head-on and transforming through them.

Can you create wealth while being partnered with someone who has a negative mindset? Yes. But let's be honest: it's harder. It's like climbing a mountain with extra weight on your back. Not impossible, but challenging.

So how do you maintain a high vibe when the person closest to you isn't on the same wavelength?

1. **Release judgment and the need to change them.**

    Stop expending energy trying to drag them onto your path. Let go of expectations and honor their free will. Everyone has the right to choose their journey, even if it doesn't look like yours.

2. **Focus on your creations.**

    Instead of using energy to fix or force, channel it into your goals, vision, and manifestations. Show, don't tell. When you embody abundance, gratitude, and self-love, you'll either inspire them to elevate or gain clarity on the alignment of your relationship.

3. **Accept them fully as they are.**

    When you genuinely accept someone without conditions, you remove the tension. Acceptance doesn't mean condoning negativity, it means recognizing that their path is theirs. Your responsibility is to stay true to your own work.

So, what happens if your relationship feels out of alignment? As you grow and evolve, it's natural to reevaluate your partnerships. Ask yourself:

- Is this relationship an energetic leak?
- Is this partnership aligned with my highest truth?
- Is this love coming from abundance and expansion — or fear and scarcity?

Ask the hard questions:

- Is this loving to me?
- Is staying in this relationship loving to me?
- Does this partnership reflect the most extraordinary vision of love I hold for myself?
- Am I showing up in this relationship as someone I'm proud of?

If it's not loving to you, I promise — it's not loving to them either.

Some relationships are meant to grow with you; others aren't.

The wealthiest decisions I've made in my life, both financial and emotional, have come from radical truth and love. They've been some of the hardest, most painful moves, but they've forged me into the woman I am today.

Your standards matter. It doesn't mean your partner has to have your exact rituals or meditate daily, but self-awareness and a desire to grow are essential. If they're not willing to elevate, they'll stay stuck while you rise, and that's a timeline you don't belong on anymore.

Reevaluate often and upgrade your standards as needed.

A Rich B$tch doesn't compromise her truth. She's here for radical love, radical wealth, and radical alignment — even when it's uncomfortable.

You are forged in the fire. Remember that.

$$\$\$\$$$

12. How do I address friends who want to know why I'm changing and why I'm distant?

Before addressing your friends, start with yourself. Take a moment to connect with your inner truth and ask yourself:

- Where are these friendships heading?
- Where would I like them to go, based on the energetic standards I now hold?

Your energy is sacred. Be selective about who has access to it.

If someone is genuinely curious and supportive of your growth, evolution, and transformation, then by all means, have an open and meaningful conversation. Let them see the light of your journey and the truth of who you're becoming.

But if their curiosity is laced with discomfort about your change — or worse, if it's tied to their projections, judgments, or unhealed wounds — you owe them nothing.

Rejection and redirection are protection.

As you grow, your social circle will evolve. Some people will fall away, making room for others who align with the frequency you're stepping into. Let it happen.

Stop holding on to relationships that have outgrown their purpose in your life. Holding on only delays the blessings that are waiting to come through. Release them with love, gratitude, and the understanding that every relationship, whether it lasts for a season or a lifetime, has served its purpose in your evolution.

Find your people. There's nothing like a sisterhood rooted in love, abundance, and shared vision. Don't settle for anything less than the deep, expansive, soul-aligned connections you deserve.

You're worth it. Trust your heart. Trust your intuition. Trust the Universe. If space is being created in your life, it's because something better is on its way.

$$$

13. When you hired your first coach and paid $20,000, you said you took out credit cards to do so. Does borrowing money affect the speed at which that money comes back? Your financial advancements sound like they have come from your own money and not from friends or family members.

Borrowing money to invest in yourself doesn't affect the timing or speed at which you manifest money or become the energetic match to wealth. The origin of the money is irrelevant. What matters is how you *feel* about the money you invest and the energy you bring to the table.

There's a saying: "When you pay more, you pay more attention." I've found this to be true, especially when the investment comes directly from your own resources. When it's someone else's money, people often don't show up with the same level of commitment. I've seen individuals invest thousands of borrowed dollars only to backslide, skip steps, or give up entirely because they didn't fully value what wasn't earned through their own effort.

It's not just about the money, it's about the energy and effort behind it. Most people value what they've worked for because they understand what it took to earn it.

Let's be clear: My success didn't come from borrowing money or relying on someone else's resources. My financial breakthroughs came from investing my own money, and not because it was "mine," but because I showed up differently when I had skin in the game.

But my seven-figure business wasn't built on money alone. It was built on **fierce courage, grit, consistency, trust**, and a willingness to face discomfort. It was forged in **learning from mistakes, implementing boundaries, raising my standards, plugging energetic leaks**, and having **courageous conversations** with myself and others.

This work isn't for the faint of heart. Success doesn't come from the external, it comes from the transformation within. Whether the money comes from you or someone else doesn't matter as much as **how you show up, how you lead, and how much you're willing to invest energetically, emotionally, and spiritually into your evolution.**

It's about claiming your truth, owning your power, and deciding *every single day* to become the Rich B$tch you know you're meant to be.

$$$

14. How do you break through the glass ceiling when you're doing everything to be aligned, but things seem to be getting worse, and you've been at it for years?

Have you ever done a juice cleanse? If you have (or even if you've heard about someone else's experience) you'll know that you usually feel worse before you feel better. Even though you're doing something incredibly healthy for your mind and body, there's a detox period, a "chaos before order" effect, when you feel discomfort before the clarity, bliss, and surge of energy emerge. Transformation, in any form, often works this way.

Becoming the energetic match to wealth can feel the same. It's a process, not an overnight switch. You might face doubts, fears, or frustration. But here's the message: **Keep going.**

This journey isn't about comparing your progress to someone else's. That often sounds like the internal chatter: "Why is it working for them and not me?" But that illusion of separation will steal your joy and your focus. You cannot compare your chapter 5 to someone else's chapter 20 or chapter 50. Every journey is unique, filled with different lessons, paths, and timelines.

Your job? Keep refining. Keep showing up. Be consistent in your effort but flexible in your approach. Trust your process.

When I moved my business online, I invested $20,000 — a decision that put me back into debt — to work with a business coach who taught me how to sell high-ticket, 1:1 coaching offers. I remember sitting on group calls where other clients celebrated $5,000, $10,000, $20,000 wins. And there I was, thinking: *WTF am I doing wrong? Why am I not celebrating wins? Why isn't this working for me?*

That inner dialogue? That was the b$tch I had to confront. The thoughts telling me I was behind. The doubts whispering, "This isn't for you." But I didn't quit. I kept going. I worked on my energy and my belief that "If it can happen for them, it can happen for me."

Even then, there were moments when I questioned the process. I thought about shifting to low-ticket group coaching, promoting multiple offers instead of focusing on just one. But then I remembered why I hired that coach in the first place — because my way wasn't working. So, I shut up, trusted the process, and committed to refining my skills, message, and energy.

And guess what? **It worked.** I closed my first 1:1 client, and the momentum snowballed from there. Once attracting and closing high-ticket clients became effortless, I expanded my offers — private readings, group coaching programs, and more. But I didn't leap before I built a solid foundation.

There's always a moment in the timeline where you'll want to quit. The work feels hard. The results feel slow. The doubts feel louder than your belief. But **you cannot break through the glass ceiling if you quit.**

Stay the course. Trust the process. Keep going — you're building the foundation of the Rich B$tch life you're destined to create.

$$$

15. How did you manifest your first paid client?

I love sharing this story because it's a powerful reminder for online coaches who are burning themselves out trying so hard to get clients: **It gets to be easy, aligned, and authentic.**

Before I moved my business online, I had a physical office where clients paid me $70 an hour. They'd find me through the *Psychology Today* directory or by word of mouth. When I decided to close that office and transition my business entirely online, I followed all the conventional advice for gaining clients. Sales calls, strategic posting, following up in DMs, implementing every suggestion my mentor offered, even though I hated it. It felt robotic, disconnected, and completely out of alignment with my intuition and heart.

Then, one day, everything shifted. I went for a run, and during that run, I felt inspired to share a heartfelt message for International Women's Day. There was no plan, no sales pitch, no carefully curated post. I simply wanted to speak from my soul for whoever needed to hear it.

Picture this: messy hair, red face, no makeup, a baggy gray sweatshirt, and sweat pouring down. Zero "perfection." And yet, I hit "live" and spoke directly from my heart. I wasn't trying to sell.

I wasn't promoting anything. I was simply being.

What happened next? A woman messaged me after watching my live and asked if I was taking on 1:1 clients. Just like that, she signed on to work with me — for $2,500 over two months. (Now, my private mentorship is a five-to six-figure investment.)

The lesson? **People aren't looking for perfection. They're looking for heart-centered leadership and embodied truth.**

When you show up authentically, aligned with your message and purpose, people feel it. The connection goes beyond strategy — it's magnetic. Your energy and authenticity do more to attract the right clients than any perfectly curated plan ever will.

Let this story remind you: **Ease and alignment will always out-perform force and perfection.** Lead with your heart, and the rest will follow.

$$\$\$\$$$

16. How did you manifest your first $100,000 month?

Celebrating my first six-figure month in Marco Island, surrounded by clients who were also attending a Dr. Joe Dispenza retreat, was unforgettable. Let me break it down and share why this milestone is significant — beyond the numbers.

THE TIMELINE:

1. **The Intuitive Leap**: Four months before that milestone, I made a bold, intuitive move: I invested my first six figures into mentor-ship. It wasn't just a decision, it was a calling. While my logical mind questioned the risk, my inner knowing felt exhilarated by the expansion. This was me trusting the process, even though it felt scary. That investment stretched me far beyond previous comfort zones and set the tone for everything that followed.

2. **Taking Action on My Dreams**: I announced my first retreat,

held in Ireland, opening spots at $17,000. Within an hour of announcing it, someone jumped in. For years, I had talked about leading retreats but never acted. My mentor called me out, asking, "What are you waiting for?" The next day, I launched the Ireland retreat — without all the details figured out but with total certainty. I had always envisioned leading retreats, and having lived in Ireland, it felt aligned. Every single attendee of that retreat came back for the next one. Moral of the story? Trust yourself and take the leap.

3. **Plugging the Energetic Leaks**: My business was thriving, but I knew I had to address a significant energetic leak (if you missed the recap, revisit Chapter 19: Rich B$tch Sisterhood). Once I closed that gap, the six-figure month naturally followed.

4. **Intuition over Strategy**: That six-figure month wasn't planned or calculated. I wasn't tracking numbers or mapping out a specific sales strategy. I simply followed my intuition about which offers felt aligned, and people kept buying.

WHY THIS MATTERS:

While content strategy, marketing, sales tactics, and offers are essential, energetics play an equally important role. **Applying the Rich B$tch principles and aligning energetically with what I desired was the secret sauce.**

For me, this journey wasn't just about hitting a revenue milestone, it was about having fun, feeling worthy, and trusting in my ability to create abundance. I wasn't just following a road map, I was writing my own, guided by intuition and self-awareness.

WHAT THIS MEANS FOR YOU:

1. **Tailor Your Path**: How I run my business won't work for everyone, and that's the point. You need to uncover what works for you based on your unique energy, desires, and strengths. Some

of my clients thrive on structured, masculine strategies, while others don't. There's no one-size-fits-all approach to success.

2. **Feel Worthy**: To create your version of a six-figure month (or whatever goal you have), you must feel worthy of receiving it. The Universe reflects your sense of deservingness.

3. **Have Fun**: Enjoy the process. When you lead with joy, alignment, and a strong sense of self, magic happens.

REMEMBER:

You are an energetic match for the moves you make. Step into your worth, act from alignment, and trust that what you desire is already in motion. It's time to claim it.

$$\$\$\$$$

17. How do I break the cycle of attracting broke clients who can't pay my fees?

There's always a dual conversation in the pursuit of wealth: **energetics** (frequency, alignment, closing leaks) and **business strategy** (content, marketing, positioning). The magic happens when these two align. Let's start with the energetics because that's where transformation begins.

THE ENERGETICS OF WEALTH:

First, get crystal clear about your worth and what you desire. Claim what you're available for, and release what you're not. If you don't believe in your ability to attract clients who pay effortlessly and joyfully, you'll unconsciously attract people who reinforce your doubt. This begins with **conscious creation**: becoming the energetic match for clients who are ready to pay in full because money isn't a barrier for them.

Here's a simple exercise:

Imagine receiving a DM from someone who says, "I want to work with you, and I'm ready to pay in full." No objections. No hesitation. How does that feel in your body? **Notice it. Amplify it.** That feeling is your map. Practice tuning into it daily until it feels like your new normal.

If you're not doing this, your energy and attention are likely focused on the people who *can't* pay you — and that's exactly what you'll keep attracting. Shift your focus. Clients who are ready to pay are abundant, but to attract them, you must believe in their existence and consistently align yourself with the frequency of receiving them. This is a practice, not a one-time event.

ASK YOURSELF:

Do I feel certain about who I am and the value of what I offer? Am I showing up with the confidence that my work is transformational and worth every penny?

A lack of certainty in who you are and the power of your work is one of the biggest reasons people struggle to attract ready-to-pay clients. **Confidence sells.** When you trust yourself, your business, and your pricing, that energy becomes magnetic.

THE BUSINESS SIDE OF WEALTH CREATION:

Now, let's talk strategy. Without seeing your business, here are the common patterns I've observed in coaches who attract clients that "can't afford it":

1. **Lack of Consistency**: Sporadic posting, sporadic selling, or inconsistent energy sends mixed signals to your audience and the Universe.

2. **Messaging to Lack**: If your content speaks to people's struggles without holding them in their power, you're reinforcing lack rather than empowerment. You attract what you speak to.

3. **Confusing Marketing**: Messaging that isn't clear about who you serve or the transformation you provide leaves potential clients uncertain — and uncertainty doesn't pay.

4. **Contradictory Boundaries**: If you want ready-to-pay clients but are giving away too much for free or lowering your prices out of fear, you're energetically leaking.

5. **Unaligned Offers**: Offers that don't excite you won't excite others. If you're creating from obligation or doubt, it shows.

THE BOTTOM LINE:

You attract ready-to-pay clients when your **energy and strategy align.**

When you shift your energy, you'll shift your experience. When you refine your strategy, you'll amplify the results of that energetic shift. Keep tuning into the frequency of wealth and embodying your highest truth.

Ready-to-pay clients exist. The only question is whether you're showing up as the version of yourself who attracts them. **Keep going.** You've got this.

$$$

18. How do you handle price objections when someone says your prices are too high?

Easily. I don't.

The price is the price. I don't make exceptions or lower it for anyone. If my pricing shifts, it's because *I* feel excited to offer something special — born out of **overflow and alignment**, not pressure or fear. Every special offer I've ever created came from an intuitive, in-the-moment spark, not a calculated need to make sales.

With that said, let's clear something up:

Never run a special offer because someone isn't buying. Never lower your price because you feel like people "need" it to say yes. That's scarcity thinking wrapped in a false sense of generosity.

Frequency first. Alignment first.

There will always be someone who charges more than you and someone who charges less. Your job isn't to cater to everyone, it's to stand in your worth and trust that your pricing reflects the transformation and energy you bring to the table.

Sure, you can create multiple pathways to cash: high-ticket, mid-tier, and lower-priced offers. That's a strategy. But your 1:1 mentorship is sacred space, and if you charge $10,000 for ninety days and someone says it's "too much," simply respond, "Okay." Let them find what feels aligned for them elsewhere.

The right clients will always find you, and they will jump into your offers when they're an energetic match.

Keep creating space for those aligned clients. Keep trusting yourself. Keep leading from truth, not compromise.

And remember: It's not your job to catch people up to speed. Stay in your power.

$$$

19. What are your thoughts on trading services in business? How does that impact what we are manifesting?

Like everything we do, **what matters most is the frequency behind it.**

If trading services feels aligned, joyful, and comes from your highest truth, it will not negatively impact your energy or manifestations. But if it feels off — if you'd rather be paid, if the exchange feels unfair, if it stems from lack instead of overflow, or if you're trading because you don't feel "good enough" to charge — that frequency creates an **energetic leak**.

That leak will eventually demand your attention, forcing you to clean it up and realign with your truth.

Personally, I don't trade services because it doesn't feel good or aligned for me. That's not to say it's right or wrong for you. It's about **what honors your truth** and feels good in your energy.

Here's an example: I paid a friend $2,222 for a one-hour session because those are her rates, and I wanted her full attention on my business. For some, hearing this might trigger the belief that "friends shouldn't charge other friends." I strongly disagree. If someone close to you has a business, they should be respected, supported, and compensated for their work.

Yes, she and I often exchange ideas in casual conversations, but on this day, I wanted **dedicated focus and professional support.** I was the one who initiated the payment because it felt aligned, joyful, and supportive.

On the flip side, a friend recently came to me drained and resentful after agreeing to a business trade. The terms weren't clear, expectations were misaligned, and she felt stuck. After coaching her through the issue, she honored her highest truth, contacted the person, and explained she could no longer move forward with the trade. The relief in her mind and body was immediate.

Your **highest truth** will always yield the **greatest results.** Honor yourself by making Rich B$tch decisions that align with your energy. When you do, you'll notice how wealth, energetic and material, flows effortlessly into your life.

LESSON: If it doesn't feel good, it's not aligned. Trust yourself.

$$$

20. I purposely don't speak about how much money I make or even about my business with people who aren't aligned. I am confused. You talk about us not having resistance to sharing what we're doing, not caring about what other people think, and how we may even inspire others. I agree, but I'm empathetic. I avoid the topic because of other people's negativity regarding money. Can you speak to this?

This is the perfect moment to remind yourself that **honoring your highest truth** comes before anyone else's advice — including mine. Trust yourself.

I love talking about money. I'm empathetic too, but empathy does **not** mean dimming your joy, excitement, wins, or self-expression for someone else's comfort.

Let's step outside money for a moment. I have large boobs. Am I supposed to wear baggy shirts and hide my body to avoid upsetting someone with a smaller chest who wishes they were bigger? Of course not. The same principle applies to celebrating your success — **you're not responsible for someone else's triggers.** Their work is theirs, and trying to take that on for them is not only impossible but also out of alignment with your truth.

In the coaching industry, it's common to see coaches celebrating money wins. Let me be clear, though; it's not something you *have* to do. However, if you **want** to share your wins but hold back out of fear of judgment or backlash, **that's where the work is.** You're not serving anyone by stifling your truth, gratitude, or joy. That's why I tell my clients, "I want more of you, not less. You're not too much. You never were."

Now, some people are turned off by money celebrations online, often because of the frequency behind the posts. Sometimes they can feel when something posed as a celebration carries undertones of selling or positioning — it feels misaligned or inauthentic.

But regardless of why, money will always be a triggering topic. That doesn't mean you should compromise your values or shrink to avoid upsetting others or being disliked.

Duality is the reality of this human experience. For every person you trigger, there will be many more inspired by you. You must decide what's most important: hiding to keep others comfortable or standing in your power.

If you want more money but are afraid of being judged for it — or worse, if you diminish or hide your success — that's an **energetic block**. Money flows where energy flows, and limiting how you show up is like telling the Universe, "I'm not ready for more."

Let's also address a critical truth: **You can't please everyone.** You will be judged whether you're making millions or struggling, whether you share your wins or stay silent. So, why not stand in your highest truth and highest love?

Finally, when the version of you online doesn't match the version of you in real life, I guarantee you're leaving money on the table. Why? Because people invest in leaders who aren't afraid to be unapologetically themselves. When you show up in your full truth, you invite aligned opportunities beyond what you could imagine.

Stand tall. Speak your truth. Create from your soul. There's magic in that. Don't dim it.

$$$

21. What does your day look like concerning business, play time, meditation, workout, etc.? I realize it can shift, but approximately how much time is spent dedicated to raising your vibration?

I added this question because, let's be honest: when we see someone creating the kind of results we dream of for ourselves, we naturally want to know their "secret sauce." What are they doing behind the scenes? Is there something we're missing?

While I've shared plenty in these chapters about how I've aligned myself to becoming the energetic match to wealth, let me pull back the curtain even more. Here's a glimpse into a typical day and the nonnegotiables that anchor my success.

MY MORNING RITUAL

I don't wake up at the same time every morning. It depends on my schedule, travel, and time zone, but it's always early — somewhere between 4 a.m. and 6 a.m. (and honestly, 6 a.m. feels "late"). The first thing I do is dive into my meditation practice.

The style varies depending on my mood, but one constant is that I use Dr. Joe Dispenza's meditations. They resonate deeply with me. I dedicate a minimum of one hour per day to this practice. It's nonnegotiable. Sometimes I'll pair it with breathwork before or during the meditation, which amplifies my connection and clarity.

MOVEMENT IS MEDICINE

After meditation, I move my body. Whether it's a workout at the gym, a long walk, or something else, I make sure to integrate movement into my morning. Success is holistic — it's about mastering all areas of life. Mind and body are equal priorities. Neglect one, and the other will eventually suffer.

TUNING INTO POTENTIAL

Throughout the day, I take intentional pauses to tune into my potential. These mini "time-outs" are usually five to ten minutes long. I close my eyes, visualize the experiences I'm creating, and generate the emotions I'll feel when they're realized.

This practice isn't random. It's deliberate. It's about connecting with the energy of creation — not just thinking about what I want but feeling it as though it's already mine.

MY HOME IS MY HAVEN

Whether I'm working at home or traveling, the space around me matters. At home, I ensure my environment is clean, clutter-free, and energetically supportive. I treat myself like the most important guest in my own space.

I burn beeswax candles daily (Big Dipper Wax Works is my favorite). I diffuse essential oils. I might burn copal, take a luxurious Epsom salt bath, or blast music that moves me while pole dancing in my bedroom.

The goal? To create a sanctuary — a space where creativity and alignment flow effortlessly.

CONNECTION AND JOY

I take breaks to play with my Dobermans, who remind me to stay present and connect with nature. Joy and connection are just as important as strategy and action.

WORK, CREATION, AND SERVICE

I pour my energy into projects that light me up (this book, for example). I meet with my team, support private clients, and run my business in alignment with my energy. If something disrupts my vibration, I stop and self-regulate before continuing. Energy first. Action second. Always.

HIGH-FREQUENCY LIVING

Every single thing I do has intention behind it. From the way I set up my workspace to how I approach my day's tasks, I infuse purpose into everything. When I work, I work. When I rest, I rest. I aim to maintain flow, not force.

If my energy dips, I don't push through. I recalibrate. Some days require more recalibration than others, and that's okay. The key is that my energy and connection to the divine always take priority.

If you don't have a daily ritual, create one. Do it with intention. Treat yourself like the VIP of your own life, because that's exactly who you are. Set the tone for yourself every single day. That's how a Rich B$tch moves through life.

Your life is your creation. Make it a masterpiece!

Congratulations! You now hold the keys to unlock your Rich B$tch era, dripping in abundance and unstoppable power, if you have the courage to claim it. Remember, knowing isn't enough; action is the currency of transformation. So, step up, break the limits of your past, and show the world exactly what happens when a woman fully owns her power. The wealth, the life, the legacy — it's all waiting for you.

If this book lit a fire within you, I'd love to hear your story! Send me a message on Instagram **@kyerakacey** or email **info@kyerakacey.com** — I want to know how it's inspired you. And when you're ready to deepen these Rich B$tch principles, click the QR code to discover the next chapter waiting for you.

At fEMPOWER, we help thought leaders and creative entrepreneurs capture their vision in the form of nonfiction books, journals, workbooks, affirmation cards, and personal growth products.

Our mission is to help our authors grow and scale a platform far beyond the book, protect their soul's work, and turn their message into a legacy!

www.fempower.pub | @fempower.pub

www.ingramcontent.com/pod-product-compliance
Lightning Source LLC
Chambersburg PA
CBHW051133120626
46547CB00012B/790